Teaching Hemingway and Gender

TEACHING HEMINGWAY
Mark P. Ott, Editor
Susan F. Beegel, Founding Editor

Teaching Hemingway's *The Sun Also Rises*
EDITED BY PETER L. HAYS

Teaching Hemingway's *A Farewell to Arms*
EDITED BY LISA TYLER

Teaching Hemingway and Modernism
EDITED BY JOSEPH FRUSCIONE

Teaching Hemingway and War
EDITED BY ALEX VERNON

Teaching Hemingway and Gender
EDITED BY VERNA KALE

Teaching Hemingway and Gender

Edited by Verna Kale

The Kent State University Press   Kent, Ohio

Copyright © 2016 by The Kent State University Press, Kent, Ohio 44242
All rights reserved
Library of Congress Catalog Card Number 2016007534
ISBN 978-1-60635-279-3
Manufactured in the United States of America

Library of Congress Cataloging-in-Publication Data
Names: Kale, Verna, editor.
Title: Teaching Hemingway and gender / edited by Verna Kale.
Description: Kent, Ohio : The Kent State University Press, 2016. | Series: Teaching Hemingway | Includes bibliographical references and index.
Identifiers: LCCN 2016007534| ISBN 9781606352793 (pbk. : alk. paper) ∞ | ISBN 9781631012518 (epdf)
Subjects: LCSH: Hemingway, Ernest, 1899-1961--Study and teaching. | Masculinity in literature. | Men in literature. | Sex in literature. | Women in literature. | Gender identity in literature.
Classification: LCC PS3515.E37 Z89165 2016 | DDC 813/.52--dc23
LC record available at https://lccn.loc.gov/2016007534

for Sandra Spanier and Susan Beegel
with appreciation

V.K.

Contents

Foreword
    MARK P. OTT   ix
Acknowledgments   xi
Introduction
    VERNA KALE   1
State of the Field: Gender Studies, Sexuality Studies, and Hemingway
    DEBRA A. MODDELMOG   7

Part One: Hemingway and Gender

In Our Time and American Modernisms: Interpreting and Writing the Complexities of Gender and Culture
    JOSEPH FRUSCIONE   27

"The Garden of Cultural Acceptability": Gender in *The Garden of Eden*, Then and Now
    PAMELA L. CAUGHIE AND ERIN HOLLIDAY-KARRE   38

Redeeming Hemingway and His Women: Periodicals as Sites of Change in the Literature Classroom
    BELINDA WHEELER   47

It *Is* Pretty to Think So: Domestic Relationships in the Nick Adams Stories
    JOHN FENSTERMAKER   58

Nick Adams and the Construction of Masculinity
    SARAH B. HARDY   70

A Very Complicated Negotiation: Teaching Hemingway to Second Language Learners of English
    DOUGLAS SHELDON   80

Part Two: Hemingway and Sexuality

"Afición Means Passion": Sexuality and Religion in *The Sun Also Rises*
    JOSHUA WEISS   93

Reading Hemingway Backwards: Teaching *A Farewell to Arms* in Light of *The Garden of Eden*
    CARL P. EBY   104

Economic Power and the Female Expatriate Consumer Artist in *The Garden of Eden*
    CATHERINE R. MINTLER   115

Part Three: Hemingway and Women

Hemingway and the Modern Woman: Brett Ashley and the Flapper Tradition
    CRYSTAL GORHAM DOSS   129

Men Without Women?: Can Hemingway and Women Writers Coexist in the Classroom?
    SARA KOSIBA   142

Katie and the Pink Highlighter: Teaching Post-"Hemingway" Hemingway
    HILARY KOVAR JUSTICE   153

Appendixes   165
Works Cited   212
Selected Bibliography and Suggestions for Further Reading   225
Contributors   233
Index   236

Foreword
Mark P. Ott

How should the work of Ernest Hemingway be taught in the twenty-first century? Although the "culture wars" of the 1980s and 1990s have faded, Hemingway's place in the curriculum continues to inspire discussion among writers and scholars about the lasting value of his work. To readers of this volume, his life and writing remain vital, meaningful, and still culturally resonant for today's students.

Books in the Teaching Hemingway series build on the excellent work of founding series editor Susan F. Beegel, who guided into publication the first two volumes of this series, *Teaching Hemingway's* A Farewell to Arms, edited by Lisa Tyler (2008), and *Teaching Hemingway's* The Sun Also Rises, edited by Peter L. Hays (2008). To promote their usefulness to instructors and professors—from high schools, community colleges, and universities—the newest volumes in this series are organized thematically, rather than around a single text. This shift attempts to open up Hemingway's work to more interdisciplinary strategies of instruction through divergent theories, fresh juxtapositions, and ethical inquiries, and to the employment of emergent technology to explore media beyond the text.

Teaching Hemingway and Gender, edited by Verna Kale, speaks to issues that continue to be of intense interest to students and scholars today: gender, sexuality, and "the Hemingway text." The expertise and insight Kale brought to her highly regarded biography *Ernest Hemingway* (2016) and her work on modernism, gender studies, and feminist theory is manifest throughout this volume. These far-ranging essays exploring Hemingway's fiction through the lens of gender and sexuality demonstrate that in today's classrooms and lecture halls Hemingway's work is being taught in more thoughtful and innovative ways than ever before. The essays showcase the creativity, wisdom, and insight from authors of varied backgrounds that are united in their passion for sharing Hemingway's modernist texts to twenty-first-century students and scholars.

Acknowledgments

Verna Kale

Teaching is always a collaborative process, and thus the list of individuals deserving to be thanked here is much too long to publish. That said, I'd like to acknowledge the following people in particular for their help in bringing this project to completion.

First and foremost, I wish to thank the contributors to this volume for their hard work and perseverance and for sharing their experience and creativity. I am grateful to Mark P. Ott, series editor, for asking me to take the lead on this volume; Joyce Harrison and Mary Young at Kent State University Press for easing this book through the gauntlet of academic publishing; and Rebekah Cotton for her careful editing of the manuscript. I am also grateful to Lisa Tyler, editor of *Teaching Hemingway's* A Farewell to Arms (Kent State 2008), for helping me sort through some of the trickier behind-the-scenes questions that arise when editing a collection, and to the anonymous reviewers who offered valuable constructive criticism. I am grateful to the provost and dean of faculty and my colleagues at Hampden-Sydney College for supporting this project with a summer research grant and other funding, the librarians at Bortz Library for their tireless assistance, and Jane Holland for her administrative support. And, as always, I offer my most heartfelt thanks and love to my family: Steele, Betty, and Julian.

The greatest debt, however, is surely to the scholars who have blazed a trail (and tolerated what Hilary Kovar Justice calls, in the essay that closes out this volume, "The Question"): the smart, imaginative, and dauntless women and men who, instead of closing the book on Hemingway, decided to help rewrite it. That list is long, and so, instead, I direct readers to Debra A. Moddelmog's Selected Bibliography.

Two of the most influential women in Hemingway studies—Susan Beegel, former editor of the *Hemingway Review,* who accepted my first scholarly publication, and Sandra Spanier, general editor of the Hemingway Letters Project, who took me on as her research assistant and has supported my professional endeavors ever since—have also been the most influential mentors in my career, and it is to them that this collection is dedicated, with appreciation.

Introduction

Verna Kale

The purpose of this book seems straightforward enough: *Teaching Hemingway and Gender* explores themes relating to gender and sexuality in Hemingway's work, and it provides a selection of approaches to teaching these themes in the secondary, post-secondary, and graduate classrooms. Immediately, however, the challenge of such a task asserts itself: to what problems does this book offer a corrective? Is Hemingway—whose reputation as "AMERICA'S No. 1 HE-MAN" still precedes him—in need of recovery?[1] Can such work be done in a way that does not turn the instructor into an apologist for the predominantly white, predominantly male ethos that so long defined "the moderns" (and the academy that canonized them)? Conversely, if Hemingway has never really left us—and his ubiquitous presence in literature anthologies and the continued scholarly interest in his work suggests that his pervasiveness is in fact the case—how can we elucidate the study of these masculinist, modernist texts to twenty-first-century students (and scholars)?

The conversation Leslie Fiedler sparked in 1960 with his famous proclamation that there are "no *women*" in Hemingway's texts (emphasis Fiedler's) spanned decades, survived the canon wars, and carries on today (316). Other critics declared that in Hemingway's works "the only good woman is a dead one, and even then there are questions" (Fetterley, *Resisting Reader* 71) and suggested that women "are not likely to see [them]selves in Hemingway's encoding of subjectivity" (Westling 100). Not yet ready to give up on Hemingway, Ann Putnam has asked, "How do female readers who have always been moved by

Hemingway's works . . . negotiate theories that insist upon the exclusionary quality of the Hemingway world? How does the female reader locate herself in a landscape where there are no women?" (110). More recently, as Nancy R. Comley notes, scholars have reconsidered Hemingway's female characters as "finely drawn figures, frustrated and limited by their social roles and one-dimensional relationship to the men in their lives." Comley suggests that the perennial view of Brett the "bitch" originates with critics rather than with Hemingway. Instead, she argues, a strong female character like Brett "demonstrates not only the social freedom accruing to women . . . but also the pressures and difficulties of women in the postwar period" ("Women" 412–13). Furthermore, as scholars now recognize, there is no single heroic code in Hemingway's work but rather an "endless concern with varieties of male experience . . . complex, troubled, and troubling" (Strychacz, "Masculinity" 277). Nevertheless, as Hemingway's private correspondence demonstrates, the author sometimes well deserves his reputation as a misogynist and homophobe.[2] With no end to this conversation in sight, should scholars and students of Hemingway "come to grips"—as our colleagues in Fitzgerald studies have done—"with the fact that our man's prejudices reflect rather than transcend the prejudices of his day"? (Curnutt 159). As the work of this volume will show with its diverse approaches, readings, and perspectives, the answer is a qualified no.

For of course there *are* women: Catherine Barkley and Brett Ashley spring immediately to mind along with Maria and Pilar. Margot Macomber generates fierce debate in class discussion, as does Jig in "Hills Like White Elephants" and Catherine Bourne of *The Garden of Eden*. As soon as we make this argument, of course, we notice that these characters can be too-easily categorized, as Fiedler argued, into versions of "Dark Lady and Fair"; indeed, sometimes the familiar tropes are provided in the character's own name (or rather, her lack of a name): "girl," "The Old Lady," "Poor Old Momma," "[the] Moorish tart."

Before we concede that Fiedler was right and abandon entirely the project of teaching Hemingway in the twenty-first-century classroom, we should acknowledge that Hemingway—both the man and his work—is irrevocably overdetermined. Students read Hemingway through us; we have, in turn, read him through critics who (rightly) questioned the hero worship of an academy largely dominated by white men "who shared World War II as their most important historic memory" (Beegel, "Conclusion" 275). Work in gender and sexuality studies has asserted a much-needed reexamination of the canon and given us the tools to reread Hemingway through the lens of gender and queer theory. Hypermasculine Hemingway is now something of an old chestnut, so much so that we risk belaboring the point. Having grown accustomed to my urging to reassess Hemingway's portrayals of gender and sexuality, my own students in an upper-level undergraduate seminar began one class discussion with feigned ennui: "Are we going to do a queer reading?" a student teased good-naturedly. Our job now as feminist critics (and at this point we are all, I hope, feminist critics) is to be aware of how the gaze—Hemingway's and our own—assumes, through these many deferrals, a host of subject positions. When we take on the task of teaching Hemingway and gender, we are not simply counting the women in Hemingway's texts (and then determining if they count); we are instead looking at how considerations of gender and sexuality in Hemingway's work might revise our understandings not only of Hemingway but of modernism, authorship, the literary marketplace, popular culture, gender theory, queer theory, men's studies, and other modes of inquiry.

Just as importantly, the project of teaching Hemingway and gender asks us to consider dynamics of our own classrooms as well. Nina Baym's 1992 essay on "The Short Happy Life of Francis Macomber" left a lasting impression on me when I began teaching Hemingway, not only for her astute reading of the story but for the thoughtfulness Baym brings to the roles of graduate mentor and undergraduate instructor. She relates the disconcerting experience of observing a class led by a graduate teaching assistant who unwittingly shut down a female student's sympathetic reading of the story from the lion's perspective. In doing so, the hapless TA "reenacted, in a nonfatal but deeply political (and ... destructive) fashion" (79) the plot of the story and, with it, "precisely the matters that the text exposes and asks us to consider"(80). Following Baym's example, the essays in this volume deal not only with our readings of Hemingway but our interactions with and assumptions about our students. The essays that follow elucidate Hemingway's emergent themes as well as the ways in which we might challenge students—and ourselves—to engage them.

The reader, then, should approach the various essays in this book with an awareness that the subject of Hemingway and gender is one inherently fraught with conflict, contradiction, and, ultimately, great promise. After all, the instructor's task is not to provide students with one correct way of reading a text but rather to teach students to read critically. Likewise, these essays provide a variety of feminist and queer readings of Hemingway as well as ways to navigate the challenges of teaching students from a variety of backgrounds. Though each essay in this volume deals with specific Hemingway texts, the ideas in this collection can be broadly applied and are part of an ongoing conversation about gender and sexuality in American literature and culture.

Debra A. Moddelmog's bibliographic essay opens the collection, providing an overview of some of the important trends in the field of gender and sexuality studies and how that work has been applied in studies of Hemingway. From Moddelmog's account, we can see how the subjects of gender and sexuality are interrelated in Hemingway's work (and in Hemingway scholarship), a connection that necessitated the editorial decision to include essays on sexuality in this volume as well.

The first section of the collection considers how gender is constructed in the Hemingway canon. Joseph Fruscione's essay looks to *In Our Time* as an accessible text to introduce students to ideas about performativity. By bringing in criticism by prominent scholars of modernism to class discussions of the stories of *In Our Time*, Fruscione encourages students to situate the performance of gender in Hemingway's text within a larger cultural framework, uncovering a "problem" with gender that encompasses not only Hemingway's work but modernism itself. Problems are good: beginning with the confession that as an undergraduate he did not necessarily like Hemingway's work, Fruscione allows for initial resistance from students who come to appreciate, and write about, the texts on their own terms.

Pamela L. Caughie and Erin A. Holliday-Karre teach Hemingway's *The Garden of Eden* to women's studies students, finding the novel useful for exploring the various conceptions of gender that spanned the twentieth century, from the 1920s (the decade in which the novel is set) to the 1950s (when Hemingway worked on it) to the 1980s (when it was heavily edited for posthumous publication). The instability of the text exemplifies the instability of cultural concepts of gender. Material concerns figure into Belinda Wheeler's pedagogy as well; presenting Hemingway's "The Short Happy Life of Francis Macomber" in its original publication context, Wheeler defamiliarizes the frequently anthologized story and its canonical author. Tasking students to consider not just the text but also its illustrations and the advertisements for beauty products that appear in the pages of *Cosmopolitan*, Wheeler encourages her students to formulate readings of Margot Macomber that view the much-maligned character against the gender roles played out in the paratextual matter.

John Fenstermaker suggests, too, that we might read one of Hemingway's best-known characters within a larger context, namely, that we should consider the various domestic scenes in which we find Nick Adams as he matures from boy to man across the entire story "cycle." Reading this Nick Adams cycle thematically and holistically, Fenstermaker argues that we come to understand Nick best in relationship to others: as son, husband, and father, and that, together, the stories offer an ultimately "hopeful" version of a masculine ideal. Sarah B. Hardy, too, entertains the possibility of a masculine ideal in Hemingway's work as part of her approach to teaching Hemingway at an all-male college. However, through a comparative reading of Nick Adams and his father in "Indian Camp" and "Fathers and Sons," Hardy's students ultimately come to question their initial "monolithic" definitions of masculinity, exchanging them for an understanding of masculinity as "contextual and constructed."

While Hardy's students confront their existing familiarity with Hemingway, Douglas Sheldon relates a teaching experience in which his students, second-language learners of English, were hindered initially by the utter foreignness of Hemingway's characters. The relatively short and accessible prose of "A Very Short Story" belies a host of complicated cultural assumptions. Sheldon's experience navigating the concerns of Saudi and Chinese students, whose proficient language skills nevertheless proved insufficient to understanding the relationship between the unmarried main characters, demonstrates how Hemingway's deceptively simple prose can provoke challenging discussions.

Because the concepts of gender and sexuality are inextricably bound, this collection offers three essays on teaching Hemingway and sexuality. Joshua Weiss relates the recurring questions his students have about *The Sun Also Rises* as they try to understand the enigmatic narrator and the concept of *aficion*. Weiss argues that the religious ceremonies and allusions throughout the novel help us to understand the triangulation of desire between Jake, Brett, and Pedro. This reading of the novel not only answers the students' specific questions but also presents Hemingway as a Catholic writer and introduces students to queer readings of the text.

Much as Caughie and Holliday-Karre used *The Garden of Eden* to explore the changing conception of gender in the twentieth century, Carl Eby finds *The Garden of Eden* a useful text to introduce students to readings of psychosexual and gender issues in *A Farewell to Arms*. Reading the posthumously published *Eden* before they read the 1929 bestseller, Eby's students are prepared to read Catherine Barkley as a "split-off other-sex" alter ego, an interpretation they might have resisted had they not first encountered the non-normative sexualities portrayed in the later text. Catherine R. Mintler, too, uses a theoretical lens to explore the character of Catherine Bourne, applying foundational works of feminist criticism to her reading of the "economically empowered consumer artist." Mintler refutes the idea that Hemingway's female characters are weak;

rather, she argues, Catherine demonstrates the author's criticism of a society that undermines women's artistic production, a feminist reading that can be applied to other characters in the Hemingway canon as well.

The last section of the collection considers Hemingway and women. Providing a counterpoint to Fenstermaker's consideration of the domestic in the Nick Adams cycle, and taking into account work by feminist theorist Lauren Berlant, Crystal Gorham Doss examines how Hemingway's female characters resist traditional female "genres" of the domestic, the sentimental, and even the New Woman and flapper in favor of a more complex identity that both resists and reflects the conflicting models of female identity available to women in the first half of the twentieth century. Sara Kosiba answers the question of whether Hemingway and women writers can co-exist in the classroom with a definitive yes. Taking a biographical approach, Kosiba looks at Hemingway's professional relationships with his female contemporaries and argues for the pairing of Hemingway and women writers in American literature syllabi. Reading Hemingway alongside Martha Gellhorn, Josephine Herbst, Dawn Powell, and Eudora Welty, for example, resists the delimiting view of Hemingway as suspicious of female influence.

Finally, we close out the collection with a personal narrative by Hilary Kovar Justice about teaching Hemingway in the twenty-first-century classroom. Justice relates one student's acquittal of Hemingway on charges of misogyny, a journey that illustrates in practice the points that Doss, Kosiba, and the other contributors to this volume theorize: namely, that it is time, perhaps, to set our preconceptions about Ernest Hemingway aside and to enjoy, at last, the critical distance—and opportunities for further critical inquiry—afforded by the nearly century-long separation between the publication of *In Our Time* and our own time.

Notes

1. For an illustrated study of hypermasculine Hemingway in the popular imagination, including the June 1956 cover of *Modern Man* magazine from which this blurb is taken, see David M. Earle, *All Man! Hemingway, 1950s Men's Magazines, and the Masculine Persona* (Kent, OH: Kent State UP, 2009), 3.

2. For a comprehensive scholarly edition of all of Hemingway's known correspondence see Sandra Spanier, ed., *The Letters of Ernest Hemingway* (Cambridge: Cambridge UP, 2011, 2013, 2015, and forthcoming).

State of the Field

Gender Studies, Sexuality Studies, and Hemingway

Debra A. Moddelmog

Considerations of gender and sexuality have been central to understanding Ernest Hemingway's life and work from the start of his career in the 1920s to today. One reason for this focus is that Hemingway's special brand of masculinity created both a fascination with and a suspicion about the author's identity and the politics of gender representation in his work. After the publication of his first novel, *The Sun Also Rises* (1926), Zelda Fitzgerald reportedly claimed of Hemingway that no one could be that masculine (Reynolds, *The American Homecoming* 46); the next year in reviewing his short story collection *Men Without Women*, Virginia Woolf called him "self-consciously virile" ("An Essay in Criticism" 54). Soon after, Gertrude Stein wrote in the *Autobiography of Alice B. Toklas* (1933), "what a book ... would be the real story of Hemingway, not those he writes but the confessions of the real Ernest Hemingway. It would be for another audience than the audience Hemingway now has but it would be very wonderful" (265–66).

Hemingway's reputation as a man's man and the concurrent view that such a persona was a mask hiding a compromised masculinity grew only more pronounced over time. In its March 1934 issue, *Vanity Fair* called him "America's own literary cave man; hard-drinking, hard-fighting, hard-loving—all for art's sake" and offered readers a Hemingway "Neanderthal man" paper doll that might be clothed as a bullfighter, a fisherman, a soldier, or a hard-drinking representative of the Lost Generation (Alajalov 29). The previous year, the critic Max Eastman famously had written in the *New Republic* that it was a "critical commonplace that Hemingway lacks the serene confidence that he *is* a full-sized man" and accused him of wearing "false hair on his chest" (96). This statement so infuriated Hemingway that four years later, when he encountered Eastman in the office of editor Maxwell Perkins, Hemingway apparently ripped open his shirt to prove he had hair on his chest, opened Eastman's to show he didn't, and then hit Eastman in the face with a book. "This image of Hemingway as he-man has proven resilient, continually seductive in the popular media," as David Earle illustrates in his examination (2009) of Hemingway's representation as a masculine ideal circulated by midcentury pulp men's magazines (4). A number of scholars have thus shown how Hemingway produced his public persona with the help of a rising celebrity and commodity culture (e.g., del Gizzo, "Glow-in-the-Dark"; Earle; Glass; Leff; Raeburn; Trogdon; Turner). At the same time, Hemingway's aggressive tough-guy image has sparked theories that he was not the man he made himself out to be; for example, in 1983, Gerry Brenner proposed that Hemingway, while clearly heterosexual, harbored a latent homoeroticism based in a fixation on his father.

Another reason why gender and sexuality have been at the forefront of critical work on Hemingway and his writing is that he put them there. Hemingway was a member of a generation that witnessed significant transformations in gender roles and conceptualizations of sexuality. Born in 1899, he grew up during what has been called the "first wave of feminism," when women fought for and gained important political rights, including the right to vote, and experienced greater freedoms in the social sphere, such as smoking, drinking, driving, and riding a bicycle. The New Woman, the "It Girl," and the flapper became notable female figures representing these expanded freedoms and opportunities.[1] Hemingway's mother, Grace Hall Hemingway, was in many ways a perfect transitional figure of this time in that she gave up a promising future as an opera singer, in part, to marry and become a mother, but she also earned her own income by giving music lessons in the Hemingway home, and she expressed her approval of feminist politics by joining the Suburban Civics and Equal Suffrage Club and attending suffragette meetings while visiting Nantucket in 1909 (Barlowe, "Hemingway's Gender Training" 122–29).

Changing roles for women meant the introduction of new models of masculinity. White men were encouraged to break with Victorian models of restrained manliness and embrace more powerful forms of masculinity, partly in response to challenges to their social dominance from women, African Americans, and an influx of immigrants from Eastern and Southern Europe as well as from Latin America, the Caribbean, and Asia. Other factors contributed to a growing sense that the social order was rapidly changing and that white masculinity might be more vulnerable than previously thought. Among these were a faster-paced way of life that was said to cause a variety of nervous disorders, especially neurasthenia; the movement of masses of people (including the "Great Migration" of African Americans) from rural areas to urban centers; the rise of monopoly capitalism in which workers increasingly became parts of a bureaucratic machine; and the enormous devastation of World War I which killed millions of men worldwide, including over 120,000 Americans.

Marching hand in hand with changing gender roles at the turn of the twentieth century were modern ideas about sexuality. Dating replaced chaperoned courting as the primary way that young men and women spent romantic time together, providing more opportunities for privacy and an acceptance of more intimate behaviors, such as petting. Marriage reformers and sex scientists argued that women's sexual desire was just as strong as men's, an idea that bolstered a redefinition of marriage as a companionate union grounded in the mutual sexual pleasure of the couple. Hemingway, like many modernist writers, became enthralled with new theories about gender, sex, and sexuality introduced by late-nineteenth- and early-twentieth-century sexologists. These sex theorists, as well as Sigmund Freud and his psychoanalytic school of thought, developed a language for sexual matters (e.g., Oedipal complex, repression, congenital) and a taxonomy of sexual types (e.g., homosexual, heterosexual, fetishist, and masochist) that governed Euro-American understanding of sex and sexuality for many years and that still have relevance. In 1920–21, Hemingway avidly recommended the works of Havelock Ellis, the well-known British sexologist, both to his friends and to his fiancée Hadley Richardson. His good friend Bill Smith claimed not to be interested in Ellis's "degenerates," and Hadley wasn't sure all those "evils and diseases" were "a right way" for her (Reynolds, *The Young Hemingway* 120). But Hemingway pursued his sexological education undeterred. Both his library and his writing reflect his lifelong exploration of the complexities of male and female desire, the so-called sexual perversions, and the sexual mores and practices of other cultures, such as the Kamba and Masai ethnic groups of Africa.[2]

The view that Hemingway's central subject was men and masculinity and that he was an influential recorder of sex, gender, and sexual norms of his age has thus characterized scholarly work on Hemingway from its beginnings until today. However, the particular slant this work has taken and the conclusions it has drawn have shifted dramatically over time for two main reasons.

First, as a field (or, more accurately, a set of interlocking fields), gender and sexuality studies has undergone major transformations since the 1970s when feminism began to produce complex theories about gender and subjectivity that were used to (re)read texts; with each critical turn, new approaches to thinking about these topics, including in Hemingway's life and fiction, have been generated. One of feminism's early central insights was that sex (male/female, man/woman) should be distinguished from gender (masculine/feminine). Sex was perceived to have biological origins (hormones, chromosomes, anatomy), whereas gender was aligned with cultural roles and norms that men and women were expected to follow. Over time feminists have critiqued various assumptions of the sex/gender formulation—for example, its presumed universality, the idea that sex is solely a matter of biology, and the notion that biology constitutes an unmediated and objective condition. To theorize and account for some of these complications, feminism has consequently developed a variety of paths for the study of women, sex, and gender: cultural feminism, French feminism (*écriture féminine*), materialist feminism, poststructural feminism, postcolonial feminism, ecofeminism, Black feminism, Xicanisma, and womanism, to name just a few.

Even the overlapping but newer fields of gender studies, sexuality studies, and queer theory have evolved dramatically since entering the critical scene. Gender studies, with origins in poststructural feminism, views gender as a social construction or a performative effect of regulatory practices and socially instituted norms rather than a biological trait or a singular cultural acquisition (Butler 23). It conceives of masculinity and femininity in the plural (masculinities, femininities) and has devoted considerable attention to female masculinity and the masculinities of men of color (e.g., Halberstam; Stecopoulos and Uebel). There is now a well-established field of masculinity studies. Sexuality studies deals with sexual identity (heterosexuality/homosexuality/bisexuality) as well as with sexual norms and sexual expression. It has a long history within feminism (e.g., debates over whether pornography is always demeaning to women) but also can be found in fields such as gay and lesbian studies, which emerged in the 1970s as an academic discipline focused on exploring the suppressed histories, experiences, and cultural work of gays and lesbians (e.g., Katz; Faderman).

Queer theory took academic shape in the 1990s as an approach that resists the identity-based politics of gay and lesbian studies in favor of messier notions of gender and sexuality that often actively challenge normalizing practices and their effects (e.g., Butler; Sedgwick; Warner). As David Halperin put it in 1995, "Queer is by definition *whatever* is at odds with the normal, the legitimate, the dominant. *There is nothing in particular to which it necessarily refers.* It is an identity without an essence ... describing a horizon of possibility whose precise extent and heterogeneous scope cannot in principle be delimited in advance" (16). Recently, a "queer-of-color critique" has arisen within the field. Proponents of this perspective, such as José Esteban Muñoz (1999), Roderick Ferguson (2003), and Ernesto Javier Martínez (2013), argue that race and class are indissoluble components of gender and sexuality, and must thus be considered central to queer analysis. They also trace their antecedents to civil rights movements of the '60s and '70s as well as to women-of-color feminism and assert the transformative value of paradigms and perspectives produced by queer-of-color artists and writers.

A second reason for the revolution of critical thinking about gender and sexuality in Hemingway's life and fiction has been the steady publication of writings that were unpublished, and often unfinished, when Hemingway died in 1961. As will be explained in more detail below, these posthumous publications—such as *A Moveable Feast* (1964; especially the restored edition of 2009), *Islands in the Stream* (1970), "The Last Good Country" (1972), *The Garden of Eden* (1986), *True at First Light* (1999), and *Under Kilimanjaro* (2005)—as well as the manuscripts from which they are drawn, have revealed Hemingway to be much more invested in transgressive forms of gender and sexuality than previously thought. This realization has, in turn, inspired critics to reconsider gender and sexuality throughout his oeuvre. The exploration of gender and sexuality in Hemingway's work and life has thus become one of the most interesting, lively, and often controversial areas of research in Hemingway studies today.

The following overview of some major trends in Hemingway scholarship takes into account these intersecting factors of new and evolving critical approaches as well as the posthumously published and archival material. The trends overlap, and interestingly, many of them never disappear completely from Hemingway criticism even though they take radical new forms, thereby reflecting the viewpoints of the times in which they have been formulated as well as the complexity and durability of competing perceptions of Hemingway and his work.

One of the most enduring arguments about Hemingway's fiction has been that it repeatedly features a male protagonist who has been wounded both physically and psychologically. Philip Young set forth the most influential version of this position in *Ernest Hemingway* (1952) and *Ernest Hemingway: A Reconsideration* (1966). According to Young, this wounding occurs most traumatically during the protagonist's service in World War I but can occasionally also be traced to his childhood where he was subjected to the unpredictable and senseless violence of the modern world. The wounded Hemingway hero (e.g., Nick Adams, Jake Barnes, Frederic Henry) is typically juxtaposed with a "code hero," the man who has found his own principled and understated (too much talking ruins things) way to deal with the misery, disorder, and violence of the modern world. The code hero exemplifies the man who lives with "grace under pressure," and part of his function is to teach the Hemingway hero how to live this way as well; the skillful bullfighter is a good example of this figure. Young's argument—that these two models of men, the vulnerable and traumatized Hemingway protagonist and the stoic code hero who, in later Hemingway works, becomes a kind of parody of his earlier incarnations (think Robert Wilson in "The Short Happy Life of Francis Macomber")—has an entrenched formula about masculinity in Hemingway's work, which has been hard to break from, even though critics have periodically revised it, have collapsed the Hemingway hero and the code hero into one, and have repeatedly pronounced its demise. The persistence of the code hero in Hemingway criticism suggests that he (or, occasionally, she) remains useful, a reminder that the modern world is one in which values must be created and not simply enacted.

Another early debate about gender and sexuality in Hemingway's work that has developed many sides over the years has to do with his portrayal of women. In 1939, Edmund Wilson observed Hemingway's "growing antagonism" toward women; a couple of years later, he distinguished a "split attitude" ("Gauge of Morale" 193), with Hemingway's heroines falling into two categories: the "submissive infra-Anglo-Saxon women that make his heroes such perfect mistresses" and "American bitches of the most soul-destroying sort"[3] ("Gauge of Morale" 194n1). This view of Hemingway's female characters became a basic premise of Hemingway criticism for decades to come. Some readers accepted the dichotomy and its gender politics, following Wilson's lead in naming characters such as Brett Ashley and Margot Macomber "bitches" (Fiedler 319) or "bitch goddesses" (Aldridge 24), "Circes" (e.g., Baker, *The Writer as Artist* 87; Gladstein 59; Moreland 186), and "castrators" (Lebowitz 195), and viewing characters such as Catherine Barkley (*A Farewell to Arms*), Liz Coates ("Up in Michigan"), and Maria (*For Whom the Bell Tolls*) as "erotic fantasies" (Rogers 248), "divine lollypops" (Hackett 33), or "inflated rubber doll" women (Bell 114). Some attributed the binary to Hemingway's inability to conceive of complex women and to his preference for homosocial environments. For instance, in 1960, Leslie Fiedler concluded that Hemingway "does not know what to do with [women] beyond taking them to bed" (*Love and Death* 317). He determined that for Hemingway and his heroes, "[o]nly the dead woman" is revered because she "becomes neither a bore nor a mother" (318).

These questions about Hemingway's women were vigorously taken up by women scholars and feminist critics of the 1970s and '80s. In an interpretation of *A Farewell to Arms* that sounds strikingly similar to Fiedler's, Judith Fetterley

(1978) concluded that male life is the only life that counts in the novel and that women reading it are given the message that "the only good woman is a dead one, and even then there are questions"[4] (*Resisting Reader* 71). Others quickly followed suit. Faith Pullin (1983), for example, insisted that Hemingway's work "reveals a progressive repudiation of people in general and of women in particular" (191). Some feminist critics measured Hemingway's women not against the "real" world but against Hemingway's own psychic struggles with women and gender differences. From this perspective, the disturbing character traits of Hemingway's women were projections of Hemingway's own fears and anxieties. Female characters such as Brett Ashley and Helen of "Snows of Kilimanjaro" (1936) became representations of Hemingway's personal challenges with his mother, his wives, or other women in his life. While such arguments added depth to an understanding of Hemingway's creative process, some feminist and feminist-influenced critics in the 1980s became disenchanted with his work, arguing for a demotion of Hemingway within the canon or even a complete ejection from it (see, for example, Buell; and also Merrill's rejoinder).

Yet, at about the same time, feminist scholars began to present a different view of Hemingway's women, finding them to be more complex and diverse than previous critics had. Although arguments for such complexity can occasionally be found in earlier scholarship (e.g., Alan Holder's 1963 article "The Other Hemingway"), these critics considered Hemingway's women within the historical, cultural, and personal contexts of the characters, suggesting that they presented positive values and/or acted out of frustration with their limited opportunities, limitations imposed either by the misguided men in their lives or by the patriarchal, sexist, and heterosexist society in which they lived. For example, in 1980, Linda Wagner-Martin proposed that Hemingway's early fiction (written before his father's suicide in 1928) featured full-fledged female characters who were admirably heroic as they dealt with serious relationship issues such as abusive husbands (Brett) or unsympathetic partners or lovers (the American woman in "Cat in the Rain," Jig in "Hills Like White Elephants"). The next year Joyce Wexler responded to Fetterley's charge of misogyny by identifying Catherine as a fully developed Hemingway hero whose own self-fashioned value system precipitates Frederic's growth and development. Sandra Spanier (1987) expanded this idea by claiming that Catherine is actually the novel's code hero, who shows grace under pressure and teaches Frederic how to live in a chaotic world by developing individualized roles and rituals.

In *Cassandra's Daughters: The Women in Hemingway* (1984), Roger Whitlow made an extended case that almost all of Hemingway's women, including his minor female characters, are "interesting, dramatic characters, who offer a vision of life that is more humane and decent than that offered by the 'heroes' with whom they spend—and often waste—their lives" (113). In "Hemingway's Women's Movement" (1984), Charles J. Nolan also argued that Hemingway's sympathies frequently lie with women who suffer a variety of mistreatments. Even Margot Macomber, whom critics had seen as one of the most unscrupulous of Hemingway's female characters, was recuperated by Kenneth Johnston's claim (1983) that she was only trying to save her husband when she accidentally shot him dead and by Nina Baym's argument (1990) that Margot's situation (as well as the lion's) asks us to consider the hypocrisies and inconsistencies of the dominant male ethos. As Jamie Barlowe noted in 1993 when summarizing the importance of feminist work in Hemingway studies, "'Hemingway' is a more complex and valuable metaphor of our culture and history when his texts and their critical contexts are also re-read and de-stabilized than when he is only read and re-read in ways which re-explain his self-explanations" (33). Thus, by the turn of the twenty-first century, it was generally accepted that women and feminist critics had been at the forefront of a radical re-visioning of gender in Hemingway's works. In their introduction to *Hemingway and Women: Female Critics and the Female Voice* (2002), Lawrence R. Broer and Gloria Holland proclaimed that women scholars have had a "salubrious impact" (ix) on Hemingway studies and have shown that "the author's portraits of women and his deepest understanding of sex and love are a continuing tribute to [Hemingway's] complexity" (xiv).

A third major trend in gender and sexuality approaches to Hemingway's work has centered on his portrayal of love as it is realized (or, more commonly, not realized) in heterosexual relationships. Early on, critics noted a pattern in Hemingway's fiction of an idealized heterosexual relationship that was prematurely ended, often through the death of one of the lovers or an insurmountable circumstance, such as Jake Barnes's genital wounding. In 1965, Robert Lewis argued that in Hemingway's early work, romantic and sexual love (eros) were destructive, whereas brotherly love (agape) held more promise for lasting union; however, by the time of his last major work, *The Old Man and the Sea* (1952), Hemingway had worked out an ethic for modern living and loving that consisted of a reciprocal blend of eros and agape. Brian Harding suggested in 1990 that Hemingway's stories repeatedly portray the failure of love but, paradoxically, attest to the value of what has been corrupted or lost (114). Scholars have also argued that Hemingway's love stories share affinities with the medieval courtly romance, with its notions of chivalry, sacrifice, passion, and a private, idyllic world (see, for example, Moreland). In 2002, Linda Wagner-Martin proposed that throughout his life, Hemingway wrote romances in which his real subject was eroticism: "What he seems to have meant by 'love' was erotic desire, sexuality blended with the chivalric concept of courtly love; he seems to have wanted both, synthesized into some all-encompassing, completely satisfying, unquestioned and unquestioning emotion" ("Romance" 55).[5]

In contrast to those who situated Hemingway's conception of love in a lost or medieval past, others insisted that his view of love and sex was firmly grounded in contemporary realities. Rena Sanderson (1996) claimed that Hemingway's works can be viewed as "studies of the lives and relationships of New Men and New Women complicated by distinctly modern problems" ("Hemingway and Gender History" 176). Prominent among these modern problems were those related to sexuality, especially since in the early twentieth-century, women had begun to assert their rights to sexual pleasure, sexual autonomy, divorce, birth control, and decision making about their own bodies. From Brett Ashley, who maintains that being unfaithful and sleeping around is "the way I'm made" (*Sun Also Rises* 62) to Marie Morgan who declares after making love to her husband, Harry, "I could do that all night if a man was built that way. I'd like to do it and never sleep" (*To Have and Have Not* 115), Hemingway's fiction is, as Michael Reynolds notes, replete with women with strong sexual appetites (*Young Hemingway* 120-24). Yet many in the modern world also found it difficult to break from Victorian standards of morality and social hygiene expectations of pre-marital "purity" and marital fidelity. Wendy Martin (2002) has suggested that these contradictions and confusions about women's and men's sexual and social roles are especially prominent in *Sun*, in which "men cry and women swear; Brett aggressively expresses her sexual desires, while her lovers wait to be chosen; she likes action . . . whereas the men appreciate the pleasure of sipping brandy in a quiet café" (56).

Although the three trends traced above have been central to Hemingway scholarship on gender and sexuality all along, it is no exaggeration to claim that in the late 1980s and 1990s, they underwent a sea change, leading to the development of several new trends as well. This re-direction was precipitated by a convergence of several factors: (1) the emergence of gender and queer studies within literary and cultural studies; (2) a biographical focus on parts of Hemingway's life that had been previously subordinated or submerged; (3) the opening of Hemingway's papers to researchers in 1975; and (4) the publication of new work, especially the heavily edited *The Garden of Eden* (1986), Hemingway's unfinished novel about gender role reversals, racial transformation, same-sex attraction, fetishism, polygamy, and other non-normative desires and dispositions.

While a few scholars, for instance J. F. Kobler (1970), had previously pointed out that some of Hemingway's fiction contains sympathetic portrayals of sexually transgressive subjects, *Garden* propelled an extensive examination of this topic not only in the novel and the manuscript from which it derived but in all of Hemingway's work. Critics noted that a number of Hemingway's short stories, many of them generally neglected by earlier scholars, deal with same-sex desire (e.g., "The Sea Change," "The Mother of a Queen," "A Simple Enquiry," "Mr. and Mrs. Elliot," "A Lack of Passion") and that almost all of Hemingway's novels include some interest in gender reversals, identity merging, and hair dyeing, cutting, or lengthening that are central to the action of *Garden*. Androgyny (Spilka 1990; J. Kennedy 1991; Broer 2011), deep anxieties about traditional gender and sexual binaries (Messent 1992), fetishism (Eby, *Fetishism* 1999), the tension between the permeable boundaries of the homosexual and the heterosexual (Moddelmog, *Reading Desire* 1999), and male masochism (Fantina 2005) were all explored as keys to Hemingway's writing, reinforcing the claim made by Nancy Comley and Robert Scholes in *Hemingway's Genders* (1994) that "sexual truths, for Hemingway, lie not at the center of 'standard' heterosexual practice ... but at the margins: in what the society of Hemingway's parents would have called perversion or miscegenation" (77).[6]

Several critics—for example, Bert Bender, Deirdre Anne McVicker Pettipiece, Debra Moddelmog ("We Live in a Country"), and Jennifer Haytock—have connected Hemingway's interest in these sexual truths to his knowledge of sex theories of his day, specifically the ideas of Havelock Ellis but also, in the case of Bender, those of evolutionary psychology. Others noted that the psychosexual concerns of Hemingway's writing are often intertwined with matters of creativity and artistry. For example, drawing heavily on the archival materials in the Hemingway Collection and in the Scribner's archives at Princeton, Rose Marie Burwell (1996) argued that Hemingway envisioned four of his posthumously published works—*A Moveable Feast* (1964), *Islands in the Stream* (1970), *The Garden of Eden* (1986), and the African book—as an extended "portrait of the artist," with dangerous families, androgyny, and other gender/sexual taboos, serving as unifying themes. Hilary K. Justice (2006) proposed that all of Hemingway's writing, published and unpublished, might be viewed as a lifelong exploration of the public (reflected in the author who writes "authentic" books based on observation) and the private (represented by the writer who works from personal experience). This exploration reaches a culminating convergence in *Garden*, which presents a "far more sophisticated understanding of the ways in which publication complicates creativity, whether textual or sexual" (7).

Scholars who examined the manuscripts of *Garden* in the Hemingway Collection at the JFK Library disclosed that a number of editorial decisions had muted some of the more radical offerings of the novel related to gender, sexuality, and race.[7] Still, the revelations of the published version were enough to convince many critics that Hemingway was not the writer they had presumed him to be, although some have since warned against drawing conclusions that the "new" Hemingway is necessarily progressive (e.g., Altman). At about the same time, the revisionary and controversial biography of Kenneth Lynn (1987) and the scholarly work on androgyny by Mark Spilka (1990) proposed that Hemingway's own early experience with gender reversal—his mother dressed and coiffed him and his elder sister as same-sex twins until Hemingway was six or seven—was the secret behind not only his compensatory hypermasculinity but also his identification with "the feminine."[8] Others downplayed or rejected the theory that the twinning had a major effect on Hemingway's psyche and advanced different reasons for his gender and sexual interests. Michael Reynolds suggested, for example, that the liberated and sensual world of Paris that Hemingway encountered in the 1920s enticed him to explore "forbidden" erotic desires (*The Paris Years* 230; see also Bonds). A few critics noted that Hemingway and at least two, possibly three, of his wives participated in their own cross-gender sexual pursuits, as revealed in a variety of sources such as Mary Hemingway's autobiography, *How It Was* (1976), Hemingway's letters, and "The Secret Pleasures" chapter of *A Moveable Feast*, published in the 2009 version of the memoir (see, for example, Spilka, "Hemingway's Quarrel"; J. Kennedy; Burwell; and Eby, *Fetishism* and "He Felt the Change").

Garden's publication in 1986 and this adjusted biographical perspective thus inspired a rereading of gender and sexuality in much of Hemingway's work, but this resurgence also relied heavily upon, and was even made possible by, theories and techniques provided by the fields of gender and queer studies, which gained footing in British and American literary studies from 1990 on. For instance, critics influenced by the premises of gender studies have proposed that masculinity in Hemingway's writing is not a self-evident accomplishment but, rather, a rhetorical or socially constructed performance. Greg Forter (2001) contended that masculinity in Hemingway's work is staged around a tension between a modern sense of fractured masculinity and a melancholic sense that there was once a heroic form of masculinity that cannot be recovered. As Thomas Strychacz has also argued (2003, 2008, 2012), Hemingway's fiction presents masculinity as a theatrical performance involving a complex negotiation between male characters, readers, and cultural codes of manhood (*Dangerous*

Masculinities, Hemingway's Theaters). Such an understanding revises our view of the code hero as well:

> Men are not born with a Code; if they are to become "men," they must acquire one and constantly renew it. Therefore a Code marks something of an existential predicament. Masculinity can no longer be whole and uncompromised: it must be represented. And representations can be temporary.... Nostalgia for a time when masculinity was undamaged and unchallenged competes with the melancholic knowledge that there never *was* such a time. (Strychacz, *Hemingway's Theaters* 279)

Daniel Worden (2011) follows this line of thinking that masculinity in Hemingway is both performative and historically situated but determines that Hemingway is most interested in a productive masculinity that comes into being when subjects "mold their emotions, bodies, and styles as if they were themselves works of art" (15). Worden then explores the formation of this stylized masculinity in *Death in the Afternoon* (1932).

Queer readings (even when not expressly named as such) of Hemingway's writings have also taken various shape and grown in prominence over time. Several scholars have examined sexual and gender inversions in *Sun* (Blackmore; Buckley; Cathy and Arnold Davidson; Elliott, "Performance Art"; and Moddelmog, *Reading Desire*), the gender-bending (Traber) and queer subplots and sensibility of *Farewell* (Cohen; Eby, *Fetishism;* Elliott, "*Farewell*"; Hatten; Hewson, "Real Story"; Mandel; Moddelmog, "We Live in a Country"; Takeuchi; Vernon, *Soldiers*), and the role that *For Whom the Bell Tolls* might have played as "a rehearsal ground for the more conscious experiments" with gender and sexuality undertaken in Hemingway's later work such as *Islands in the Stream* (1970) and *Garden* (Hewson, "Matter of Love or Death" 172; see also Vernon, *Hemingway's Second War*). John S. Bak (2010) has applied the insights of queer theory to Hemingway's *Sun* to argue that Jake is a "queer heterosexual" (215) man whose desire and performed gender does not reveal the truth about who he is—to others and, at times, to himself. Valerie Rohy suggests that *Garden* reveals that "the story of heteronormative masculinity has its own queer moment" ("A Darker Past" 118), its own "prehistory of perversity" (119); and more recently, she has proposed that critics have pathologized non-normative gendering and male femininity in Hemingway, despite evidence that he was receptive to these possibilities ("Hemingway, Literalism, and Transgender Reading"; see also Long). It is also important to consider that at least some of this new queer critical work is focused not so much on Hemingway or his male characters finally being pulled out of some kind of "closet," but on the societal and scientific limitations placed around gender and sexual expression that created a closet in the first place (e.g., Tanimoto, "Queering" and "Subversion"). Much of Hemingway's work, but especially his posthumous writing, reveals that he endeavored to counter the authority of sexological, psychoanalytical, religious, and social understandings of his and his characters' behaviors and desires.

The posthumous works have also sparked a reconsideration of Hemingway's views of race as it intersects with gender and sexuality. Over the years, some critics have condemned Hemingway's portrayals of the "racial Other," such as the American Indian girls Trudy and Prudy, who are eager sex partners of Nick Adams in stories such as "Ten Indians" and "Fathers and Sons," or the "emasculated" Jewish Robert Cohn. But since the publication of *Garden* with its focus on African sexuality and racial change, examinations of race throughout Hemingway's work have become more common; and his perspective on race, especially in relation to gender and sexuality, has increasingly been viewed as complex rather than simplistic or stereotypical.

In 1992, Toni Morrison explored Hemingway's investment in "Africanism—the fetishizing of color, the transfer to blackness of the power of illicit sexuality, chaos, madness, impropriety, anarchy, strangeness, and helpless, hapless desire" (80–81). Morrison's influential argument focused on male "black nurses" who either enable or impede the white male protagonists of Hemingway's works, and on the cross-gender story of *The Garden of Eden* that plays out within an "Africanist field." Several scholars have shown how Hemingway's heroes, such as Harry in "Snows of Kilimanjaro" (1936) and Francis Macomber and Robert Wilson in "The Short Happy Life of Francis Macomber" (1936), forge their masculinity by exercising their white (and often colonial) privilege over racialized others (Moddelmog, *Reading Desire*; DuCille). Others have suggested that white masculinity in Hemingway's work is constituted in opposition to some kind of "lack" or "threat" assigned to the racial or ethnic other. Ian Marshall (2012), for example, maintains that Hemingway's construction of masculinity is limited to white men because black men are never granted the will or the capacity for choice that must precede risk taking. On the menacing side of the equation, Keith Gandal (2008) has proposed that the social and sexual threat that Cohn poses to Jake Barnes is a consequence of the egalitarian practices of the U.S. military during WWI which gave ethnic American men like Cohn increased status and created a sense of masculine competition in white writers like Hemingway who had seen no actual combat action.

Other readers have argued that the politics of racial representation and its intersections with gender and sexuality in Hemingway's work and life tell a more complicated story than that of a modernist author simply immersing himself in the "mythos of white superiority" (Dudley 7), ignoring the humanity of racialized others, or investing in primitivist notions. For instance, a decade after Morrison made her famous argument, Cary Wolfe (2002) countered that she had overlooked the way in which Catherine's apparently stereotypical view of African sexuality is undone by her recognition (crystallized in her response to David's elephant story) that the white, patriarchal, colonial enterprise functions on a "sacrificial economy" (255) that links women, blacks, children, and species. Identifying a subversive potential of the Jewish Robert Cohn, Jeremy Kaye (2006) has proposed that Cohn performs white masculinity so well that he exposes it as a construct rather than an essential identity (51). Marc Dudley (2012) posits that early on Hemingway discerned that race was a "construct," and many of his works reveal him "turn[ing] conventional knowledge on its ear as he transposes the civilized and the savage and skillfully shifts the color line" (11), thereby deconstructing the superiority of the great white man.

Critics have also reconsidered the role of race in Hemingway's own psychosexual makeup, especially since the publication of his "African book," produced first in abridged form as *True at First Light* (1999) and then in a more comprehensive version as *Under Kilimanjaro* (2005). Hemingway sometimes tried to adopt other racial identities; several times he insisted he was part American Indian, and during his 1953–54 African safari, recounted in *True* and *Kilimanjaro*, he was so serious about joining the Kamba ethnic group that his wife, Mary, had to remind him that he was a respected white man who must give up the fantasy of changing his race (see, for example, Strong; Eby, *Fetishism* and "He Felt the Change"). According to some critics, Hemingway's desire to join the African "brotherhood" was an effect of his exhaustion with the overly masculine persona that had become his public identity by the 1950s. As Suzanne del Gizzo puts it, in insisting on becoming Kamba, Hemingway made "a thorough-going attempt to distance himself from seemingly non-negotiable identity markers" (23) such as whiteness and masculinity, which were central to his commodified image as "America's No. 1 He Man" (18) and literary star. Others have proposed that Hemingway's second safari to Africa transformed his views of race, gender, sexuality, and colonialism. For example, Jeremiah Kitunda (2008, 2012) suggests that in Africa, Hemingway had a *"transvaluation* of experience" ("African Book" 113) in which he created new standards and principles for evaluating cultural norms, including those related to gender roles and sexuality, such as norms about remarriage and polygamy (see also Kitunda, "Love is a Dunghill"). Nghana Lewis (2006) makes a similar argument in claiming that Hemingway's second African trip inaugurated a "fictional reverse migration" (462) through which he finally apprehended the material realities of the African people and developed a "sexual antiphony" (465) with Debba (his African "fiancée") based not in primitivist or colonialist myths but in an understanding of her identity and agency as an African woman. In his African book, we thus find Hemingway contemplating the relativism of Western gender and sexual "truths," given that homosexuality, miscegenation, and polygamy are an accepted part of life in some areas of the world.

There are, of course, other interpretive approaches that have produced important new ways of understanding Hemingway and his oeuvre—e.g., animal studies, disability studies, ecocritical studies, and postcolonial studies—and, as the above review indicates, many of these approaches have been embedded in or combined with feminist, gender, and queer perspectives (see also, for example, Beegel, "Santiago" and "Second Growth"; Tyler; Fore; Moddelmog, *Reading Desire*). Even Hemingway's style and aesthetics, supposedly well-worn topics, have lately been the subject of some exciting new work. Given that Hemingway's minimalist style has been viewed as constitutive of the model of heteromasculinity that his writing promotes, it's not surprising that some of the recent work on gender and sexuality has reconsidered the causes, meaning, and "affect" of this style (e.g., Haralson; Strychacz, *Hemingway's Theaters*; St. Pierre). The in-progress publication of all of Hemingway's letters, over 6,000 by Cambridge University Press under the general editorship of Sandra Spanier, promises to offer additional insights into the complexity of gender and sexuality in Hemingway's life and writing.

This essay began with the observation that gender and sexuality have been central to the study of Hemingway from the beginning of his career; clearly, the diverse criticism and scholarship in this area have been invaluable in helping scholars identify, grapple with, and even appreciate *el nuevo Hemingway*, which from the 1980s on has replaced "the Hemingway [we] were taught about in high school" (Comley and Scholes 146). But the transference of this revisionist Hemingway into classrooms has been slower to follow. There are a number of likely reasons for this: for example, it is the job of scholarship to "cut the edges" of new thinking, whereas the classroom is typically focused on other, more conservative tasks; the scholarship on the "new" Hemingway has taken many directions, thus making it difficult for an instructor to consolidate this work into a coherent approach; the public image of Hemingway as a macho bully or a masculine model (take your pick) is still alive and well, thus predisposing both students and teachers to analyze Hemingway's work in traditional ways. But surely another reason is that the transgressiveness of the new Hemingway creates pedagogical complexities for teachers who may be uncertain about how to introduce this material to students. Yet, as this overview of the scholarship shows, the gender- and sexuality-focused study of Hemingway opens up all sorts of fascinating and contemporary questions about the processes and practices by which masculinity, femininity, heterosexuality, homosexuality, queerness, interracial or intercultural desire, and other societal norms, values, and variations are articulated, circulated, and frequently challenged in our world. Recent scholarship has thus revealed just how relevant Hemingway's work is to the social realities of our time. Our classrooms can do the same.

Notes

1. For more on the changing views of gender and sexuality that Hemingway was exposed to as a young man, see Rena Sanderson, "Hemingway and Gender History," in *The Cambridge Companion to Hemingway*, ed. Scott Donaldson (Cambridge: Cambridge UP, 1996), 170–96; Jamie Barlowe, "Hemingway's Gender Training," in *A Historical Guide to Ernest Hemingway*, ed. Linda Wagner-Martin (Oxford: Oxford UP, 2000), 117–53; Thomas Strychacz, "Masculinity," in *Ernest Hemingway in Context*, ed. Debra A. Moddelmog and Suzanne del Gizzo (Cambridge: Cambridge UP, 2012), 277–86; Debra A. Moddelmog, "Sex, Sexuality, and Marriage," in *Ernest Hemingway in Context* 357–66; and Nancy R. Comley, "Women," in *Ernest Hemingway in Context* 409–17. For more on masculinity in the early twentieth century, see Gail Bederman, *Manliness and Civilization: A Cultural History of Gender and Race in the United States, 1880–1917* (Chicago: U of Chicago P, 1995); Michael Kimmel, *Manhood in America: A Cultural History* (New York: Free Press, 1996); and Anthony E. Rotundo, *American Manhood: Transformations in Masculinity from the Revolution to the Modern Era* (New York: Basic Books, 1993).

2. Some of the sexual research and theory books in Hemingway's library include Anton Kristen Nyström, *The Natural Laws of Sexual Life: Medical-sociological Researches* (1919); a four-volume edition of Havelock Ellis, *Studies in the Psychology of Sex* (1936); Eugen Steinach, *Sex and Life: Forty Years of Biological and Medical Experiments* (1940); Alfred Charles Kinsey, Wardell B. Pomeroy, and Clyde E. Martin, *Sexual Behavior in the Human Male* (1948); Gordon Westwood [aka Michael George Schofield], *Society and the Homosexual* (1953); George W. Henry, *All the Sexes: A Study of Masculinity and Femininity* (1955); and Theodor Reik, *Of Love and Lust: On the Psychoanalysis of Romantic and Sexual Emotions* (1957). See James D. Brasch and Joseph Sigman, comp, *Hemingway's Library: A Composite Record* (New York: Garland, 1981) and Michael Reynolds, *Hemingway's Reading, 1910–1940: An Inventory* (Princeton: Princeton UP, 1980), both now available at jfklibrary.org, the website of the Ernest Hemingway Collection at the John F. Kennedy Presidential Library.

3. Wilson's division of Hemingway's women into two categories was not part of his original essay; it appeared in the version published two years later in his collection *The Wound and the Bow*.

4. The chapter in which Fetterley makes her argument, "*A Farewell to Arms:* Hemingway's 'Resentful Cryptogram,'" was originally published in *Journal of Popular Culture* 10.1 (1976): 203–14; this version did not include the famous line about the only good woman in Hemingway being a dead woman.

5. Wagner-Martin later clarified her position in this essay by claiming that Hemingway's women exist mostly in relation to his men; when these women are superior, it is only because they have something to teach the men (57).

6. Spilka began his investigation of androgyny in Hemingway's work in 1978, but his full-length book on the topic appeared in 1990, after the publication of *Garden*, which, he argued, had provided "the retrospective vision" of androgyny "as a wounding condition . . . against which Hemingway's artistic bow has always been manfully strung" (5).

7. These arguments can be found in the various essays collected in Suzanne del Gizzo and Frederic J. Svoboda, eds., *Hemingway's* The Garden of Eden: *Twenty-Five Years of Criticism* (Kent, OH: Kent State UP, 2012).

8. Burwell notes that in Grace Hemingway's scrapbooks, there are no photos of Hemingway in clothing that is unmistakably feminine after October 1904, when Hemingway was five years old (194). However, as unused material from drafts of Marcelline's *At the Hemingways* makes clear, he and Marcelline continued to be twinned, sporting Buster Brown haircuts, overalls, and boy coats, until he was around seven years old (Burwell 192). The effect of this twinning on Hemingway has been variously explained, and some of these explanations have sparked controversy and rebuttals within the field. Some biographers and critics downplay and even dismiss the substance or the effect of the twinning, noting that young boys of the early twentieth century were often dressed in gowns for ease of toilet training. Others point out that the deliberate twinning of Hemingway with his sister created confusion on the part of both siblings, with Hemingway asking his parents at three years old whether Santa would know he was a boy and Marcelline experiencing such anguish over her boy's haircut when she was around eight years old that she tried to trim it herself and was punished by Grace by being forced to wear a child's bonnet to school (see Mellow 11; and Burwell 20–21, 192–94). Some biographers, such as Mellow, who recognize the gender confusion caused by the twinning, do not necessarily think that the experience negatively affected Hemingway in his youth and maintain that it "quite probably inspired the ambiguous combinations of sexual play between heroes and heroines in his novels" (Mellow 11); see also Eby, *Fetishism*.

Part One

Hemingway and Gender

In Our Time and American Modernisms

Interpreting and Writing the Complexities of Gender and Culture

Joseph Fruscione

I start with a confession.

As a high school and then undergraduate student, I disliked Hemingway, specifically *The Nick Adams Stories* and *The Old Man and the Sea*. The writing style and content felt forced, unappealing, and plodding. Hemingway's pared-down aesthetic, for instance, seemed simple compared to Woolf, Faulkner, Shakespeare, García Márquez, and others in my undergraduate curriculum. When I entered academia, first as graduate student and then as professor, I realized that Hemingway's work was richer and more complex than I'd given him credit for, such as the nuanced, evolving masculinity Nick Adams exhibits in the early stories. Reading *In Our Time*—especially the opener of the 1930 edition, "On the Quai at Smyrna"—in a graduate seminar reinitiated me into Hemingway studies. In two pages, I'd seen what I'd been missing in the past: rich imagery, subtle style, complex depiction of gender, and overall immediacy. I have often shared these early experiences with my own students to demonstrate that Hemingway requires patience and *re*reading. Acknowledging potential resistance to the author's image and interpretive challenges also helps turn a negative into a positive. Students occasionally need reminding that we educators, too, once struggled with material that did not necessarily appeal to us.

In Our Time is a very versatile Hemingway text and has worked well in undergraduate courses as part of a cluster of works exploring constructions of race, class, and gender in the modernist era. I want to focus here on using *In Our Time* as one of several post-WWI works addressing what Janet Lyon has called "the modernist problem of gender" (230). Lyon explores this "problem" in *The Garden of Eden* and "The Sea Change," but her interpretive model applies equally well to *In Our Time*. I have taught *In Our Time* in upper- and mid-level undergraduate courses typically titled "American Modernisms" or "Multiethnic American Modernisms." *In Our Time* is especially teachable when studied in conjunction with other modernist texts that reveal a spectrum of manhood and womanhood, such as William Faulkner's *As I Lay Dying* (1930), Jean Toomer's *Cane* (1923), Gertrude Stein's *The Autobiography of Alice B. Toklas* (1933), F. Scott Fitzgerald's *The Great Gatsby* (1925), and Kate Chopin's *The Awakening* (1899). Stressing gender as fluid and changeable—a process, spectrum, or performance—when teaching these works helps prevent (or correct) students from seeing it as always stable, binary, or biologically determined.

In this essay, I address the kinds of classroom strategies that buttress my pedagogy for teaching Hemingway, gender, and modernism. I sketch out interpretive and compositional approaches to help students first understand, and then complicate, their connotations of *Hemingway*. Having students do some kind of writing almost daily—most often a short, focused response to a specific prompt that can evolve into a paper and/or research topic—is a cornerstone of my teaching. Below, I focus on how using key moments and omissions in *In Our Time* deepens students' conceptions of masculinity and femininity, both in Hemingway's texts and in literary modernism. This kind of work also foregrounds patience, rereading, and careful analysis of text, culture, and context as important elements of student learning. I also address how I encourage students to understand the sequences of *In Our Time*'s gender relationships: such as parents/children, strained lovers, and bonding males.[1] Relatedly, isolating stories (e.g., "Cat in the Rain" or "Cross-Country Snow") for extended treatment develops students' reading and writing skills, giving them space to deepen an analysis of one or two texts. By closely studying Hemingway's work, reading it aloud, and juxtaposing it with that of selected contemporaries, educators can broaden students' understanding of gender in/of the modernist era. I foreground *In Our Time* as a key text with which to explore gender, culture, and modernism, specifically considering Hemingway's conflicted performance of masculinity among his contemporaries.

It may be, as Bonnie Kime Scott has written of the era's gender constructions, that a "crisis in gender identification... underlies much of modernist literature" (2). Whether it is articulated as a "crisis" or, in Lyon's terms, as a "problem," gender in *In Our Time* allows students to understand that "masculinity" and "femininity" are rarely cut-and-dried concepts, especially with this and other Hemingway works relying on subtlety and multilayered gender roles. Although we discuss *In Our Time* collectively, "The End of Something," "The Three-Day Blow," "Cat in the Rain," and "Cross-Country Snow," with their rich dialogue and interactions, are particularly helpful in understanding gender in terms of a masculine-feminine dynamic (as opposed to simply tracking how women and men are portrayed individually).

Our discussions of *In Our Time* generally begin with a question about what Hemingway connotes for the students, based on past readings and the author's cultural legacy. When they know his work—which is slightly less common now than in previous years—students tend to bring up his war experience, aura of machismo, apparent male chauvinism, expatriate life, marriages, and apparently "easy" or "simple" writing. (Some have mistaken Jake Barnes's injury for Hemingway's, but quickly realize their mistake when I remind them that he had three sons.) From here, I reveal how this foundational text complicates the Hemingway cultural imaginary in terms of the various performances of genders, such as Nick's evolving masculinity from "Indian Camp" to "Cross-Country Snow." I then shift discussion to *In Our Time* (which typically spans two or three classes) by twice reading aloud "On the Quai at Smyrna" as a prologue for the style, themes, and cultural issues we will discuss. Students often understand texts better when reading them aloud. Ideally, in-class reading is a *re*reading, since they've presumably done their homework. In many cases, students noted that they saw new things when speaking Hemingway's words in class.

In-class prompts deepen students' knowledge of how gender undergirds *In Our Time*, the Hemingway persona, and modernism. For example, paired readings of "Cat in the Rain" can highlight Hemingway's subtlety. I ask students whether the story's man or woman is more sympathetic to them. I then choose two groups of three (man, woman, narrator) to read the story with different intonations, reflecting where their sympathies lie. "The End of Something" and "Cross-Country Snow" benefit from similar interactive treatment, depending on the students' readings of Nick's views of Marjorie and Helen, respectively. (I'm thinking specifically of how many ways one could speak Nick's "Yes. Now" (111) in response to George's question about Helen's pregnancy.) Such focused work underscores complexities in characterization and the narrator's role.

In Our Time teems with nuanced hetero- and homosocial dynamics in the stories and inter-chapters. The ways in which, for instance, Nick and Bill interact late in "The End of Something" and throughout "The Three-Day Blow" suggest Hemingway's exploration of dual masculinities—Nick's more emotional character contrasts Bill's more stoic one when "that Marge business" comes up. That Nick "said nothing" in response to Bill's criticisms of marriage reveals to students how close reading can clarify gender constructs—here, that Nick keeps his anxieties about Marjorie to himself to project a controlled aura expected of a postwar man (46–47). This triangulated relationship—Nick, Bill, Marjorie—develops character and theme. One sees the same triangulation in "Out of Season" (the American couple and Peduzzi) and "Cat in the Rain" (the American couple and the hotel keeper), suggesting *In Our Time*'s rich intratextuality—which students tend to see more clearly when rereading and writing about the stories. That Marjorie is linguistically present in "The Three-Day Blow" indicates how Hemingway outlines Nick's nuanced masculinity: namely, as Marjorie's (former) romantic companion and as Bill's male-bonding and drinking companion. Even in stories in which women are not present in the scene, only talked about—such as "The Three-Day Blow" or "The Battler"—students can see how Hemingway offers an interactive model of gender—namely, how what is "masculine" and/or "feminine" is fluid and socially contingent.[2]

To encourage a meaningful literary-critical dialogue, I highlight a scholarly claim and then encourage students to repurpose it with a different text. For example, we extend Janet Lyon's idea about the "fungibility of sexuality and gender" (230) in "The Sea Change" to such stories as "The Doctor and the Doctor's Wife" or "Out of Season."[3] I ask students, *How does Hemingway reflect and complicate gender as something unstable? How does Hemingway help us question Dr. Adams's conflicted masculinity in relation to his wife and Dick Boulton?* Along these lines, Nancy Comley and Robert Scholes give a persuasive reading of "Mr. and Mrs. Elliot" in *Hemingway's Genders* (1994) that we extend to other *In Our Time* pieces highlighting "the interaction—and occasional conflict—among . . . cultural codes," such as those concerning sexuality, morality, and marriage (83). In their section on Nick Adams's growing awareness of marriage and parent-child relationships, Comley and Scholes conclude with a claim that students can apply to specific stories: "If Hemingway's male figures are organized around a problematic opposition of boyhood to fatherhood, his females may well be deployed in a manner that is the shadow of this one, in which the space between girlhood and motherhood is scarcely fit for human habitation" (19). After unpacking Comley and Scholes's claim—a key first step when using scholarly criticism in class—the students focus on specific characters and their gender roles to determine whose worlds are and are not "problematic" and "scarcely fit for human habitation." The unnamed mothers of "Indian Camp" and "Cross-Country Snow," in conjunction with Marjorie, Mrs. Elliot, and Mrs. Adams, give students different kinds of girls and mothers—to use the Comley and Scholes binary—to discuss as they come to understand gender as socially constructed and dynamic. Students can also explore and debate the male-male relations of "The Doctor and the Doctor's Wife" and "The Three-Day Blow" and/or male-female relations in "Cat in the Rain" and "Indian Camp" through the claims of Comley and Scholes.

Another relevant critical work accessible to undergraduates, Rita Barnard's "Modern American Fiction," usefully contextualizes the "structural disjuncture," "rituals of masculinity" (56), and "extreme immediacy" (57) of *In Our Time*. Students read this essay early in the semester and then read *In Our Time* vis-à-vis postwar avant-gardism and gender relations. In both cases, students connect Barnard's sense of "extreme immediacy"—which I read as a complement to the text's palpable content, imagery, and style—to the gender themes of "The End of Something," "Indian Camp," and several inter-chapters of the text. Barnard's multilayered approach helps prevent compartmentalization that, for instance, might not account for how *In Our Time*'s story/vignette arrangement complements its manifold gender roles.

To join context and content to structure, I have groups of two or three students do focused work with a two-page sequence of *In Our Time* to understand the interrelationship between the text's themes and the order of vignettes and stories. (Students do similar work with other fragmented modernist texts, such as *Cane* and *As I Lay Dying*.) Students who choose a vignette and the beginning or ending of an adjacent story are better able to analyze the vignettes as textual bridges that comment on the stories. For instance, students can connect Chapter X ("They whack-whacked the white horse . . ." [89]) and the preceding "Mr. and Mrs. Elliot" in terms of the indecision shown by both the bull and Mr. Elliot. The unnamed soldier's anxiety in Chapter VII ("While the bombardment was knocking the trench to pieces at Fossalta . . ." [67]) at some level anticipates the problems of readjustment Harold Krebs experiences in the following story "Soldier's Home." Such close work with the stories' themes and structure helps students make connections within and among modernist texts. While the unnamed soldier in Chapter VII is not Krebs per se, the story and vignette telescope the issues of war and postwar masculinity that Hemingway explores throughout the text, issues that students encounter initially through the interpretive model Barnard offers.

Having initially come to understand *In Our Time* on its own as a signature text of Hemingway's exploration of gender, students then situate it with and against other modernist works. For instance, we explore gender and sexuality in *The Awakening*, *The Autobiography of Alice B. Toklas*, and "Mr. and Mrs. Elliot." *In Our Time* also gives readers numerous instances of men looking at—and sometimes objectifying—women, such as in "The End of Something" and "Cross-Country Snow." Juxtaposing these stories with "Karintha" and "Bona and Paul" in *Cane* or depictions of Addie and Dewey Dell Bundren in *As I Lay Dying* reveals how the authors imagined gender as a continuum partly defined by the male gaze. This practice, again, gives students some useful critical language to describe something they see often: men gazing at women.[4] Faulkner's pregnant, unwed Dewey Dell in some respects echoes the unwed waitress in "Cross-Country Snow" who serves Nick and George. "She's got that baby coming without being married and she's touchy," George observes. He continues: "Hell, no girls get married around here till they're knocked up," suggesting a consequence of sexual activity that Hemingway would weave into "Hills Like White Elephants" (1927) and other works. Continuing to define gender dynamically, Hemingway has Nick and George wishing "[they] could just bum together" shortly after discussing the pregnant waitress, suggesting an idyllic masculinity free of the fatherly responsibility she symbolizes (*In Our Time* 110–11). Hemingway again clarifies a key unspoken moment: Nick's seeing the pregnant waitress seems to trigger the thoughts—and attendant anxieties—about how Helen's pregnancy is working against the men's freedom.

When reading Toomer's *Cane*—often right before *In Our Time*—students discuss a similar power juxtaposition in such stories as "Karintha" ("This interest of the male, who wishes to ripen a growing thing too soon, could mean no good to her" [5]) and "Theater" ("Above the staleness, one dancer throws herself into it. Dorris. John sees her. Her hair, crisp-curled, is bobbed. Bushy, black hair bobbing about her lemon-colored face" [52]).[5] When read consecutively, *Cane* and *In Our Time* show students how such multi-perspective modernist texts offer a diversity of gender performances. That these and other texts are more complementary than imitative of each other enables students to develop nuanced arguments about gender and aesthetics as they function across literary modernism.

At key moments within *In Our Time*, *Cane*, and *As I Lay Dying*, the authors reverse this male gaze, giving female characters a greater degree of feminine autonomy and self-confidence. The beginning of Toomer's "Bona and Paul" shows Bona eyeing Paul in romantic qua erotic terms: "He is a candle that dances in a grove swung with pale balloons," she thinks while she "sees" him play basketball and "[t]he dance of his blue-trousered limbs thrills her" (70). Relatedly, in *As I Lay Dying* Addie Bundren's affair with Reverend Whitfield telescopes her sexual autonomy, resistance to a mother/wife role, and sense of self: "While I waited for him in the woods," Addie remembers in the novel's only chapter in her voice, "waiting for him *before he saw me,* I would think of him as dressed in sin" (175–76; emphasis added). Initially, at least, Addie does the looking in remembering her erotic relationship with Whitfield, a kind of culmination of Bona's eyeing Paul. The gendered, erotic gaze here is mutual and in keeping with modern constructions of gender, such as the New Woman. It aligns Addie with a woman like Kate Chopin's Edna Pontellier, another unhappily married character who unapologetically violates the cult of true womanhood. Making such thematic connections helps students see these and other modernist works in sequence and in context, as opposed to in a proverbial vacuum on the pages of an anthology.

In "The End of Something" Marjorie, too, works against Nick's gaze after their breakup: "He was afraid to look at Marjorie. Then he looked at her. She sat there with her back toward him. He looked at her back." Nick's other, more commonly masculine pursuits—fishing, soldiering, male bonding—notwithstanding, his sensitivity toward Marjorie counterbalances the freedom he envisions after the breakup. Bill's asking "'Did she go all right?'" suggests that Nick had told Bill his plans (*In Our Time* 34–35). Bill can be said to embody what Janet Adelman has called in another context an "absent presence" throughout "The End of Something," since he is presumably biding his time before night-fishing with Nick.[6] That Nick still thinks fondly of Marjorie in "The Three-Day Blow" when talking with Bill reverses this important absence of a gender-inflected character and again helps (re)define Nick's masculinity. To fill in the spectrum of womanhood that connects our course readings, I ask the students to situate specific texts' characters in relation to those in previous readings—such as how Mr. Adams's role as husband and father relates to those of Anse Bundren, Léonce Pontellier, and Tom Buchanan, or how the wife in "Cat in the Rain" compares to other modern women—*is she more of a . . . Daisy? Jordan? Edna? Addie? Bona?*

Through these and other examples, students see evidence of some resistance to patriarchy, perhaps not too bold by contemporary standards but progressive when contextualized in Hemingway's time. I encourage students to explore these intertextual and contextual connections more deeply in their writing, which extends our in-class discussions and group work. Rather than simply allowing students to note similarities between *In Our Time* and *Cane*, for instance, I encourage them to look at the texts collectively and to build an argument around what Hemingway and Toomer endorse or challenge about different masculine-feminine relations of the modernist era. Addressing these kinds of questions in class and early in the writing process helps students create a meaningful synthesis between course texts and contexts.

To begin applying our modes of interpretation and contextualization in their papers, students spend some class time prewriting about *In Our Time* and other readings, in part to enable them to plan out their writing, research, and argument. Because I approach Hemingway's work from the standpoint of a professor of both literature and writing, I balance out our treatment of literary readings with emphasis on college-level writing and research methods. For example, introducing the concept of an analytical lens (in this case, that of gender studies) helps students narrow their approaches to *In Our Time*, deepen their analysis of it, and focus their research options. I require a primary lens—such as gender, sexuality, genre, history, race, or ethnicity (among other possibilities)—for all papers, a requirement that has enabled a more controlled treatment of selected literary texts.

I often use critical works, such as essays from *The Cambridge Companion to American Modernism*, as both class readings and secondary sources for papers to deepen students' writing. I sometimes choose an essay (such as Rita Barnard's, discussed above) as the lone reading for the day, which ensures focused analysis of a scholarly work as an interlude between literary readings. Students also have the option of using one or two assigned scholarly works in their essays. As they move from reading to writing assignments, students will typically write two to three papers in a semester (ranging from six to eleven pages), each of increasing length and difficulty. Literary analysis papers require at least one scholarly source not directly about the author or text. We move toward creating synthesis between literary and scholarly works (e.g., through close analysis and questions), as well as toward introductory rhetorical analysis (such as studying the scholar's analytical lens, use of secondary sources, method of argumentation, and bibliography). This enables students to explore a historical and/or theoretical work germane to their argument. Their research project (spaced over six to eight weeks) requires one or two period sources, such as advertisements or other primary media, which contextualize a particular gender construction relevant to *In Our Time*. I demonstrate how to use online archives of such materials (such as The Modernist Journals Project or "Historic Newspapers" through the Library of Congress) and then encourage students to use these or other digital sources.

In conjunction with the selected critical views of Hemingway and gender from Rita Barnard, Janet Lyon, and other scholars, the intratextual patterning of *In Our Time* makes this kind of work productive in transitioning from class discussion to writing. I encourage students to continue this critical reapplication with other secondary texts in their papers, a tactic that works to eliminate "quote and run" or "information dumping" approaches. For many students, this exercise is an important—though challenging—learning moment. Beginning to recognize that a scholarly source does not have to be directly about their literary text helps them use it meaningfully in their writing and understand that a source can offer a model, theory, or lens in addition to a compelling interpretation. Such advanced application of a critical source gives students confidence that they are part of a larger scholarly conversation about their chosen texts and themes, as well as an understanding that their writing has an audience outside our classroom.

When time and enrollment allow, I devote parts of class to workshop, helping students generate a multilayered thesis section and two or three "why"-based questions to explore in their writing tasks. I stress that such questions should be triply "-able": Arguable (instead of plot or factual summary), Researchable (with a variety of secondary works), and Manageable (within the student's allotted scope and page length). Such interactive attention to writing is particularly useful in an intermediate or gateway course comprising students from various disciplines; for English majors, I stress that this kind of layering and "why" emphasis leads to good literary analysis. Sharing samples that I have written through a Google Drive or Blackboard wiki further enables me to add text or emphasis to the models, while streamlining how I share them with students to review later. We discuss how the positive thesis and question models (see the Appendix) match the "-able" criteria through such critical keywords as *successfully* and *period*. I stress that understanding how texts *reflect* and/or *complicate* a key theme (as opposed to simply how they *depict* or *show* it) allows for a debatable argument analyzing the *why* of gender in Hemingway's text.

Providing a thesis anti-example further helps students move beyond a more report-like model of writing about *In Our Time*; I note that *depicts*, *portrays*, and other such words can lead to a fact-based argument that summarizes plot and makes nonspecific statements. I use comparable word counts for each example to demonstrate that the quality of the thesis section does not simply mean greater quantity. I give students time to draft their own thesis section and questions using the "why" language I offer them. Such guided in-class work time is generally successful, because it helps strengthen the dialogue between the students' reading and writing approaches, while encouraging them to embrace writing as an extended process. Many students enter the class thinking that a thesis can be only a single sentence that can never change during the writing process; my emphasis on an evolving thesis section is often liberating for such students since it allows for more critical inquiry and argumentation about the complexities of *In Our Time* and other modernist works. This writing component of teaching *In Our Time* can of course be adjusted depending on the nature of the course—perhaps emphasized in a seminar or writing-intensive class for majors, or applied to shorter assignments in a survey.[7]

Consistently getting students to the "why" requires patience and explanation, but regular work with the interpretive and writing/research approaches helps advance their ways of meaningfully understanding—and then writing about—Hemingway's work. Students eventually see that such critical questioning leads to workable thesis sections about *In Our Time*, and thus to focused writing and research. Students often have so much they want to say about our readings that their writing can become labored and unfocused. I often hear variations on "I keep changing my mind and thesis about my topic, and Hemingway writes about so many themes . . ."; I require the two or three questions for writing assignments to help contain such thought.

The final lines of "On the Quai at Smyrna"—"My word yes a most pleasant business"—make for a nice closing for our reading of *In Our Time* (12). Ending discussion of the text by reviewing the prologue story gives the students a sense of symmetry and closure since it reiterates motifs and the complexities of narration present in the work as a whole. That it is accessible, debatable, and versatile helps enrich student writing, researching, and (re)reading. Working with such a nuanced text, as we know, is part of the constructive challenge of teaching Hemingway, particularly through a text richly complex in its form, aesthetic of omission, and multiple gender constructs. That I continually stress the plurality of our course themes—that is, modernisms, sexualities, genders, and so on—underscores the importance of keeping *In Our Time* and other Hemingway texts in dialogue with the complementary works of the modernist era.

Notes

1. For further discussion of Hemingway's attention to the domestic, see John Fenstermaker's essay in this volume.

2. Two stories in the first half of *In Our Time*—"The Doctor and the Doctor's Wife" and "The Battler"—reveal a complex interaction of manhoods, racial difference, and potential interracial conflict. The myriad conflicts between Dr. Adams/Dick Boulton, Nick/Ad Francis, and Bugs/Ad overlap masculinity and racial identity. Toomer and Richard Wright—in, respectively, *Cane* and *Uncle Tom's Children* (1938)—offer similarly complex interactions of genders and races. For Toomer and Wright, though, the violence is actualized in the forms of more direct conflict and lynching.

3. Similarly, one could also use excerpts from Thomas Strychacz's *Hemingway's Theaters of Masculinity* (Baton Rouge: Louisiana State UP, 2003), Keith Gandal's *The Gun and the Pen* (New York: Oxford UP, 2008), and other scholarly texts in the same way.

4. An accessible and foundational text for introducing students to the idea of the "male gaze" is Laura Mulvey's article "Visual Pleasure and Narrative Cinema," *Screen* 16.3 (1975): 6–18.

5. *Cane*'s patriarchal gaze is more manifestly white than Hemingway's, given the racial othering of Dorris by John and, in a later story, Paul by Bona and others curious about his light-skinned, multiethnic appearance. Margaret E. Wright-Cleveland's recent essay on Hemingway and Toomer, "*Cane* and *In Our Time*: A Literary Conversation about Race," makes further connections. See *Hemingway and the Black Renaissance*, eds. Gary Holcomb and Charles Scruggs (Columbus: Ohio State UP, 2012), 151–76.

6. See Janet Adelman, *Suffocating Mothers: Fantasies of Maternal Origin in Shakespeare's Plays*, Hamlet *to* The Tempest (New York and London: Routledge, 1992), 104, *passim*. Adelman specifically discusses the symbolic presence of the dead queen in *King Lear*, but her notion of a character's "absent presence" is applicable to other texts, particularly Hemingway's, that operate via meaningful omission.

7. If necessary, I encourage constructive self-reflection by having students write their answers to the questions about process and intellectual challenge on the back of the papers they submit. In many cases, such writing about writing helps students advance their approaches to course readings and assignments. I remind them that they're addressing both themselves and me in their reflective writing; in many cases, this equips students with the tools appropriate to quality academic writing.

"The Garden of Cultural Acceptability"

Gender in *The Garden of Eden,* Then and Now

Pamela L. Caughie and Erin Holliday-Karre

Ernest Hemingway has long been revered as "a masculine icon," on the one hand, and accused of sexism and homophobia, on the other. This reputation makes him an excellent choice for a course like ours, "Topics in Feminist and Gender Studies," which covers feminist, gender, and transgender theories from the early twentieth century to our contemporary era. Hemingway's posthumously published *The Garden of Eden* (1986) is all the more relevant to this course for both English and women's and gender studies majors given that the novel is set in the 1920s, was written in the 1950s (sometime between 1946 and Hemingway's death in 1961) and was published in the 1980s (Fleming).[1] This rather unique and, for us, auspicious expanse of time allows us to explore different cultural conceptions of masculinity and femininity in these different historical eras. This publishing history also provides us the opportunity to call attention to the way editors, publishers, and critics advance certain notions of gender and sexual identity through the editorial and interpretive choices they make. We thus challenge our students, as potential scholars and teachers of literature, to become accountable for the value-laden notions of gender and sexual identity promoted—subtly, even unconsciously—in their academic scholarship and pedagogy.

Our first objective in the course is to bring students to understand gender and sexual identity as cultural rather than innate, as historically specific and rhetorically laden concepts, and not some truth about the body (Hausman 476). Even if many of our students have come to talk in terms of gender as a social construction rather than a biological given, they retain a notion of gender as sexual *difference*—male versus female, femininity versus masculinity, men versus women—a notion that dominated early feminist theory (when feminist critics focused on women's culture or feminine writing, for example) and that still remains dominant in the wider culture.

To challenge this comfortable notion of gender and sexual identity as binary constructions, we read a number of theorists—including philosophers, biologists, anthropologists, sociologists, historians, and literary scholars—from the 1980s and '90s, such as Michel Foucault (*The History of Sexuality*, vol. 1, 1978; *Herculine Barbin*, 1980), Sandra Bartky ("Foucault, Femininity, and the Modernization of Patriarchal Power," 1988) and Judith Butler (*Gender Trouble*, 1990; *Undoing Gender*, 2004). These theorists have offered a way of conceiving both sex and gender as products of various cultural discourses, including literature and film, psychology and psychiatry, endocrinology and gynecology, legal documents and biology textbooks. To be sexed, these theorists argue, is to be subject to the discourses that categorize sex, and, in Susan Bordo's words, to the "cultural grammar of gender" (23). "The body [is] not only a physical entity," writes Bordo, but also "a cultural form that carries *meaning* with it" (26). She continues, "The way we experience our bodies is powerfully affected by the cultural metaphors that are available to us" (38). Students are not surprised to find a literary scholar like Bordo talking of gender in terms of grammar and metaphors, but they are surprised when they read this language in the work of anthropologists such as Emily Martin, and biologists, such as Anne Fausto-Sterling and Joan Roughgarden. "If the state and legal system has an interest in maintaining only two sexes, our collective biological bodies do not," writes Fausto-Sterling. "If nature really offers us more than two sexes, then it follows that our current notions of masculinity and femininity are cultural conceits" (31).

Postmodern theories of sex and gender were gaining prestige (or notoriety, depending on your viewpoint) at the time *Garden* was being edited for publication. Through reading about changing notions of sex and gender in the 1920s, however, students come to see that our contemporary notions of identity, as constructed or discursive, have as much to do with the historical conditions of the modernist era as with the sexual theories of the postmodern. Challenges—legal, political, social—to sexual dimorphism in the late nineteenth and early twentieth centuries had a profound effect on concepts of gender and sexual identity in the 1920s, the era in which *Garden* is set. "Homosexuals," only recently named, were showing up in ever increasing numbers, writes Alice Dreger, and with the rise of gynecology more hermaphrodites were being discovered as well.[2] Medical discoveries of sexual variations, and social developments in sexual politics, such as women's agitation for suffrage and access to the professions, aroused concern that "physical sexual confusion" could "amplify social sexual confusion" (6), Dreger says. Thus medical definitions of sex maintained clearly demarcated lines between sexes, protecting the two-sex system. New definitions of sex, as Foucault writes, "made it possible to group together, in an artificial unity, anatomical elements, biological functions, conducts, sensations, and pleasures," and social meanings (*History of Sexuality*, 154). Once this artificial unity is in place, it becomes the *cause* for the very things that had been grouped together to create the concept in the first place, the secret to uncover, the key to identity. Everybody came to have a "true sex," prompting Foucault to pose his provocative question in the introduction to *Herculine Barbin:* "Do we *truly* need a *true* sex?" (vii). The reiteration of *true* raises doubts for our students about the naturalness of sex, as does the first line of Virginia Woolf's *Orlando:* "He—for there could be no doubt of his sex" (13). The emphasis on what should be obvious makes it seem unnatural.

The kind of social sexual confusion Dreger refers to was pervasive in the early twentieth century. In the 1910s, anthropologists were writing about the Native American "Berdache," men living and dressing as women. In the 1920s, transsexual surgery was being performed in Germany. On the social scene, the New Woman, a cultural icon of this era, was cutting her hair, wearing pants, smoking in public, playing sports, and traveling alone—challenging traditional notions of femininity. Androgynous fashions of the day, such as pants for women and the sheik look for men (based on Rudolph Valentino's 1921 screen performance) made it difficult to tell "who is who or what is what," as the popular 1926 song, "Masculine Women, Feminine Men" put it.[3]

A highly publicized trial in Britain in 1929 captures the anxiety created by changing understandings of sexual and gender identity. Colonel Victor Barker, known previously as Valerie Arkell-Smith, was tried for perjury for passing as a man. In this case, the identity of his "true" sex was not in dispute, nor was his sexuality at issue, even though he, born female, was married to a woman. (Unlike male homosexuality, lesbianism was not a crime.) The perjury trial centered instead on what we now call gender identity, raising questions about how to classify this anomalous woman. Was Barker a sexual invert? A pervert? A New Woman?[4] Reading about this trial, students are surprised to learn that what we now call "transgender identity"—the social phenomenon of people living a gender identity other than that assigned to them at birth—was being practiced in the early twentieth century, though termed "androgyny" at that time, a term that retains the binary that transgender undoes. It's no wonder

Virginia Woolf wrote in 1929, "No age can ever have been as stridently sex-conscious as our own" (99).

When we turn to Hemingway's novel, then, students have some sense of the larger public world in which the novel was set. In teaching the novel, we focus on the ways in which Hemingway's experience and his writing are produced in response to the "cultural grammar of gender," not just in the 1920s but in the 1950s when he was writing the novel. The published version of *The Garden of Eden* centers on a newlywed couple, David and Catherine Bourne, who, during the course of their honeymoon, begin to experiment with gender roles. David becomes the "girl" in the bedroom, while Catherine plays the role of the "boy." Eventually their role-playing escalates to a point in which Catherine and David decide to bring another woman, Marita, into their relationship. The climax of the novel occurs when, in a jealous rage, Catherine burns David's manuscripts and leaves him. Because of her reckless behavior, Catherine's mental stability is thrown into question, while David discovers that he is madly in love with the more traditionally feminine Marita. That Catherine's and David's sexual inversions raise questions about their normality, maturity, and, in Catherine's case, her sanity has as much to do with the dominant narratives of the 1950s as with the social reality of the 1920s. If they go too far, writes Debra Moddelmog in *Reading Desire*, they risk being cast out of "the garden of cultural acceptability" (74). But that garden was tended differently in the 1940s and 1950s. In psychiatry, as in popular culture of that era, male rebelliousness was seen as immaturity, and tainted with homosexuality. Susan Bordo in *The Male Body*, Michael Kimmel in *Manhood in America: A Cultural History*, and Barbara Ehrenreich in *The Hearts of Men* all argue that fear of homosexuality kept men tied to the breadwinner role in the 1950s and to a hyper-, and hetero-, masculinity. In the 1920s, D. H. Lawrence may have argued that the new "cocksure" woman was making men "timid, tremulous, rather soft and submissive" (229), but not until the 1950s was the henpecked man at risk of being labeled homosexual. As Kimmel remarks, "The etiology of homosexuality was . . . to be sought in the sinews of gender-role acquisition" (209). It is the etiology of sex, sexuality, and gender in historically specific cultural discourses, including literature, that we trace with our students in this course.[5]

Yet no matter how savvy students become in discussing sexuality and gender as culturally constructed concepts as we move through the theoretical essays, when it comes to the literature, their readings tend to be thematic and author centered, especially with an author as familiar to them as Hemingway. We start our discussion of *The Garden of Eden*, then, by gathering a general consensus about our students' conclusions. We ask questions such as: How and why does Catherine play with sexuality? Why does David participate in this play? How does Marita fit into their sexual experimentation? Does the ending of the novel subvert or uphold traditional notions of gender? What do you expect from a novel authored by Ernest Hemingway? Among the responses generated from class discussion are the ideas that (1) Catherine Bourne is crazy and that this is the reason behind her erratic and confusing behavior; (2) in the end, David chooses Marita because he loves her, and not because Marita subscribes to the socially desirable feminine roles of docility, selflessness, and transparency; and (3) Hemingway promotes hetero-normative gender identities through re-inscribing traditional gender roles in the novel's final scene. These conclusions become cast iron in student minds not only because there is overwhelming textual evidence provided to support their findings, or because students commonly desire to uphold the author's intention, but also because of the publisher's insistence in a note preceding the preface that "beyond a very small number of minor interpolations for clarity and consistency, nothing has been added [to Hemingway's manuscript]."

Although it is possible to complicate these initial conclusions through the use of *The Garden of Eden* in its published form, we have found that using the text on its own only *slightly* alters students' perceptions: their original conclusions are still fixed even as the more critically minded express the possibility of doubt. Bringing in scholarship on the manuscript, such as Moddelmog's *Reading Desire*, which exposes editor Tom Jenks's numerous and highly selective cuts, turns this intangible uncertainty into a full-blown crisis over these unwavering positions, ultimately leading many students to the realization that meaning is both culturally and socially constructed. Because of its accessibility, we find it useful to bring Robert Fleming's article "The Endings of Hemingway's *Garden of Eden*" into our classroom discussion. Students generally find Fleming validating because of what they see as a shared desire for authorial intention. That is, Fleming finds the Scribners ending suspicious because the final scene of the published novel is uncharacteristically happy. And, according to Fleming, Hemingway never intended for the novel to end with David in a state of pre-lapsarian, sun-drenched repose with the proverbial Eve by his side, the written words flowing like wine. Fleming's article aims to provide textual support for reader expectations: he wants us to experience the cynical and depressing Hemingway that scholars have come to know and love. But our aim in utilizing Fleming's article is not to uncover Hemingway's intentions so much as it is to have our students question their assumptions about Hemingway as well as their acceptance of socially prescribed sex and gender categories. Questioning editorial decisions made by Scribners, Jenks, and Hemingway's widow thus serves to bear fruit in Hemingway's *Garden*.

Fleming begins by addressing the fact that while nothing may have been *added* to Hemingway's text, the published novel is one-third the length of the manuscript. The published version of the novel certainly provides evidence for the argument that Catherine Bourne is crazy, a conclusion most students subscribe to: Catherine's father is said to have suffered from mental illness, suggesting a hereditary predisposition; Catherine repeatedly admits to "craziness" of her own volition; and burning David's writing is something that students find appalling (thus "crazy"). But knowledge of the larger manuscript leads students to question whether Catherine's actions indicate mental instability or suggest a larger social issue. Fleming informs us that the manuscript contains at least two other subplots and three other characters who are left out of the published novel—characters who *also* experiment with sexuality, role-playing, and infidelity. While Catherine and David affect short, bleached hair in the published novel, the manuscript includes the characters Nick and Barbara Sheldon who likewise display matching haircuts, though they grow their hair long rather than cut it short. In class we talk about the fact that the elision of what Fleming calls "The Sheldon variant" imposes meaning on the novel. Isolating Catherine in what we see as an obsessive desire for gender bending is, in itself, the first indication that something is "wrong" with Catherine. When, for example, Catherine first goes to the barber shop to have her hair cut short "like a boy," she implicates the reader in her assertion to David, "Stupid people will think it is strange." Later David informs us that "No decent girls had ever had their hair cut short like that in this part of the country and even in Paris it was rare and strange and it could be beautiful or could be very bad" (16). Through close attention to the language, we show students how we, as readers, are instructed by the text to read meaning into Catherine's haircut. She is "strange," "indecent," and *possibly* "very bad." Catherine's actions are thus seen to be uncommon. Later evidence, such as Catherine's pyrotechnic act of vengeance, will only provide support for these early assertions.

The incorporation of Nick and Barbara, however, would suggest that gender fluidity and sexual experimentation were not uncommon during the time period and not limited to the individual experience of Catherine and David. Catherine's assertion that she and David "are not like other people" (27) is amplified by the fact that there are no other people in the novel who practice gender fluidity. Catherine becomes "crazy" to the extent that she stands alone in a heteronormative world. Most students agree that the incorporation of other characters who also reject gender norms would make Catherine a more sympathetic character. Catherine's experience would be seen as reflective of a more general social anxiety about the restriction of fixed sexual identities, particularly when one considers that the character Barbara, who professes to be infatuated with Catherine—in whom she sees lesbian tendencies—is set to take her own life in one variant ending of the novel. The character Barbara would, in effect, lead us to reconsider Catherine as similarly a victim of social constraint rather than a societal menace or as suffering from a hereditary disease. Burning David's manuscript, the quintessential act that solidifies Catherine's mental instability, becomes a reaction against the heteronormative underpinnings supported in David's written identification with the elephant-slaying patriarch.

Fleming's discussion of Hemingway's alternate endings unintentionally challenges students to consider the possibility that the published version of *The Garden of Eden* was chosen for its cultural acceptability and in conjunction with an effort to keep the novel consistent with a literary-critical focus on Hemingway's machismo. The end of the novel is consistent with Hemingway's other works to the extent that David learns to love, accept, and admire the masculinity of his father, a man he once saw as sexist, brutal, and cruel. It seems fitting then that Catherine, the character who questions the naturalness of sex and gender, should unexpectedly depart on a train while David begins a life with Marita, who likewise revels in her socially given gender role. Although Hemingway did write the words that we now come to consider the last chapter of *The Garden of Eden*, Fleming stresses that this section was never intended to be the end of the novel. In fact, in one provisional ending, David is lounging on a beautiful beach with Catherine (where they contemplate taking their own lives as Barbara did), while Marita is inexplicably written out of the novel. This revelation is a particularly enlightening moment in our discussion, especially in response to those students who stake their lives on the fact that David *loves* Marita. This particular unpublished ending suggests an acceptance of fluidity and a desired freedom from the social constraints of heteronormativity.

However, this ending is not consistent with our accepted notions of Hemingway as patriarch, as "Papa Hem," as the embodiment of masculinity. Although Fleming acknowledges that the published ending was never the intended ending, he still maintains that Scribners editor Jenks "got most of the good material that was in the manuscript and cut out many distracting elements" (261). Thus, like the editor at Scribners, Fleming exposes a desire to uphold the popular notion of Hemingway. Fleming's article, then, provides for us a dual function: students are left contemplating the social and cultural construction of sex and gender *and* the "objectivity" of authorial intention.

For the paper assignment in this unit, we offer several possible topics to guide students on connecting the theoretical material with the novel. For example:

- Through a close reading of a few passages in Hemingway's novel, show how Butler's and Foucault's understanding of gender and sexual identity can help us understand this narrative. Where does Hemingway seem to present a notion of gender or sexuality as historically constituted and culturally mediated? How does such a reading challenge popular views of Hemingway?
- The song "(You Make Me Feel Like) A Natural Woman," made famous by Aretha Franklin, suggests not only that what is supposedly natural is a metaphor or trope, but that a woman can *be* only in relation to a "you," understood to be male. The construct "woman" is formed within a discourse of heterosexuality that links sex, gender, and desire in a causal relation. Through a close reading of a few passages in Hemingway's novel, illustrate this notion of "woman" as it functions in (or as it is challenged by) the narrative.

Writing in response to such prompts, as well as in the class discussions outlined above, students come to see how the manuscript opens up the discussion of gender and sexuality, whereas the publisher, and even critics like Fleming, would have us close that discussion down.

Our teaching of Hemingway's posthumous novel brings home to students the importance of thinking about gender and sexuality as historical concepts, and the significant role editors, publishers, and critics play in promoting certain ways of thinking about gender and sexual identity. The published version of the novel (and its correctives, like Fleming's), we argue (following Moddelmog), reinforces the very notions of gender that Hemingway's manuscript challenges. Given that ambivalence toward gender identity and sexuality was not simply pervasive but *encouraged* in the 1920s when Hemingway was producing his first major works, it is not surprising to find that Hemingway's novel would self-consciously explore the ambiguity of gender norms and sexual desire. What is surprising, however, to most of our students is that resistance to this gender ambiguity persists eighty years later in contemporary scholarship on Hemingway's posthumous novel.

Notes

1. While the published version of *The Garden of Eden* is only 247 pages, the actual manuscript takes up more property in the John F. Kennedy Library than any of Hemingway's other manuscripts. Where the published version includes thirty chapters, the actual manuscript is forty-seven chapters, exclusive of copious handwritten notes, inserts, and provisional endings. Robert Fleming suggests that the published novel is a third the size of the original manuscript, but this is a conservative estimate at best.

2. Studies of homosexuality and gender inversion date to the late nineteenth century. As early as 1886 Richard von Krafft-Ebing was studying gender divergence among homosexuals, for which he coined the term "gynandry." His *Psychopathia Sexualis*, first published in 1886 and expanded through twelve editions, is often cited as the first use of the term "homosexual." Havelock Ellis published *Sexual Inversion* in 1897, using the terms "eonism," or "sexuo-aesthetic inversion" for Krafft-Ebing's "gynandry." Magnus Hirschfeld, himself a homosexual and transvestite (to use Hirschfeld's terms), coined "transvestism" and "transsexualism" in 1910 and 1923, respectively, and is considered the pioneer in medical treatment of transsexuality. For more on the history of homosexuality and transsexuality, see Dreger, Foucault, and Meyerowitz *How Sex Changed: A History of Transsexuality in the United States* (Cambridge MA: Harvard UP, 2004).

3. What struck many anthropologists in the 1920s as a sexual perversion, the Berdache, so named by colonialists who saw them as homosexual transvestites or male prostitutes, were called *la'mana* by the Zuni tribe, and "two-spirit people" in many Native American cultures today. See, for example, Elsie Clews Parsons's 1916 essay, "The Zuni *La'mana*." The first transsexual surgeries, performed at Magnus Hirschfeld's institute in Berlin, began with the removal and transplantation of sexual organs. In the spring of 1930, Lili Elbe (born Einar Wegener) was referred by Hirschfeld to Dr. Gohrbandt in Dresden for the first of four sexual reassignment surgeries performed over 16 months. For more on transsexual surgeries, see Meyerwitz. On the phenomenon of the New Woman, see Martha H. Patterson, *Beyond the Gibson Girl: Reimagining the American New Woman 1895-1915* (Urbana: U of Illinois P, 2005).

4. For more on this trial, see Pamela L. Caughie, "Passing as Modernism," *Modernism/modernity* 12.3 (2005): 385-406.

5. For a longer overview of this course, one that includes a reading of another modernist novel—namely, Virginia Woolf's *Orlando*—see Pamela L. Caughie, "'Passing' and Identity: A Literary Perspective on Gender and Sexual Diversity." In *God, Science, and Sexual Diversity: An Interdisciplinary Approach to Christian Ethics*, ed. Patricia Jung and Aana Vigen (Urbana: U of Illinois P, 2010): 195-216.

Redeeming Hemingway and His Women

Periodicals as Sites of Change in the Literature Classroom

Belinda Wheeler

With its "showcasing of heroic white manhood" (duCille 39), Hemingway's popular short story "The Short Happy Life of Francis Macomber" has been closely scrutinized by feminist scholars. In her landmark essay, "Actually, I Felt Sorry for the Lion," Nina Baym encourages readers of Hemingway's short story to listen to the voices of the lion and Margot because their voices and silences occupy "so much of its space" (79). Both characters have often been dismissed or maligned by some critics, but Baym warns readers that if they introduce this line of thinking in the classroom they will simply be indoctrinating themselves and their students "into an ethos, a self-styled male ethos" that does not examine the various "murderous hypocrisies and inconsistences" (80) taking place within the story. Given Hemingway's history and our students' difficulty approaching the text objectively in a postfeminist world, updated teaching strategies that engage students actively with the text are increasingly needed.

Baym's essay provides an excellent analysis of the short story and effective strategies teachers can use in the classroom, but, as she noted over twenty years ago, her essay was written largely for those "student readers unaware of the standard interpretation of 'The Short Happy Life of Francis Macomber,' who also know little or nothing about the Hemingway mystique" (72). Today's students usually have a general opinion of Hemingway and his work before entering the classroom, either because they are familiar with the Hemingway who is a fixture of popular culture or because they have easily found summaries of Hemingway's biography or his works online. Most of those opinions, particularly those of my female students, have been negative. Trying to circumnavigate these strong negative opinions before we even examine a text by Hemingway has previously been a challenge for me. Also challenging is that my students immediately focus on the male characters because they concentrate on the short story's title and how the male characters treat Margot. Consequently, they begin their analysis feeling that she is a woman who has been stripped of all power. They also struggle to understand the historical and cultural context of the story, which limits their understanding of how the characters may be conforming to or departing from traditional gender roles. However, by looking at the story in its own context in a mass market periodical, I have students immediately engage the text itself (without focusing on Hemingway's mystique) and concentrate primarily on Margot's character and how she successfully challenges gender roles without being the "bitch-woman" (Baym 71) so many critics love to label her.[1]

Before Hemingway was a canonical figure in American literature he was an up-and-coming writer trying to obtain an audience. He, like many other authors during that time, began his publishing career in various literary magazines. Writers found this outlet attractive because they could share their work with an engaged audience, it sometimes paid quite well, if not in cash then in exposure and prestige, and it was often the first step in the larger publication process. As Lawrence Rainey noted in his 1998 article "The Price of Modernism: Publishing *The Waste Land*," if a writer could build a solid reputation on the pages of a magazine, he or she would be in a good position to secure a limited edition by a small press and, finally, a mainstream edition by a commercial press. Examining Hemingway's publishing history, we can see that he followed a trajectory similar to that of T. S. Eliot, Ezra Pound, and James Joyce, contributors to the "little magazines" of expatriate Paris.

I have always found it exciting to look at the first publication of any text, but when I am covering Hemingway in my classroom it is essential to revisit that moment when a widespread readership first encountered a now-familiar literary work. By carefully tailoring my classroom lectures and discussions I am able to re-create the scenario many 1936 readers had when they first encountered "The Short Happy Life of Francis Macomber." It is vital that a similar scenario occur in my classroom so that Hemingway's celebrity and/or notoriety—a persona largely, though by no means entirely created in the 1940s, 1950s and beyond—does not overshadow students' initial engagement with the text.[2] Students respond favorably to the novelty of viewing the original text because most of them are used to reading a piece of literature in an anthology. The process of looking through an original 1936 magazine—a vibrant historicized document that includes not only the story but articles, advertising, and eye-catching layout, all for a cover price of 25 cents—enables them to have a clearer understanding of the time period, gender dynamics, and consumer culture. In order to have original documents in class for my students, I usually purchase an issue in advance from an online auction site, browse the web for images of the magazine, and/or work with my university's library or with local libraries to bring the magazine to my classroom or to bring my students to the library.[3]

Before students learn what text they will be reading, in this case "The Short Happy Life of Francis Macomber," we devote class time to studying the original September 1936 issue of *Hearst's International combined with Cosmopolitan*. I do not initially list the story on my syllabus so that students do not read ahead (or use online study guides like Shmoop) prior to our discussion. To assess the magazine's target audience, students explore the magazine's cover art, advertisements, contents, layout, and other paratextual elements. Although I have used digital images of the magazine in the past, I prefer to provide an original physical copy of the magazine so students can touch it, further connecting them with the materiality of the text. Before I place the magazine on our classroom document camera, I hide the small subheading advertising Hemingway's short story, "Novelette by Ernest Hemingway," and because I do not want students to make snap judgments about the magazine's target audience (they may be familiar with today's *Cosmopolitan* magazine), I obscure the *Cosmopolitan* reference. With that information removed, students can focus on the unfamiliar image and text as their only clues to identifying the magazine's 1936 audience.

The first characteristic of the magazine's cover that my students comment on is the illustration that covers roughly 90 percent of the page (see Fig. 1). The illustration is by American artist Bradshaw Crandell, noted for his glamorous depictions of movie stars. The color drawing depicts a beautiful, tanned, young, slender white woman waist deep in the ocean. Students note that she is wearing a bright yellow swimsuit and holding a large, colorful beach ball. Her body is in profile to the viewer, but she is looking to her left so that her face is to the audience. With her rosy pink cheeks, well-manicured eyebrows, full eyelashes, smiling red lips, pearly white teeth, and well-kept dark hair peeking out of her swimming cap, she could be mistaken for a movie star. Often when students are assessing the woman's beauty, they agree that she would be considered just as beautiful today as she was in the 1930s. To further complement this "ideal" image, at the bottom of the magazine's front cover is the slogan "Special Vacation Issue."

Fig. 1

In this image, Crandell employs the concept of "glamour"—a distinctively modern idea—to address the magazine's public. As Judith Brown notes, glamour is "an experience that moves one out of the material world of demands, responsibilities, and attention to productivity, and into another, more ethereally bound, fleeting, [and] beautiful" (5). Glamour is clearly being marketed on the magazine's front cover, bringing together a "range of aesthetic objects [image and text] to seduce, enchant, and revise" (8). After we have examined the image, students then study the other text on the page: the issue date, price, and a small subheading advertising the first installment of a serialization by a now-forgotten author.

At this point I invite my students to determine the target audience for this magazine. Common student reactions are that the magazine would appeal predominantly to white women between the ages of 18 and 35 who strive to better themselves. When I reveal the obscured *Cosmopolitan* reference we usually have a larger discussion about how the initial identification of the magazine's target audience closely fits *Cosmopolitan*'s primary demographic today. The confirmation that their initial assessment of the magazine's target audience matches the current *Cosmopolitan* on newsstands motivates the students to further investigate the magazine, though students are usually surprised to learn that, from its nineteenth-century beginnings through the 1930s and beyond, it was primarily a literary magazine and featured work by such illustrious writers as Mark Twain and Willa Cather.[4]

After viewing the magazine's cover we look at the opening pages. In some magazines the table of contents appears first. In a magazine like *Cosmopolitan*, however, high-priced advertising usually fills at least the first two pages. In this particular issue, the advertisement on the inside of the magazine's front cover is for Coca-Cola. Tying in seamlessly with the beach scene on the front cover, the Coca-Cola advertisement displays a large refreshing glass of Coca-Cola set against an image of an iceberg and water. The first words of the advertisement read, "Cold . . . ice-cold every day in the year." Immediately opposite the Coca-Cola advertisement, on the right side of the magazine, is an advertisement for Mum deodorant, offering advice on how women can stay cool. This advertisement opens with the suggestion that women need to listen to men's opinions about hygiene: "Suppose we listen to **the MEN** awhile" (original emphasis). The advertisement continues, we "decided to ask several hundred men what feminine quality appealed to them most" and they responded with the "daintiness of person." According to the advertisement, "The smart woman knows that the greatest danger to this essentially feminine quality of freshness, immaculateness of person, is the ugly odor of underarm perspiration." To the right of this text are five facial images of well-groomed white men with quotes next to them. Some of the quotes read as follows: "I can't forget it—or forgive it—when a woman offends with perspiration odor"; "I sometimes wonder if a woman thinks a pretty face can make up for a fault like this"; and "Perspiration odor contradicts everything I want to think about a woman." Near the end of the advertisement are the words, "Let's listen to the men and ensure our daintiness of person by the daily Mum habit! ... MUM takes the odor out of perspiration" (original emphasis). My students are usually incensed about the lecture women are receiving from men and are eager to analyze stereotypical gender roles in the 1930s. Before I engage discussion on that topic, however, I move to another advertisement on page 10.

The advertisement on page 10, "Beginnings of Wisdom," is sponsored by *Cosmopolitan*'s Education Department. This advertisement appears opposite the "*Cosmopolitan* Education Guide" promoting various schools, colleges, academies, and seminaries throughout America, Canada, Mexico, and France. With an equal number of male and female images appearing in the "Beginnings of Wisdom" advertisement, many of my students initially believe the magazine is placing women and men in an equal position; i.e., both can obtain a rigorous education. On closer examination, however, students notice that the opportunities available to students are separated by gender. For example, the image that accompanies the caption "All round physical development" showcases an all-white male rowing team; similarly, the image that has the accompanying caption "An atmosphere conducive to quiet study" features three white men studying in a library. In contrast, there are two images that feature white women and claim that women will find fulfillment "working for speed in transcription" and painting female colleagues in "art class."

Other advertisements throughout the magazine promote products such as facial cream and beauty secrets, insurance coverage for families, cleaning products, cigarettes, alcohol, soap, toothpaste, and food items for the family. By this point I have opened up the discussion to gender roles in 1930s America, and students compete with each other to add their voices to the discussion. Overall, the students usually contend that the advertising in the magazine strongly pushes for the ideal image of American womanhood—with perfect hygiene and a pretty face, well groomed, and knowledgeable about food and other products around the house that will benefit her family. (And, notably, always white.) Furthermore, the absence of hard-hitting journalistic pieces in favor of various short stories, poems, serials, and nonfiction features prompts my students to argue that the magazine holistically promotes a woman's place in American society. As Michele Ramsey discusses in her analysis of early twentieth-century automobile advertisements, these *Cosmopolitan* advertisements focus "on issues of appearance," represent women's household activities as "non-serious and appropriate only in service to others," and link women's purchases for the family home to "good mothering," inviting "women to spend their time in pursuing social status rather than political or economic status" (26).

REDEEMING HEMINGWAY AND HIS WOMEN 53

After we view the various advertisements in the magazine, I ask my students to investigate whether a short story in the magazine also parallels many of the themes we have identified so far. Before turning to "The Short Happy Life of Francis Macomber," I again ensure that Hemingway's name and the title of the piece are obscured from the students' view. Usually students do not notice the omission of the author's name, but if they ask about the title of the piece I simply state that I have removed it temporarily so as to focus the discussion not on the title but on the contents of the short story.

Even before my students begin delving into the text, they are confronted by the large full-page color illustration on the right side of the magazine: an image of a white woman, approximately 30 to 35 years old, in an outdoor setting leaning over a person lying on the ground. Though there are three male figures in the picture and a caption, "He lay face down, not two yards from where the buffalo lay on its side" (Hemingway, "Short Happy Life" 31) most of the students gravitate toward the woman. Placed off-center on the right side of the magazine, the woman is the only one whose posture and face are turned slightly toward the reader (see Fig. 2). Her rosy cheeks and lips are marginally lighter than the

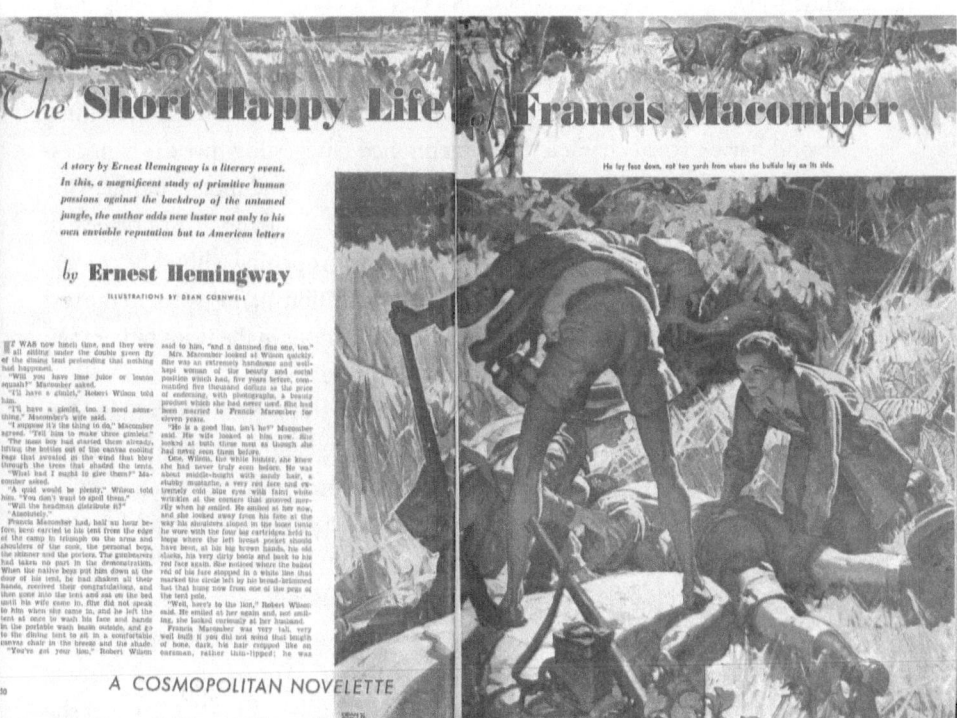

Fig. 2

red shrubbery off to the distance, and she is adopting a nurturing position over the body lying on the ground. Almost always my students quickly note how the woman's facial features are similar to those of the woman on the magazine's front cover. The short "teaser" that appears prior to the beginning of the short story promises: "In this, a magnificent study of primitive human passions against the backdrop of an untamed jungle, the author adds new luster not only to his own enviable reputation but to American letters" ("Short Happy Life" 30). Of course, at this point the students do not know who this author is, but they do not seem perturbed because our discussion has been focused on the text itself and how it is being "marketed" to its audience.

From the opening moments of the short story, students see Mrs. Macomber as the epitome of the 1930s woman who appears in many of the advertisements throughout the magazine: "She was extremely handsome and well-kept woman of the beauty and social position which had, five years before, commanded five thousand dollars as the price of endorsing, with photographs, a beauty product which she had never used. She had been married to Francis Macomber for eleven years" (30). In previous classes when I did not introduce this short story to my students via the magazine, students immediately cringed at the oversimplification of Mrs. Macomber: no first name given (she is the property of Mr. Francis Macomber); a woman who is only appreciated for her beauty (her endorsement is always accompanied by a photograph, as if her word is not enough); nothing beyond her personal characteristics mentioned (suggesting that she is not especially smart); and a woman appearing manipulative and money hungry (she misrepresents herself by endorsing products that she does not use or believe in for financial gain). When they read the short story's opening within the context of the magazine, however, students focus their attention on the words in the text and their relationship to perceived societal expectations in the 1930s rather than simply dismissing the story and its author as misogynistic.

As my students delve further into the short story, they learn that Mrs. Macomber does indeed have a first name, Margaret, and a nickname, Margot. They also learn that while there are moments when she displays stereotypical "feminine" characteristics, such as sentimental crying for the dead lion her husband has killed and directing anger toward him for his part in the animal's death, she is capable of exercising power over her husband. For example, she insists on coming to the next day's hunt despite comments from the professional hunter, Robert Wilson, dismissing her sentiment: "Women upset. Amounts to nothing" (32). Furthermore, she ignores her husband in bed; instead she has sex with Wilson, and she chooses the solitude of sleep when her husband insists on talking. Students also learn that some of the power dynamics in this 1930s relationship still resonate over eighty years later: "Margot was too beautiful for Macomber to divorce her and Macomber had too much money for Margot ever to leave him" (169).

Though Mr. and Mrs. Macomber appear to understand one another quite well after eleven years of marriage, it is clear that women continue to mystify Robert Wilson. He notes to himself early on in the story that American women are "the hardest in the world; the hardest, the cruelest, the most predatory and the most attractive and their men have softened or gone to pieces nervously as they have hardened"; "Or is it," he thought, "that they pick men they can handle?" (166). Later in the story, after he has slept with Margot, he still feels that women dominate the men around them: "women did not feel they were getting their money's worth unless they had shared that cot with the white hunter. He despised them ... but he made his living by them; and their standards were his standards as long as they were hiring him" (170). At this point in the discussion, students note how Margot cleverly reverses the male-female power dynamic: She pays for sex, while the hunter must consent because he is economically dependent on her. Students are intrigued by this character, and they often reread different sections of the text to uncover other displays of Margot's power.

Students are excited about the possibility of discovering a postfeminist character, but when they read and reread the story's ending they start to question Margot's reaction to her accidental fatal shooting of her husband. Where students before viewed Margot's silence as her circumventing of prescribed gender roles (unlike her mourning of the lion's death, now she resists expressing any sentiment), some come to believe her long pauses show that she is first processing, then acknowledging, her limitations in her current predicament. Here, some of my students argue, she needs to re-adopt societal expectations in order to be exonerated at the inquest. She must now say "please" and let Wilson gather the necessary information so that she will be "perfectly all right" at the inquest (172). To some of my students, Margot—like the women in the various advertisements in the magazine, including the Mum deodorant advertisement—has to "ensure ... daintiness" and the power dynamic shifts, putting Wilson in charge. I allow students to meditate on this point for a moment before I play devil's advocate and ask them whether Margot might be saying please and revealing her vulnerability to Wilson as a way to get what she wants: her perceived weakness will allow her to be exonerated. The students often pause before a larger debate begins as they consider a question that scholars, too, have yet to answer definitively, namely, whether the shooting was an accident or a murder.

In my classroom there are no right or wrong answers as long as the students can adequately support their positions with convincing textual evidence. When the subject of Margot's behavior in "The Short Happy Life of Francis Macomber" has almost been exhausted, I then reveal the short story's title and its author. In addition, I usually briefly mention some of the politics around Hemingway's portrayal of women in his short stories. This new information prompts renewed discussion of the story and its characters. By the end of the discussion, the students often are defending Hemingway and defending Margot against the critics.

There is certainly a place for those critics who take offense with the story's gender politics. However, in order to engage our twenty-first-century students, we need to re-envision how they approach this text to allow for dynamic readings. The paratextual material of the September 1936 *Cosmopolitan* offers readers a number of examples of men and women conforming to expected and prescribed gender roles. Hemingway, with his journalistic eye, observed such performances in real life and reproduces them in his short story. Reading the story in its original context allows students to read Margot Macomber, Francis Macomber, and Robert Wilson among the white men and women featured in the magazine's advertisements and editorial pages. That Margot herself had once advertised a product she did not use indicates Hemingway's critique of the economies that drove the mass market magazines to which he himself contributed.

This approach would work with other stories serialized in periodicals as well, such as "The Butterfly and the Tank," a lesser-known story published in the upstart men's magazine *Esquire* (1938) or "A Clean, Well-Lighted Place," published in the widely circulated literary magazine *Scribner's Magazine* (1933), and it could even be used for excerpts from a novel, such as *Across the River and into the Trees* (*Cosmopolitan*, 1950) or a story in one of the highbrow "little magazines" of 1920s Paris (providing the instructor can procure a facsimile of the issue), such as "Work in Progress"—later known as "Indian Camp"—in the April 1924 *transatlantic review*). The students are closely engaged, their reactions to major and minor characters are broad and deep—and unbiased, at least by Hemingway's reputation—and they deftly connect the material to its historical context by situating it within the preserved bibliographic code.

Notes

1. Baym notes: "As for Margot, she commits adultery virtually under her husband's nose and then kills him at the very moment when his belated entrance into manhood (through blood sport and male bonding) threatens her dominance. It is not surprising that a feminist short story anthology [*Images of Women in Literature* (1973)] has featured it, through four editions, as a leading example of the 'bitch' stereotype . . . a reading that is likely more the critics' than the author's construction" (72).

2. For a discussion of the role of 1950s pulp magazines in the development of Hemingway's hypermasculine persona, see David Earle, *All Man! Hemingway, 1950s Men's Magazines, and the Masculine Persona* (Kent, OH: Kent State UP, 2009).

3. I purchased the September 1936 issue of *Cosmopolitan* a few years ago on eBay for about $40. Though it is more expensive now, at about $100, it is still comparable in cost to many textbooks; unlike most textbooks, however, the 1936 *Cosmopolitan* is likely to appreciate in value, a circumstance that might justify the expense to instructors who pay out of pocket or to the department chairs or librarians who approve such purchases. In any case, the students see the magazine in class only: by using a document camera rather than circulating photocopies, I am able to keep the students on task (postponing the "reveal" that the author is Hemingway), and in so doing I also remain well within the bounds of fair use for educational purposes.

4. For a thorough history of *Cosmopolitan* see James Landers, *The Improbable First Century of* Cosmopolitan *Magazine* (Columbia: U of Missouri P, 2010).

It *Is* Pretty to Think So

Domestic Relationships in the Nick Adams Stories

John Fenstermaker

Easily three-quarters of Hemingway's short stories deal explicitly with gender, many more specifically with the domestic—that is, the "family" side of the "family/workplace nexus" of the private and public spheres (Kimmel, Hearn, and Connell 292). Male/female relationships in Hemingway often produce distressed pairings ("Out of Season," "Hills Like White Elephants," "The Sea Change," "The Short Happy Life of Francis Macomber," *The Sun Also Rises*) and, in turn, severe critical dicta. At Hemingway's death, Leslie Fiedler famously proclaimed that "There are . . . no *women*" in the works and that no other writer considers "childbirth more customarily . . . the essential catastrophe" (316–17). A generation later, Michael Reynolds ventriloquized Hemingway: marriage usually "bitches a man" and "either kills him or cripples his work" (*Young Hemingway* 201).

Such ideas necessarily impacted classrooms. Wayne Booth concluded, "Surely ANY teacher who teaches *A Farewell to Arms* without inviting . . . critical consideration of Hemingway's heroes as human ideals, and of his portraits of women as reflecting a peculiarly maimed creative vision, and of his vision of the good life as a singularly immature one—surely any such teacher is doing only half the job" (301). Nina Baym described students' debating Margot's shooting of Francis ("The Short Happy Life of Francis Macomber"). A male instructor, asserting a "dominant male ethos" by advancing Wilson as the story's moral authority, "silences" a woman unsympathetic to Wilson: "Now you sound like Margot" (79). Baym's article offers a necessary correction: fault lies with the instructor, not Hemingway. By century's turn, published criticism and, more slowly, classroom interrogations of Hemingway on gender approached equipoise, trending along lines urged by Rena Sanderson:

> When Hemingway arrived at young manhood, there was a struggle... between men and women over personal and sexual freedom, economic independence, and political power... [affecting] his thinking and writing about women.... [A]nyone who wants to understand the confused history of gender relations in twentieth-century America would do well to read him closely. ("Hemingway and Gender History" 172)

•

I first studied Ernest Hemingway formally in the 1960s under Fitzgerald authority Matthew J. Bruccoli. His *awful* and *wonderful* (root meanings) seminar glossed artistries, biographies, and editing/publication/sales/reception data. Fledgling scholars, we found his polymath Hemingway exciting: "hunter, fisherman, soldier, aesthetician, patriot, military strategist, yachtsman, drinker, womanizer, gourmet, sportsman, philosopher, naturalist, intellectual, anti-intellectual, traveler, war correspondent, boxer, big-game hunter—and author" (xix).

Today, I teach Hemingway in English and honors classes, graduate seminars, and thesis/dissertation projects. I emphasize a domestic vision in Hemingway, absent from Bruccoli's broad-stroke sketches. This interest developed from reading the texts; from scholars of Hemingway and gender—Sanderson, as well as Linda Patterson Miller, Sandra Spanier, Linda Wagner-Martin, and others; and from a specific predication by Susan Beegel, then distinguished editor of *The Hemingway Review*. Speaking at the Oak Park Hemingway conference in 1999 in celebration of the centennial of the author's birth, Beegel described being recently asked by a female reporter how she could "devote [her] professional life to a known misogynist whose words and works deprecate women." Beegel responded politely—devastatingly: "To which Hemingway works specifically might you be referring?"[1]

The male-chauvinist Hemingway of Beegel's interviewer still exists. Hence, I introduce Hemingway to students via representative historical and fictional "moments" that parallel his era with ours. Students soon discover that gender issues in Hemingway arise continually, central in individual works and fundamental to his broadest cultural critique. My essay tracks students' investigation of Hemingway and gender, primarily in the Nick Adams narratives. The Adams cycle appeared across three story collections, 1925–1933. We follow Nick in the *Complete Short Stories*, Finca Vigía edition.[2]

Our historical/fictional orientation begins with the stories of *In Our Time* (1925). The intertextuality fascinates students. Terrifying images in "On the Quai at Smyrna" (added 1930) "introduce" the stories and vignette chapters. Nick appears in seven stories and chapter VI, the domestic pronounced in each. We emphasize Nick, but careful readers also recognize marriage/family issues in the other stories: "Mr. and Mrs. Elliot," "Cat in the Rain," and "Out of Season" have long been considered a "marriage" group; marriage prospective ("A Very Short Story") and desirable ("Soldier's Home") extends this grouping, as do father-son relationships, literal ("My Old Man") and metaphoric ("The Revolutionist"). Women initiate major action. Motherhood constitutes a primary role, and pregnancy, birth, or a child's presence, actual or potential, underscores family issues; traditional marriages undergo stress, in "Mr. and Mrs. Elliot" evolving into a queer family of three. Indeed, five decades' work in feminist and queer theory reveals that women in *In Our Time* (as different as Marjorie and Mrs. Elliot) often transcend traditional roles, allowing readers to reconsider broader issues of gender and sexuality within American culture.[3]

Structure, particularly among the vignettes, also proves rhetorical—for example, imaging the domestic ravaged by war. In the introductory narrative and in certain vignette chapters, women remain powerless: in "On the Quai at Smyrna"—mothers screaming on a pier birth and hold babies dying and dead; in chapter II, the first vignette with women characters, childbirth dominates—a tearful girl in an overloaded wagon during a forced evacuation deflects pouring rain from a woman's otherwise unassisted birthing, "[S]cared sick looking at it" (*Complete Short Stories* 71). In chapter VII, carnal violence rends on multiple levels as a coward soldier finds succor from a government-supplied prostitute. The unarticulated, perhaps inarticulable, fates of such voiceless women and mothers poignantly touch traditional religious and domestic chords—home, family, fidelity. Awareness of women at both momentous and ordinary events enables students at the outset to grasp gender as a primary Hemingway subject. Watching Nick Adams mature from childhood to early middle age across historical events and, especially, in familial roles—son, husband, father, friend, observer, writer—we explore a specific dimension of Hemingway's gender awareness: his domestic vision.

When first encountered, Nick is a young boy; last seen in "Fathers and Sons," he is thirty-eight, and his commitment to family runs deep, centered in an exceptionally sensitive family member—a son not yet twelve years old. Although Nick's family is dysfunctional and miscommunication and violence complicate his experiences with gender, these stories constitute a chorus on domestic relationships.

A child in Michigan in "Indian Camp" (*In Our Time* 1925), Nick (with Uncle George) assists his doctor father with an emergency cesarean, performed without anesthetics, using only fishing gear. During this excruciating ordeal, the woman's injured husband commits suicide in the bunk above. The shocking surgery fascinates Nick less than the father's self-inflicted violence. Answering Nick's "why?" Dr. Adams successfully generalizes—"He couldn't stand things, I guess," and soon, nature restores normalcy: sun rises, bass jump, father rows (*Complete Short Stories* 69).

In "The Doctor and the Doctor's Wife" (*In Our Time* 1925), "half-breed" Dick Boulton, arriving with his son to work off his wife's medical debt, calls the doctor a thief. Withdrawing after an ill-advised response, Dr. Adams loses face and payment. Boulton exerts control before his son, as Nick's father had in "Indian Camp." Humiliations continue: unopened medical journals embarrass; Mrs. Adams, mouthing religious pieties, denies her husband's Boulton narrative: "Dear, I don't think, I really don't think that anyone would really do a thing like that" (75). Thus dismissed, father joins son seeking black squirrels, both ignoring mother's request that Nick attend her. This story also closes with father-son bonding in nature.

Partially a paean to the domestic, "Ten Indians" (*Men Without Women* 1927) confirms the Adams family dysfunctionality. Traveling by wagon following Fourth of July celebrations, Mrs. Garner banters affectionately with her husband. Alert to teachable moments for sons Frank and Carl, she disapproves the drunken Indians collapsed roadside. When Carl compares Nick's Indian girlfriend to a skunk, however, she interjects: "I won't have Carl talk that way" (*Complete Short Stories* 254). Mr. Garner offers Nick fatherly advice: "[W]atch out to keep Prudie, Nick" (254). Later, each Garner assumes responsibilities—unloading the wagon, stabling the horses, starting the fire—a family functioning. Returning home, Nick finds supper—chicken, milk, pie—cold, the atmosphere soon foreboding. His father's outsized shadow ominously dominates the wall; Huckleberry pie suggests Huckleberry Finn's cruel Pap. His father reports stumbling upon Prudie and another boy in the woods "having quite a time" (256).

A technician but no rhetorician, Dr. Adams's tough-love exposure of Prudie's unfaithfulness hurts Nick. The doctor presses his tearful son: "Have some more?"—pie? Prudie details? (256). Moreover, Nick's mother's absence eliminates potential support, a loss intensified because it is juxtaposed with Mrs. Garner's conscientious shaping of her sons' racial sensitivity. Nature again protects: "a big wind blowing and the waves...; [Nick] was awake a long time before he remembered that his heart was broken" (257).

Young Nick observes, but much domestic interaction exceeds his comprehension: women initiate consequential events; life overcomes the Indian father; Mrs. Adams humiliates her husband; he, elsewhere, crushes Nick. Moreover, failed fathers highlight strong mothers: fighting for her baby even as her husband self-destructs, the Indian woman screams and bites, never giving up nor passing out; wife and mother, Mrs. Garner (overshadowing Mrs. Adams) voices moral authority, eliciting her husband's support in mentoring her boys—and Nick.

Nick attempts adulthood in "The End of Something" and "The Three-Day Blow" (*In Our Time* 1925). He has planned to find work and marry Marjorie, nearly his equal in boating and fishing. Yet something about that decision threatens his resolve—perhaps, his parents' marriage; definitely, friend Bill's misogyny: "Once a man's married he's absolutely bitched"[4] (*Complete Short Stories* 90). One moonlit evening, unable to explain why love "isn't fun any more," Nick ends the relationship—awkwardly, hurting them both (81). Surprised, but her dignity intact, Marge ably rows away, leaving Nick a victor without spoils.

"The Three-Day Blow," awash in alcoholic and verbal spillage, exposes immaturity and ignorance. Nick and Bill philosophize, their misunderstandings loosed in aphorisms, clichés, epigrams: Giants manager McGraw wants Heinie Zim because "he loses ball games"; drunkards develop from "opening bottles," and not from "solitary drinking"; "Everything's got its compensations.... It all evens up"; pertinent to Nick and Marge, "Nothing was finished. Nothing was ever lost" (*Complete Short Stories* 86, 88, 89, 92). Further, Bill stereotypes the domestic in Marge's parents, describing how marriage would "bitch" Nick: "around the house all the time and going to Sunday dinners at their house, and having them over to dinner, and her telling Marge all the time what to do and how to act" (90). Midwestern family mores, despite Bill's prejudiced rendering, do not compromise Marge as potential life partner—a young woman capable, sensible, adult.

Nick's immaturity surpasses Bill's. In a bizarre twist of thought and language, he claims that Marge's fishing excellence, developed at his hands, necessitates their breakup: "You know everything"; "I've taught you everything.... What don't you know anyway?" (81). Later, in "The Three-Day Blow," after Bill's father has hunted alone for hours during stormy weather and following the boys' heavy drinking, Nick dangerously directs: "Let's take the guns... and go look for your dad" (92). With Marge and Bill, Nick disregards fundamental verities concerning man in nature—immature behavior particularly disturbing because modeling such "masculine" truths constitutes Dr. Adams's principal father-to-son legacy. Traditional female domestic roles prospective in a strong woman center action in both stories: Marge singularly attractive, the boys inexperienced, their masculinity fledgling.

Resolved to establish male independence, Nick rides the rails in "The Battler" (*In Our Time* 1925). As earlier, a man's self-inflicted ruin fascinates him, and again a strong woman controls action. Ad loved his wife; despite beatings in the ring, he became unstable only after his marriage failed. Innocent Nick misses the danger Bugs presents and the homoeroticism in the black man's description of Ad's wife: "She was an awful good-looking woman. Looked enough like him to be twins. He wouldn't be bad-looking without his face all busted. . . . She's a mighty fine woman" (*Complete Short Stories* 103). Nick's failure to "see" and "hear" unspoken realities eases the blackjack-wielding Bugs's concern about his fiefdom being exposed.

Ad's wife radically modifies the traditional domestic. She still loves, accepting the emotional duress of funding an interracial, same-sex, domestic companionship (Monteiro 224–25). Moreover, physical absence intensifies her presence, a rhetorical motif throughout the cycle. Women speechless, nameless, often absent—the pregnant Indian, Boulton's wife, Prudie, Ad's wife, and, later, the major's wife, Nick's wives, others—initiate significant action, thereby becoming crucial female "presences" effecting critical commentary.

Still in Michigan, traveling, in "The Light of the World" (*Winner Take Nothing* 1933), teenage Nick, with Tom, encounters the irrational expressed in verbal violence: Calling the boys "punks"—midcentury slang for a male prostitute—a bartender threatens; wanting to amuse them, a lumberman harasses a gay cook; usurping control with her "soft voice," 350-pound whore Alice stuns Nick.[5] Alice's voice flays fellow professional, "Peroxide," then, modulating to "poetic," intones a corrupt lover's encomium, "You're a lovely piece, Alice." Nick, unmanned, succumbs to timbre over content: "prettiest face . . . smooth skin . . . lovely voice" (*Complete Short Stories* 297). Worried, Tom hustles into flight two confused naïfs, their sexuality challenged, even imperiled.[6]

Nick's quest for independence, self, and adulthood finds him on the road near Chicago in "The Killers" (*Men Without Women* 1927). Beginning with the Marge breakup, his has been a world characterized by the failure of love, even of simple male/female communication; loss of personal control; irrationality and violence. Even so, no previous threat or actual harm has approached the horror surrounding impersonal murder. In "The Killers," Nick, George, and Sam avoid violent deaths only because a professional "hit" evaporates. When finally free, Nick rushes the targeted Andreson with impotent logic, rationality: "see the police," "it was just a bluff," "get out of town," "fix it up some way" (*Complete Short Stories* 221). Scared, Nick again fails "to see," to comprehend, genuine evil: Andreson gives up, and hirelings will soon kill him—impersonally. As had "The Battler" and "The Light of the World," "The Killers" ends with an unfocused, still-naïve Nick in flight. His moving on is not without irony here. Nick soon commits to soldiering—a traditional male rite of passage—his war involving unprecedented impersonal killing. Nick's effort to shape an adult male self now centers in a demonstrably impulsive patriotic act—one completed even before America enters the war.

Nick first appears as a soldier in chapter VI in *In Our Time* (1925). An Italian army volunteer, seriously wounded and supported by a church wall, Nick takes stock. Beyond, a bedstead hanging from an exploded bedroom with pink walls cries out for its nameless, wordless, absent child, a powerful domestic image. Now an experienced combatant, Nick remains idealistically committed no longer. He speaks unequivocally to a wounded fellow soldier: "Senta, Rinaldi ... we've made a separate peace.... Not patriots" (*Complete Short Stories* 105).

Nick's injuries and slow recovering(s) in "In Another Country" and "Now I Lay Me" (*Men Without Women* 1927) and "A Way You'll Never Be" (*Winner Take Nothing* 1933) induce reflection, distill candor, engender maturity. "In Another Country" investigates courage. Although wounded, Nick is not a hawk: "very much afraid to die, wondering how [he] would be" returned to the front (208).

He befriends a major who corrects Nick's Italian grammar. One day, the major responds angrily to Nick's "hope" to marry: "A man must not marry. ... If he is to lose everything, he should not place himself in a position to lose that" (209). The young wife the major married only after being invalided from the war has died. Describing his feelings, he falters; soon, however, he appears in dress uniform, "carrying himself straight and soldierly, with tears on both cheeks and biting his lips" (209). The domestic emerges powerfully. Suffering humanizes both men while redefining courage. Nick must ponder the civilizing discipline of grammar and duty and, within the masculine, the role of love and emotion. Again, a wife—nameless, wordless, absent—brings gender issues into focus.

"A Way You'll Never Be" records Nick's instability following a head wound. It includes battle fright, hallucinations, and language flowing uncontrollably. Also, it includes grit; Nick tries to "hold it in" (314). War includes violence to women. Though no woman speaks or appears here, propaganda postcards scattered among the dead depict soldiers raping young women; photographs and letters between lovers and among family express domestic bonds now extinguished. Nick bicycles through this grotesquerie. Later, he denies being brave: "I know how I am and I prefer to get stinking. I'm not ashamed of it" (309). In memory episodes, Nick interpolates Paris night scenes, celebrities, and multiple battle terrains, and even "saw" himself shot (314).[7] Pulling himself together after one such major break, he moves forward, again bicycling through the domestic holocaust.

Recovering from shell shock and afraid of sleep in "Now I Lay Me," Nick hones a writer's imagination, creating streams more real than waters he fished as a child: "I made up streams. . . . Some . . . I still remember and think that I have fished in them, and they are confused with streams I really know" (277). Extensive recall—people, events, details from his youth—equips Nick to write, to tackle troubling experience: for example, his mother burns his father's Indian artifacts. The child's prayer of the title underscores how childhood shapes adulthood, here specifically touching the domestic: Nick's parents' relationship subconsciously dims his "hope to marry," threatening this traditional domestic male role. Responding to his orderly's exhortation to marry, Nick realizes, after reviewing girls he has known, that unlike fishing—continuously new—the girls "blurred and all became rather the same" (282). Nick's imagination sharpens and deepens, unfortunately outpacing other dimensions of his recovering mental health.

The war ends and time passes. In "Cross-Country Snow" (*In Our Time* 1925), a dramatically take-charge Nick skis with George in Switzerland. Outside the narrative frame, Nick has chanced with Helen traditional love, marriage, fatherhood. Here Nick and George ski, share drinks, and discuss Nick's beloved. Despite Michigan parallels, these men are not Nick and Bill: they drink moderately; they accept responsibility; neither regards Helen as coming between best friends. Moreover, Nick and Helen function as equals—they experience no rivalry as skiers (unlike anglers Nick and Marge); both regret leaving European slopes but agree that the baby must be born stateside. These decisions constitute successful communication, solidarity, a mature couple becoming family. Now glad about the baby, Nick effectively denies Bill's marriage critique in the earlier story.

A writer returned to the Michigan woods in "Big Two-Hearted River" (*In Our Time* 1925), Nick first controls responsibilities—"the need for thinking, the need to write, other needs" (164). Then he sets forth to reclaim paternal roots and to restore equilibrium. Taught to find pleasure and pattern in nature, Nick honors his father's wordless rites—domesticating a campsite, fishing well. Hoping "nothing could touch him," he neatly transcends the singular loss years earlier of fishing buddy, Hopkins (167). Emotion flows uncontrollably only when a huge trout breaks his line—an event shaping behavior, vocabulary, progress. Self-aware, Nick avoids the swamp: there fishing would be "tragic" (180). Leaving the swamp to another day, Nick, at peace and with two fine fish, splashes ashore—a writer and a veteran of war and numerous of his era's violences. Mature now, at home in nature and focused on the future, Nick brings his postwar masculine self successfully to order.

The maturity in "Cross-Country Snow" anchors "Alpine Idyll" (*Men Without Women* 1927). Nick, returning from skiing, observes an odd burial scene: a peasant mourner relieves the sexton, carefully spreading the earth himself. Later, the peasant appears at an inn, buys the sexton a drink, speaks to no one, then departs. Nick, intrigued, encourages the innkeeper, who willingly shapes his narrative—"All these peasants are beasts" (265). Olz's wife died of a heart condition when winter weather prohibited transport and burial. Her frozen form near the woodpile, Olz, getting wood, routinely hung a lamp from her mouth, causing serious disfigurement. Challenged by the appalled priest, Olz insists: "*Ja,* I loved her. . . . I loved her fine" (266). The unusual/unnatural in these acts attracts Nick the writer. Olz caringly manicured his wife's gravesite; he "loved her fine." Surely Nick nods affirmatively at the innkeeper's final question, "You understand it all about his wife?" (266).

"A Day's Wait" and "Fathers and Sons" (*Winner Take Nothing* 1933) center on family and close the Nick Adams cycle. In the first story, Nick has remarried following a divorce, and his nine-year-old son from his first marriage is visiting from France. The boy confuses Fahrenheit and Celsius. Fear of certain death from misunderstanding his seemingly elevated temperature prompts the child's stoic bravery. From bed with his wife, Nick rises and discovers the ill child. Arranging for a doctor, he attempts comfort—talking, reading stories. The boy appears inattentive. Believing him lightheaded, writer Nick misses the obvious: strange looks, non-sequitur responses. During a lull in medicating, Nick hunts quail. The ground is "varnished with ice." The dog "slipped and slithered," and "I fell twice, hard, once dropping my gun and having it slide away" (333). Nick's foolishness highlights the boy's courage, "holding tight onto himself." Understanding, then relief—for father and son—quickly follow

Schatz's question: "About how long will it be before I die?" (334). Inept and embarrassed, Nick embraces the domestic as loving caregiver for his sick child.

In "Fathers and Sons," thirty-eight-year-old Nick reflects as writer and father on his family. Estranged from his mood-driven father while still young, the mature Nick possesses perspective: each family member "betrayed" his father "in their various ways." Yet always beyond the conflicts came the hunting and fishing. Nick "loved to fish and to shoot exactly as much as when he first had gone with his father" (370). Not yet able to write about him, Nick can speak: "What was it like, Papa, when you were a little boy and used to hunt with the Indians?" (375). Startled by the boy—previously asleep on this car trip—Nick describes a superb hunter, who had lived among Indians.

Earlier, the Ojibway occupied his own thoughts: Trudy (the reader recalls her as Prudie in "Ten Indians" in *Men Without Women*) and carefree sex; later, the tribe's decline. Mentally, writer Nick streamed words, first, framing the good—Trudy: "tightly, sweetly, moistly . . . fully, finally, unendingly, never-endingly, suddenly ended, the great bird flown." Then, memorializing the bad: "when you go . . . where Indians have lived you smell them gone and all the empty painkiller bottles and the flies . . . do not kill the sweetgrass smell, the smoke smell, and that other like a fresh cased marten skin. . . . Long time ago good. Now no good" (376). Dr. Adams's son, Nick, masters *his* profession—powerfully imaging in words new meanings.

Nick praises grandfather to grandson: "I'd rather see him shoot than any man I ever knew." The boy's interest deepens. The peerless marksman who walked with Indians preoccupies the child, nearing the age to have a shotgun: "Why do we never go to pray at the tomb of my grandfather?" (376). Nick is caught off guard. His son presses; he worries, too, about his father's burial. Nick gently concedes: "We'll have to go. . . . I can see we'll have to go" (377). Nick's words close the cycle on a domestic note stressing family, encompassing all three Adams generations.

Nick loves his son. Ironically, Nick's responses parallel Dr. Adams's comforting answers long ago to his young boy following the suicide in "Indian Camp." Deferring to his son strengthens the father-son bond. Moreover, it potentially (re)shapes family history: the boy's desire to preserve grandfather's and father's memory affirms family in time present; touching time past, it validates the original Edenic dream of Dr. and Mrs. Adams for family summers in Michigan. The boy himself embodies hope for the Adams family in time future.

The Nick Adams cycle offers an often marred but ultimately hopeful vision of the traditional domestic—touching love, marriage, family.

•

Domestic issues intersect all major themes across the stories and the widely taught novels. In *The Sun Also Rises* (1926), for example, Jake Barnes struggles over losing his Catholic faith and his failure to elicit a lover's commitment from Brett Ashley. She blames his sexual incapacity from a Great War wound. Brett, too, carries war wounds: her first love died of dysentery; later, her husband, Ashley, suffering PTSD, continually threatened her.

Concluding the Jake/Brett discussion, I ask students: Why does Jake note consistently, albeit cursorily, women unknown to him—all in traditional roles, female characters often wordless, most nameless, even outside the novel's frame? These women include Aloysius Kirby's daughter, Katherine; Krum's wife and family; the couple passing while Jake and Bill admire Notre Dame; the American family and the pilgrims on the train; the Spanish nurses tending children; the lovers on the raft. This metonymic chorus shapes a question: subconsciously, how broad is Jake's personal domestic dream? Does it include love, marriage, family?

Most students believe that Jake's domestic dream includes the spiritual and underscores his normality: he works and socializes, plays tennis and fishes, follows boxing and bicycling, embraces the bullfight tradition, visits several churches. Emotionally hurt, he cries in the night. Jake's dreams hover about the traditional domestic: religion, love leading to marriage, family. Thinking of his tomorrows, we remember that Jake's life initiates the central Hemingway question: how does one discover in a world of discredited, destabilized, and shifting values and traditions the way to live now?

Significantly, in families traditional and queer, troubled and in harmony— Hemingway offers an array of possibilities.

Notes

1. For another account of Susan Beegel's enduring this oft-repeated question, see Hilary Justice's essay in this volume. For a narrative glimpse of the incredulity and challenges lobbed at female Hemingway scholars, see Linda Patterson Miller, "In Love with Papa," in *Hemingway and Women: Female Critics and the Female Voice*, Lawrence R. Broer and Gloria Holland, eds. (Tuscaloosa: U of Alabama P, 2002). Justice is optimistic, however, that as the distance between Hemingway's generation and the students' own broadens, so do their preconceptions of him as anything other than an important author from the past.

2. Philip Young's *The Nick Adams Stories* (1972) includes all these stories, as well as previously unpublished materials, and fits the stories together in a neat chronology that sees Nick grow from boy to man, but Young's ordering is idiosyncratic. For example,

Young asserts without evidence that Nick is married in "An Alpine Idyll" and excludes "A Day's Wait," thereby eliminating a father/son story and the presence of Nick's new wife. These editorial decisions destabilize the domestic theme that arises holistically when the stories are read individually.

3. For example, Debra Moddelmog's essay on "Queer Families in Hemingway's Fiction" in *Hemingway and Women* argues that "family is not missing from Hemingway's fiction but is present in a form different from the one readers expect to find" (173) and that these "queer families" "not only . . . stand in for the biological family . . . but also that they often stand in opposition to this family" (174).

4. See also, Michael S. Reynolds, *The Young Hemingway* (New York: B. Blackwell, 1986).

5. The first-person narrator is not named, but readers and critics are in general agreement that the story should be included—along with "An Alpine Idyll" and "In Another Country," also featuring unnamed protagonists—among other Nick Adams stories. Following this convention, the protagonists of all three stories are referred to as "Nick" in this essay.

6. Paul Smith, in *A Reader's Guide to the Short Stories of Ernest Hemingway* (Boston: G.K. Hall & Co., 1989), notes that an earlier manuscript is even more overt in its threats of sexual violence. The lines "Ever interfere with a cook? . . . You can interfere with this one" originally offered "bugger" in place of "interfere" in the typescript, and "You know where" originally read "Up your ass" (Smith 257–58). In an alternate ending that Hemingway ultimately rejected, the protagonist decides to return to Alice and then stops, admitting that he is "spooked" (Smith 257).

7. An earlier draft of the story includes a pair of soldiers scolded—but not punished—after being "caught in a homosexual act" (Smith 271).

Nick Adams and the Construction of Masculinity

Sarah B. Hardy

> "How exciting it is to get started reading one of the greatest writers of all time! Like the rest of the world, I've been reading Hemingway for some time and can't get over his writing. I feel it is almost a cliché to say that I like Hemingway, but I do."
> —Student posting in an online course forum

When I teach Hemingway, I often start with what I hope is a gentle intervention. I ask my students to list images and ideas that come to mind when they think of the author Ernest Hemingway, and without comment, I write their list on the board. "Big game hunter." "Bullfights." "Alcohol." "Divorce." "Expatriate." Sometimes someone will contribute "suicide." We then look for patterns or common threads, and I add those to the board. "Adventure." "Toughness." "Manliness." I ask if there are any conflicts or internal tensions worth noting on our list, but other than an occasional suggestion that suicide is not a sign of manliness (a concern I ask them to bracket until later), usually the students find the profile that we have created to be internally consistent and coherent.

Essentially, we have generated a popular portrait of the author. It tends to be the same from one year to the next, and it is popular in more than one sense of the word. As the student comment at the beginning of this essay suggests, many students in my classroom are happy, and perhaps relieved, to be reading Hemingway. Whether in the context of an upper-level modern novel course, an entry-level course on fathers and sons in literature, or—as will be my focus here—a 300-level course on the modern short story, my students expect to like Hemingway, to understand him, to identify with him. Perhaps this is not altogether surprising given that I teach at Hampden-Sydney College, one of the only all-male liberal arts colleges in the country. Though our student population grows more diverse each year, we are a college that maintains a gun locker at the campus police station, presumably for the hunters in the student body, and in fact it is not unusual to see someone arrive for class in camouflage on the opening day of deer or spring gobbler season. Other forms of normative masculinity are evident in the fraternities that dominate the college's social life and in the way that the few students who choose military leadership as a career are singled out with a commissioning ceremony on stage at commencement. A popular bumper sticker distributed by the admissions staff says simply "Man Up. Hampden-Sydney College." In this context, initial discussions of Hemingway are perhaps bound to prompt a distilled masculinist version of the author and his work.

Ben Knights, in his introduction to *Masculinities in Text and Teaching*, points to what he calls the "peri-text" of any artistic work, "the buzz of conversation which surrounds the text as an enactment of social meanings" (11). Even if the peri-text of (Papa) Hemingway is more likely to be embraced with enthusiasm at Hampden-Sydney, I suspect it is present in college classrooms everywhere. The figure of Hemingway that presides in students' collective popular imagination is persistent—even insistent—in its conventions of masculinity. This persistence might seem to run counter to Michael Kimmel's argument in "Integrating Men into the Curriculum" that "there is a general failure to see men, or more accurately masculinity, at every level of the educational endeavor.... At every stage of the process, men are invisible" (181). After all, what could be more visible than this abiding performance of manhood? I would argue, however, that the hypermasculine imaginary that students bring to their reading of Hemingway paradoxically provides a rich opportunity to make masculinity visible to them, possibly for the first time.

Once we have made our list, I ask the class what dangers there might be in reading texts written by someone who is already so fixed in our imaginations. An English major in the room might pipe up that we should be careful not to confuse the author with the narrator or the characters, and I will of course agree. I also point out that there are other problems, one of which is to take for granted the idea of a coherent portrait in the first place, whether of an author or of a character. In the context of the modern short story course, we have already read Chekhov, Joyce, Kafka, and Bowen and had extensive discussions of modernism and the limits of realism.

One of my goals as we read Hemingway's short fiction is to extend those discussions to consider modernism as it complicates representations of masculinity. We start our encounter with Hemingway, then, with a series of open questions. How do we construct the idea of a real or fictional character? Do omissions in a fictional representation direct us to supply the "right" interpretation, or can they function as places that open up the story to multiple voices or points of view? What are we tempted to infer about masculinity as a monolithic idea in Hemingway's stories? What might the stories actually be saying instead?

> "It seems like a lot of the stories we read include scenes of people hunting for or searching for something. When characters find what it is they are looking for ... they are ultimately met with unsettling ends. Sometimes they find things they are not looking for, such as a story they'll never write (like in "Snows") or a suicide victim ("Indian Camp")."
> —Student posting

At Hampden-Sydney, the brick gates at the college entrance bear a sign reading *Huc venite iuvenes ut exeatis viri*, translated on the website as "Come here as youths so that you may leave as men." The study of Nick Adams and his growing up thus seems especially apt for this student population, but Nick Adams is interesting to any teacher or student who is thinking about literary gender constructions. As we see not just in the fiction of Hemingway but in that of Joyce, Mansfield, Faulkner, and others, the emerging subjectivity of childhood offers up spaces for experimental approaches to narrative. Nick Adams also demonstrates that boyhood in modernism allows for a range of depictions of masculinity—from the predictable to the subversive.

Nick has long been seen as Hemingway's fictional alter ego. In a character profile, Harold Bloom connects Nick to American rugged individualism and describes him as someone who loves nature, "is an expert hunter and fisherman; is preoccupied with notions of toughness; likes being alone and free; and becomes wounded physically and psychologically" (161). But in terms of masculine identities, Nick is perhaps most interesting for what he is not: he is not fully formed as a male character, and much of what we see of him shows that he has not finished his own transition from boy to man. He embodies a focus in Hemingway singled out by Nancy Comley and Robert Scholes: the problem of maturity, "dominated by the possibility of there being a position between fatherhood and childhood" (12). As he dwells in that possibility, Nick often seems to be searching for something, as one student points out above, even if he doesn't know exactly what he is hoping to find.

Although my short story class reads a selection of Hemingway stories, including several that are not about Nick, here I'd like to focus on "Indian Camp" and "Fathers and Sons" for considering Hemingway's representations of masculinity. With the nine-year gap in their publication history, these two stories work to bookend a larger narrative of Nick's maturation. Both are stories about learning, about transmission from one generation to the next (or the failure thereof). Both involve examinations of growing up in explicitly gendered terms. In my experience, they are compelling as classroom texts in that they provide reflective moments for students to think about boys, men, and gender, not just in the context of modernism, but over and against their own experiences.

"Indian Camp" provides an excellent example of Hemingway's technique as a short story writer while it introduces readers to Nick's exploration of gender identity. Though we see much of the story through his perspective, this young Nick has almost no agency. He is a child dragged along by his father, with little explanation, on a terrifying house call. The story's world is one of fragments of images and information, fragments that Nick has a hard time processing, in spite of his father's commentary. For a substantial part of the narrative, Nick tries not to see what is happening. He spends a lot of time "not looking," and "his curiosity had been gone for a long time" (69). The mimetic discourse of the text ties our experience of the story to Nick's blinkered and partial observations, though we do not share the same age limitations. A good class discussion of what might be implied by the surface of "Indian Camp" will often articulate underlying issues of race and class, as well as dynamics of medicine, education, and power. Depending on the context of a given group of students, they might tease out Uncle George's ambiguous relationship to the Indians or explore the implications of the logging that has been changing the landscape. As readers who have more life knowledge, we all find ourselves supplying information that Nick does not have. And indeed, our inferences are a direct response to Hemingway's well-known aesthetic of omission, his use of limited point of view and the modernist fragment as they invite us to participate in a sharply elliptical short story form.

Stories with a child protagonist are likely to highlight moments of learning and attempts at interpretation; the final moments of "Indian Camp" redirect our focus accordingly as we read how Nick tries to understand what has just happened. His questions about childbirth and suicide show that he is trying to interpret the shocking events of the story through the lens of gender. Nor is Nick wrong:

after all, he has just been exposed to an "awful mess" in which two bodies—one female and one male—were subjected to forms of violence that resulted in both life and death. Nick's response to what he has experienced reduces the situation to binaries of men vs. women and life vs. death: "Do many men kill themselves, Daddy? . . . Do many women?"(69). His oversimplification leaves out the racially inflected relationships in the story, just as it overlooks the poverty they have left behind. His father's answers to his questions sustain Nick's framework without expanding or complicating it, which may not be surprising given that his father appears to live within categories of gender and race that grant him authority. Nick's interpretive efforts, and his father's comforting masculine presence, lead him to the false conclusion that he will never die.

Students who are reading this text for the first time frequently mention how jarring the ending is for them. In the short story class, we have seen false epiphanies before and discussed what they show us about the subjective space of a character. Nick's conclusion reminds us of his immaturity while it underscores a distance between this character, the other characters, and the readers. Because Nick is young, we may experience this distance sympathetically rather than ironically. Even so, the story insists on a site of reading that includes multiple points of view that cannot be reconciled. In a class discussion of these points of view, we can tease out varying perspectives on Nick's interpretive terms.

Finding a stable perspective in the story turns out to be difficult, and this can be made clear with a class exercise that asks students to make sense of the shifting designations for Nick's father (from "his father" to "the doctor" and back). As Thomas Strychacz points out: "The rapid transformation of roles in the cabin . . . suggests the friable, temporary, and constructed nature of masculine (and feminine) roles. . . . Nor can we distinguish forms of paternal authority on the basis of racial difference, for even in 'Indian Camp' the doctor's authority is not absolute" (*Hemingway's Theaters* 58). Nick's father seems to offer answers, but the events of the story make clear that both his medical and his paternal authorities are flawed. Uncle George shifts from being magnanimous and celebratory to wounded and derogatory to mysteriously absent. The Indians' perspectives are present but mostly ignored, as is any female voice; Dr. Adams tells Nick that he does not hear his patient's screams because "they are not important." The doctor's discovery of the husband's suicide reminds us of an overlooked male point of view with violent eloquence. And when Nick finally turns to his father for help with interpreting what has happened, the adult responses to the boy's questions are staccato and incomplete.

Students sometimes want to dismiss the conclusion Nick reaches in "Indian Camp" as the mistake of a child, but asking what this story is suggesting about masculinity challenges readers to take a step back. Nick's binary, gendered lens invites a view of the world that is obviously faulty, and "Indian Camp" starts to interrogate assumptions about gender, more specifically about masculinity, through this young boy's encounter with unresolved perspectives. Here is a story with no "code hero" or clear model of hegemonic masculinity, which in turn challenges popular expectations for a Hemingway fiction.[1] With no good model in sight, this story's take on masculinity seems open-ended, if not openly critical.

"When reading Hemingway, I can't help but be reminded of the way Bowen wrote about those 'obscure crises' with which humans deal on a day-to-day basis. These are obscure in that, although many of us experience these kinds of things, we often don't think about them too much. I believe that Hemingway does a great job of elucidating these crises, especially through his use of dialogue.... In 'Fathers and Sons,' we see it with regards to a young boy's grappling with his own masculinity in his explanation of what he would do if Eddie Gilby tried to make a pass at his sister Dorothy."
—Student posting

In the context of this course on short fiction, "Indian Camp" fits into a group of modernist stories about boyhood. Clearly, in stories about boys growing up, there are likely to be moments when those boys confront new masculinities and have to decide what to do about them. These stories, and the narrative openings they create, frame a crisis point around gender identity. The older Nick we encounter in "Fathers and Sons" goes through several such moments of crisis, but he is harder to dismiss than the Nick in "Indian Camp," and this story can help students identify a pattern of constructed masculine selves.

Nick remembers confronting masculine identities for which he was not fully prepared, as we see in his humorous responses to things his father taught him (or didn't teach him) about sex. When Nick calls a squirrel that has bitten him "a dirty little bugger," his father explains that a bugger is "a man who has intercourse with animals," and "Nick's imagination was both stirred and horrified by this and he thought of various animals but none seemed attractive or practical" (371). Later he and his father talk about a singer who has been caught "mashing," which Nick's father describes as "the most heinous of crimes." Nick again responds with his imagination, picturing "the great tenor doing something strange, bizarre, and heinous with a potato masher to a beautiful lady who looked like the pictures of Anna Held on the inside of cigar boxes. He resolved, with considerable horror, that when he was old enough he would try mashing at least once." These scenes in turn occur in the context of fragmented recollections of his father, which start to set his father's approaches to being a man against Nick's own in ways that make him uncomfortable and that are "not good remembering" (371). In this part of the text we see strange, disquieting, or at least unforeseen versions of masculinity being introduced into the young character's consciousness. There is a lot Nick doesn't understand about adult male behavior, and he responds to these gaps in his knowledge by creating narratives in which he is the masculine protagonist.

The narrative's response to openings of masculine possibility thus seems to be to follow them up, even to shut them down, with a more normative masculinity. As Nick thinks back to his own early sexual education, the story turns to the memory of his relationship with the Ojibway girl Trudy, one that crosses ethnic lines while maintaining racial and gender hierarchies. As the white boy in the relationship, Nick is the one who owns the gun and literally calls the shots. Sex with Trudy is followed in Nick's thoughts by a scene of masculine bravado after he finds out that Trudy's older half-brother Eddie wants to sleep with Nick's sister. Nick constructs an imaginary scenario, illustrated with a real gunshot, in which he dramatically shoots Eddie then scalps him and feeds him to the dogs. As Linda Helstern points out, Nick's reaction asserts a new distance from Trudy at the same time that it asserts certain tropes of white masculinity and power: "Nick instantly assumes the role of Indian killer and defender of white womanhood, apparently using one of his three very real and very precious twenty-gauge shotgun shells to blow an imaginary hole through 'that half-breed bastard Eddie Gilby'" (73–74). Trudy, understandably, is upset about this possibility, and begs Nick to spare Eddie, so Nick relents: "Nick had killed Eddie Gilby, then pardoned him his life, and he was a man now" ("Fathers and Sons" 373).

Perhaps because of the compelling (and hypocritical) combination of sex and violence, this scene often makes a big impression on my students, and it is useful to analyze it in class for what it is showing us about Nick's masculinity. This moment serves as a declaration of masculine identity, but it underscores the extent to which Hemingway's masculine selves are constructed comparatively. Nick needs the idea of Eddie and the presence of Trudy to claim his own manliness; at the same time, his representation of masculinity is also a representation of race and sexuality, so his "manliness" is decidedly heterosexual, empowered, and white.

Nick's reaction to the threat of Eddie is also consistent with Strychacz's reading of masculinities in Hemingway and other modernists as theatrical representation or performance. Drawing in part on the work of Judith Butler, Strychacz argues that "under the trope of masculine self-fashioning, masculinity is held to be theatrical, rhetorical, and relational; it is a pose, a demonstration, an act of persuasion, a temporary state developing out of the relationship between a man performing and an evaluating audience" (*Dangerous Masculinities* 22). Nick's heroic pose at this point in "Fathers and Sons" has several audiences: Trudy and Billie, who are present; Eddie, who is being sent a threatening message; Nick himself as he recalls the scene; and the story's readers. Each audience refracts the performed masculinity in a different way, and students can analyze the degree to which these audiences are persuaded—and why. For instance, Trudy seems to believe the demonstration while Billie's glum response shows that even if he knows he is watching a performance, the power relationship being asserted is an unfortunate part of his own reality: "He better watch out" (373). Eddie should abide by Nick's masculine hierarchy, at least according to his siblings.

The older Nick who is remembering this scene is author, actor, and audience for the performance, and in the larger context of the story (and the Nick Adams narrative), we can see that this adolescent declaration of manhood is "a temporary state." It is also quite clearly, through the ironic lens of Nick's recollection, a fiction. After a careful discussion of this scene, the class can step back to review what Hemingway seems to be saying about Nick's claim to masculinity—that it is comparative, theatrical, short-lived, and imaginary. With very little prompting, students who have read other Hemingway texts will often connect Nick's response to other scenes of constructed masculinity, such as central moments of dialogue in "The Short Happy Life of Frances Macomber" or various scenes from *The Sun Also Rises*.

> "To me, Nick is emotionally cold to his son. The final dialogue suggests a desire to dismiss the subject of his father's tomb rather than an actual promise (or desire) to take his own son to visit the site. In this way, Nick's relationship with his father is being repeated with his own son; therefore Hemingway is calling for a way for men to express emotions rather than simply conforming and perpetuating."
> —Student posting

Both Nick and the reader are considering Nick's memories in the context of multiple generations, a context that invites us to ask whether his confrontations with masculine identity constitute lessons that can be transmitted. I like to conclude our discussion of Nick Adams by asking the class some simple questions: Has anything changed over the course of these stories? Is Nick a better father than his father was? Is his masculinity static, or has he become a different kind of man?

These questions prompt some real debate over issues that take us back to the first day we discussed Hemingway and masculinity. Some students express frustration with Nick's answers to his son's questions. Many critics would agree: as Paul Wadden phrases it, Nick seems "not equal to the task—indeed, to this potential initiation, for if the son is old enough to ask perceptive questions then he is old enough to learn" (126). Not unlike his father, Nick is withholding information, giving a fragmented picture of friendship with the Ojibways. As the above posting shows, however, even the frustrated students in the class are willing to see some critical distance between Hemingway and Nick, distance they were not quite ready to see before we looked closely at the stories. Nick's shortcomings, this student suggests, allow Hemingway a space for critique.

Other students are willing to give Nick more credit for being different from his father, particularly if they compare the conversation in the canoe at the end of "Indian Camp" to Nick's conversation with his son in the car. Nick's answers imply continuity from grandfather to father to son, but they also allow for change. When his son asks if he will ever live among the Indians, Nick replies, "I don't know.... That's up to you" ("Fathers and Sons" 376). Though this is the last Nick Adams story published in Hemingway's lifetime, the frame narrative in a moving car could suggest that Nick and his son are still in transition, that their story is ongoing, with another trip—"I can see we'll have to go"—on the horizon (377). A more positive reading of Nick's fatherhood reveals him to be more interactive and engaged with the ideas of others. In such a reading, the ending implies a more dynamic and fluid masculinity, one that is reflective and self-aware, and one that is still on a threshold.

Regardless of where students fall in their ultimate reading of (or personal liking for) Nick Adams, close attention to these stories makes clear that his masculine identity, for all its apparent individualism, is contextual and constructed. Through Nick—both within the individual stories and by virtue of Nick's appearance as a recurring character—Hemingway is showing us that any single idea of masculinity is a momentary fiction and not a timeless given.

In his argument for making men—as men—more visible in the curriculum, Michael Kimmel urges educators to be aware of how hegemonic (white, heterosexual, athletic, middle-class) masculinity came to be the norm and to acknowledge at the same time multiple masculinities that differ from that norm ("Integrating Men" 189). In my experience, Hemingway proves surprisingly useful for both undertakings. As Knights observes, "interaction with narratives (literary and otherwise) is one of the ways in which masculinity is produced. But the arena of higher education study could simultaneously be one where that very process could be held up to the light" (17). Given the demographic changes in academia and beyond, such inquiries are crucial at a men's college that hopes to prepare students for a broader world.[2] But the changes are manifest everywhere, and Hemingway's fictions can afford students a fresh look at masculinity and at themselves that may be all the more pertinent today.

Notes

My thanks go to all of the students in my spring 2013 English 230 course on the modern short story. Though I have taught this course many times, I learned new things from them. In particular, I would like to thank (in alphabetical order) John Bishop, Turner Blake, Mack Keasler, and Walter McCoy for permission to include excerpts from their Blackboard discussion forum postings. I am also grateful to colleagues Mary Prevo and Janice Siegel for their advice and expertise when I needed it.

1. For a brief explanation of the Hemingway "code hero," as well as references for further reading, see Debra A. Moddelmog's essay in this volume.

2. Professors have gender, too, of course. Colleagues and friends are sometimes surprised to learn that I, a white middle-aged feminist, enjoy teaching Hemingway and include him on several syllabi. To them, I can only say that if they don't understand why someone like me would want to teach Hemingway, then they aren't giving him close enough attention.

A Very Complicated Negotiation

Teaching Hemingway to Second Language Learners of English

Douglas Sheldon

Teaching a composition class populated by young adults who, in just one semester's time, must be brought up to speed on academic writing styles is daunting for any instructor, but it is a task made even more challenging when the classroom is made up of students whose first language is *not* English and their various native languages share no close ancestry with any European language system. They are expected to follow specific writing conventions of standard U.S. academic discourse, building essays based on thesis and support, and they must navigate cultural differences in what the word "plagiarism" means. These are just a few of the anticipated difficulties facing second language learners of English (and their instructors); however, other problems derived from these linguistic and cultural differences present themselves in subtle and surprising ways. What follows is an account of how Hemingway's "A Very Short Story" raised unexpected questions of difference for international students, and how I reworked an approach to meet the learning outcomes of communication, comprehension, and critical thinking.

    The course, a fifty-minute lecture, was held each Monday, Wednesday, and Friday in a computer-based classroom. The reading list included two main texts: *Subjects and Strategies: A Writer's Reader* (2010), which provided composition basics; and the 2003 Scribner paperback edition of *In Our Time* (1925) by Ernest Hemingway. Each class period was designed around the required reading assigned the class before, and students completed a brief reading questionnaire using Blackboard Vista, a course management system, before the next meeting when we would negotiate, as a class, the meaning and purpose of the story. My intention was for the students to use skills-based techniques to understand the text—an authentic example of American English written by a native speaker for native speakers—as a conversation between reader and writer.

The student population was composed of those who had scored high enough on the institutional Test of English as a Foreign Language (TOEFL) examination to take their first undergraduate course. In preparing for the course, I followed the model explained by language education researcher William H. Walcott. Walcott offers an operational definition of "communicative competence" for the classroom:

> Communicative competence includes grammatical competence (sentence level grammar), sociolinguistic competence (an understanding of the social context in which language is used), discourse competence (an understanding of how utterances are strung together to form a meaningful whole), and strategic competence (a language user's employment of strategies to make the best use of what s/he knows about how a language works, in order to interpret, express, and negotiate meaning in a given context). (1)

The college writing course thus makes certain assumptions about the competency of the learner. The instructor may well assume that the students have "grammatical competence" because they could not have otherwise have achieved the prerequisites of the course. Yet sometimes, when working with second language learners, educators make the assumption that "sociolinguistic . . . discourse . . . and strategic competence" will follow naturally (Walcott 2). As my experience demonstrates, however, this may not be the case.

In theory, I was doing everything right. My personal teaching methodology aligns with Dwight Atkinson's definition of sociocognitive second language acquisition. According to this sociocognitive model, language is viewed as a "default state of affairs" (143) and "a tool for social action" (146); in other words, people learn a language by using language. This model does not separate thought from action (or interaction) within language use. In adopting this sociocognitive model in practice, however, I should not have assumed competence based on previous testing or instruction but rather seen the opportunity to nurture confidence through a mix of language and writing instruction drawing upon students' questions about the text.

Using a story that was created by a first language user of English (Hemingway) to communicate to a first language audience (Hemingway's contemporary readers), the second language reader can open doors to social and thought-based contexts that shape his or her everyday English-language world. A short story that makes the student examine gender roles and societal conventions is a good place to start. The text of "A Very Short Story" involves an unnamed wounded soldier from the First World War having a short love affair with Luz, his nurse. The relationship blossoms while he is in the hospital but falls apart when he returns stateside and she takes up with an Italian officer. The more talkative students, who happened to be the Saudi men, made some interesting guesses about the text and the relationship between the unnamed protagonist, "He," and Luz. We finished that day's discussion, and, after the students had expressed no desire to ask any more questions, I gave them their next reading assignment to be completed over the Labor Day weekend and dismissed the class.

After the relay of students wanting early grade reports had dissipated, I walked back to my office. Sitting outside my door was one of my Saudi students, a woman about twenty-five years old. She was the only student who, up to this point, had successfully completed all assignments on Vista. She asked if she could discuss the story a bit more with me. I let her into my office and she took a seat at the desk adjacent to mine. Resting her bag on her lap, she pulled out *In Our Time* and, wrapping her arms around the sides of the bag, began to thumb over several yellow and pink tabs that highlighted the pages of the story. I could see Arabic translations of words dotting the page and arrows uniting paragraphs with the same vocabulary.

"I am sorry to bother you, Mr. Doug," she said.
"It's no bother. I guess you want to discuss today's reading a bit more?"
"Yes, I am confused about something."
"Is it vocabulary related? Did you check your glossary?"
"I am fine with that," she said, pulling the glossary from the back of the book.
"I have a question about the man and Luz."
"Oh, OK." At this point I, admittedly, panicked a bit.
"They spend much time alone and traveling. Then it says that they acted like they were married. Couldn't they have their documents sent from home? Why would they only act like a married couple and not get married?"[1]

In Hemingway's story the man and woman are unchaperoned and the man gets a sexually transmitted disease from a salesgirl—significantly, a woman working outside the home—circumstances that caught my students off guard, so it was my responsibility to look at how such issues are discussed in my students' first-language cultures (if they even are) and to reconcile these contingencies with my conversational American style of instruction. This was the first time in years I had stumbled over my words as a teacher. I tried my best to answer her question. I noted the effect of the war on the emergence of new gender roles, but the more I talked, the more she looked at her book and just nodded, turning pages, and gripping her bag. What I had forgotten about the communicative language approach is that language is not just the system of communication but a cultural device defined by the people who use it.[2] I had assumed that certain competencies would occur naturally since the student's grammatical proficiency was so high.

Luckily, it was Labor Day weekend.

"You know, I will look all this up and let you know over the weekend what we will do in class," I said before this very worried student stuffed her book back into her bag and sealed it shut to keep the warm September rain from making the pages swell.

She smiled a goodbye and left for the long weekend. I shut the door to my office and brooded for several minutes about how I had failed. The questions my Saudi student asked me were not questions of basic grammatical reading competence—they were cultural. It hit me that I did not know enough about these cross-cultural attitudes toward gender roles to really inform my student in ways sensitive to her home culture. I had basic ideas about patriarchal societies, but as my understanding was rooted in my own American cultural heritage, I knew my current efforts did not meet a communicative goal. I did not want to come across as condescending, ethnocentric, intolerant, or uninformed.

The Saudi student could not be the only one who was confused. She was the best student in the class so far, displaying the highest levels of proficiency. The other students must have felt like they were drowning. I had made a rookie error that I have done my best since not to repeat: I had assumed comprehension skills could be defined by skills-based testing.

I emailed the class, canceling the next reading assignment and asking them to review once again "A Very Short Story." Over the next two weeks we would develop a project around understanding this piece of writing from both a cultural and textual standpoint. I gave them a Vista assignment to make sure they actually reread the story. This time, however, I required them to ask questions about actions the characters take in the story and to consider if these actions would be greatly different in their cultures.

I had the long weekend to gather everything I needed. I started doing some basic research on the native cultures of my student population. Since my students comprised only two nations of origin, this task was less complicated than I had feared but still required some serious deliberation. The class was made up of twenty-three students: six Saudi men, three Saudi women, eight Chinese women, and six Chinese men. It should be noted that since the cultures represented in my class included only two countries, it was a relatively low-stress task. Other classroom situations have had as many as seven nations represented, and such a demographic would require much more time out of class for this project to be successful—or, perhaps, could be best accomplished by opening up the research task to the students themselves as part of the assignment. To focus the next few sessions closely, I chose a particular set of issues for students to examine. Inspired by my meeting with the student in my office, I decided to discuss gender roles in "A Very Short Story."

With no time to spare, I turned to the campus library for expert advice on cultural differences. Despite its rather off-putting title, Margaret K. Nydell's *Understanding Arabs: A Guide for Westerners* (2002) offered helpful insights,[3] suggesting that in Saudi culture "the public display of intimacy between men and women is strictly forbidden by the Arab social code, including holding hands or linking arms or any gesture of affection such as kissing or prolonged touching" and that "Middle Eastern gender roles have traditionally been governed by a patriarchal kinship system that had already existed in the regions to which Islam spread" (35). My further reading suggested that these differences are not just religious: "The symbolism of Islam combined with the uniqueness of heritage of Saudi Arabia . . . continue[s] to be center to the Saudi Identity and therefore to many Saudis' sense of political and social stability" (Yamani 133). Traveling together, the unnamed protagonist ("He") and Luz would be in direct violation of these traditions; no wonder the story raised some questions for my student about the relationship.

I investigated similar cultural factors that could have led to confusion on the part of my Chinese students. In *Understanding Chinese Families*, C. Y. Cyrus Chu and Ruoh-Rong Yu state that "since one purpose of marriage is to form a strong social network, it is likely to be an assortative one, with the bride and groom usually from families of comparable class, wealth, socio-economic status, etc." (87). They note that traditional "marriage was [historically] considered a means of lineage continuation . . . predominantly arranged and facilitated by the parents of the bride and groom." Since the approval of family seems so prevalent in this tradition, I wondered if my Chinese students might have seen the protagonists' desire to marry so quickly and without either his or the woman's family present as reckless or strange (Chu and Yu 2010). So, too, might be Luz's engagement to an Italian.

Beyond their knowing that the text says the couple "felt as though they were married" (65), and that statement bringing to mind the students' own ideas of what it means to be in a marriage, students still had trouble trying to explain why the pair traveled together. Further contextualization of the prescribed gender roles of American women during the time of the story's setting was required. In our subsequent discussions, I brought in information from Kimberly Jenson's *Mobilizing Minerva: American Women in the First World War*, which explains that in Hemingway's time

> the military had called nurses to assist in war but not to be warriors, and because they were entering a hierarchal institution, their "difference" meant inequality.... Women nurses were subject to military discipline and regulations but had no official rank in a hierarchal system that depended on it.... Nurses were "hired extras" in the business of war, invited to accompany the military because they were women practicing the indispensable women's work of nurturing. (120)

This passage illustrates for the students how the service life of military nurses mirrored the home front. Alex Vernon, too, sees "the military and the war actually subvert[ing] the possibility for autonomous agency and self-definition" (*Soldiers Once* 81). If Luz, being a nurse under military contract, must conform to the nurturing-servant identity prescribed by her superiors, she sees her relationship with "He," the unnamed protagonist, not only providing possible emotional or physical satisfaction but as denying the ability of the military to determine her fate. Luz's relationship with the story's "He" can be viewed as a rebellion against these authorities. This context explains the dynamic between the protagonist and Luz and also challenges the students' own implicit concepts of gender and courtship that they bring to a reading of the story.

Nancy R. Comley and Robert Scholes argue similarly about *A Farewell to Arms* that a woman (like the nurse Catherine Barkley in that novel or, relevant to our discussion, like Luz) who wanted to define her own relationship standards would have attempted, with the story's male character, "to establish a world of their own, a world of oneness, as they move further from society" (39). If Luz can be viewed as a character intentionally subverting the social conventions of her time, the ESL student might, as Comley and Scholes suggest, interact with "the larger text of the cultural codes that are active in the thought of any writer as alert and sensitive as Ernest Hemingway" (9). These codes shift over time and within cultures, and foreignness may actually allow for new avenues of exploration. Furthermore, Debra A. Moddelmog argues

Fig. 1. Ernest Hemingway with nurse Agnes von Kurowsky (second from left) and two other American Red Cross nurses at the San Siro horse racing track in Milan, Italy, 1918. Von Kurowsky was a prototype for the character Luz in "A Very Short Story." (Ernest Hemingway Collection. John F. Kennedy Presidential Library and Museum, Boston.)

in *Reading Desire* that issues like gender must not be viewed as "standards but as socially devised and politically potent narratives" and the examination of these narratives "is a necessary step for comprehending social power and relations" (140). In short, the questions my students had were important ones that I, as a native speaker, too easily overlooked.

Even when the students' cultural differences are taken into account, the instructor still must contend with the questions of historical context that baffle twenty-first-century college students, including first language speakers of English, who are mostly unfamiliar with World War I and 1920s Chicago. I found it helpful to bring in biographical criticism as well. Using Michael Reynolds' *The Young Hemingway* and Carlos Baker's *Ernest Hemingway: A Life Story*, I created a lecture based around Hemingway's doomed relationship with Red Cross nurse Agnes von Kurowsky and how it mirrors elements within the story itself. Using a document camera and projector, I showed students images of Hemingway lying injured in his hospital bed in Italy, walking on crutches, and standing side by side with Agnes in her nurse's uniform (see figure 1). I also modified a map of Italy at the time of the First World War to follow the action of the story. Three lines were used to mark the map: red for the man's journey from the hospital to the United States, green for Luz's journey within Italy, and blue for their journey together. To see the characters' movement across a geographical landscape helps students better visualize the story and the movement of the relationship between the two characters.

With these primary and secondary sources offering helpful contextualization, students came to understand that gender relations were subject to determiners such as time, culture, and political power. Moddelmog writes in "Sex, Sexuality, and Marriage," a chapter in *Hemingway in Context*, that, in Hemingway's fiction, couples often act "on the presumption of mutual sexual pleasure, which was the foundation of companionate marriage and also of many sexual encounters outside of marriage, given the modern view that women's sexual pleasure was just as important as men's" (364). Thus Hemingway's story illustrates how shifting gender roles were spurred by dramatic cultural upheavals like the First World War. Luz's job as a nurse under military authority conflicts with the evolving viewpoints at the time that a woman's desire is equal to that of her male counterpart.

Following these discussions, the students were then asked to look back at their written response, specifically at what they had said about the relationship between the man and Luz, and to use the new information to explain how these societal pressures would affect the romantic relationship. A short in-class writing assignment helped students to better understand the couple's relationship and to reconcile their own culture's concepts of marriage with the ones presented in the Hemingway text. I asked the students to write at least two paragraphs describing what conflicts they anticipated when an unmarried couple travels together and how the students' own preconceptions affected their reading of the story. It is important here to mention to TESOL students that you, the instructor, are not looking for a 100 percent right answer. This writing assignment is a chance for them to put their ideas into written English. In the discussion that followed the writing assignment, I provided information that allowed a negotiation between their cultural practices and the norms of the story's time.

The students' written reactions to the discussion about gender were overwhelmingly positive. Many of the male students, to their credit, empathized with Luz. While there was sympathy for the male character, the male students really saw Luz as a voice of independence and agreed that if she wanted to change her mind about the relationship it was her right to do so. Many female students said that they saw Luz as very independent, and one specifically mentioned that she hoped Luz would have gone on to open her own hospital with other women from her wartime experience. The Saudi woman who had been so confused about the pair's travels together suggested that these constraints might have driven Luz to go to another city to start a hospital. Traveling together was no longer seen as a detriment to the formation of a relationship; it *was* the relationship. While this answer is not fully explicable in the text, it shows that the students were applying their grammatical fluency to sociolinguistic and discourse skills.

Reading, discussing, and writing about fiction in the second language classroom provides not only opportunity for critical examination, but also an authentic text (a document originally intended for first language users of English) displaying first language cultural representations in a social context. Elisabeth Gareis, Martine Allard, and Jackie Saindon claim that "students' intrinsic interest in narrative and plot makes it easier to cover the skills usually taught in reading class including prediction, identification of main ideas and supporting details, skimming, scanning, and inferring" (139). Students can then move beyond simple, direct description and use literary texts to expand reading and writing skills, cultural awareness, and critical thinking. I employed the students' reading of "A Very Short Story" as a method of "playing out negotiations of otherness within this eminently national framework," acknowledging how "its characters and their relations are situated in a highly particularized time, place, and set of interests" (Palumbo-Liu 70). Using texts to negotiate meaning across cultural borders allows the ESL composition class to balance both university expectation and cultural arbitration.

Jonathan Picken argues that second language examination of literature "benefits students in the longer term by improving their processing skills and making them more independent as interpreters" of texts that possess multicultural and multi-experiential expositions of meaning (145). Such a learning outcome was met in the case of our study of "A Very Short Story." Our consideration of how perceptions shift over time and across cultures produced for the students an understanding of why Luz might have opportunistically used the relationship to negotiate an escape from the military's social authority over nurses—and then why she might have balked at returning to the United States with the solider, instead choosing to enter into another relationship. Thus Luz's actions became for our class a discussion point on the larger question of gender. The use of fiction allowed my students to consider narrative and explication in order to think critically in this second (or subsequent) language and to ask themselves, too, how concepts of gender affect their everyday lives.

As any instructor knows, the students were not the only learners. In my instruction of "A Very Short Story" I decided to take a negotiative approach to language teaching, a collaborative approach that allows both the instructor and the learners to use new understandings of cultural identities—in our case how gender roles are performed—to mediate the students' reading. Atkinson posits that "the richness of the context, that is, the deep, multiplex embedding of language activities in the lush social world" allows for an interaction with text that must be grounded in the students' (and instructor's) reality (528). Using a text like *In Our Time* in the ESL composition classroom gives the learners a common topic on which to base their study of American English language and culture. The common topic of gender roles drew my students into a conversation that allowed them to consider their culturally imbedded perceptions with those in Hemingway's text. Ultimately, students achieved the communicative goals set out in the course—grammatical, sociolinguistic, and discourse—and practiced the critical thinking that they should retain after their full release from the university's ESL Center takes them into their undergraduate majors.

Notes

1. While this is not a verbatim quotation of the conversation, I have sought in good faith to reconstruct the moment to provide context to my rationale in altering my curricular perspective and to convey my own and the student's temporary frustration.

2. For more on communicative language teaching see Klaus Brandl, *Communicative Language Teaching in Action: Putting Principles to Work* (Upper Saddle River, NJ: Pearson/Prentice Hall, 2009) and James Lee and Bill VanPatten, *Making Communicative Language Teaching Happen* (New York: McGraw-Hill, 2003).

3. An updated version of Nydell's book (2012), now in its fifth edition, offers additional commentary on the current political climate.

Part Two

Hemingway and Sexuality

"Aficion Means Passion"

Sexuality and Religion in *The Sun Also Rises*

Joshua Weiss

Having taught *The Sun Also Rises* at a couple of very different institutions—one, a small community college in the Washington, D.C., metro area and the other, the University of Chicago—I am continually struck by the similarity of questions that arise in my students' minds semester after semester. Many of these questions have to do with cultural differences and the seemingly vast gulf between the early twentieth century and the early twenty-first century. But a few seem particularly important, and students at all levels pick these out immediately: "What's going on at the club at the beginning?" "Why is Jake always going into churches?" "What is *aficion* exactly?" Above all other issues, though, my students have wondered why Jake explicitly sanctions the sexual relationship between Brett and Pedro Romero. All of these questions, of course, have their separate answers. But upon hearing the same questions again and again, I began to think of them in aggregate; I began to wonder whether these weren't separate questions at all, but rather one big question.

This essay is the result of these ruminations. It explicates the action of the novel in terms of its wider contexts like religion and sexuality, reducing students' feelings of estrangement. I take the sequence at the dancing club in the beginning of the novel as my springboard to investigate the eroticism that forms the foundation of Jake Barnes and Brett Ashley's relationship, and how this eroticism, transformed, leads to the consummation of a sexual relationship between Brett and Pedro. Ultimately, my reading suggests that the triangulation of desire between Jake, Brett, and Pedro is not only informed by but *depends on* the religious traditions represented in the background of the text. An exploration of the interconnected relationships of religion, sexuality, and aficion in the text offers answers not only to the students' question of *why* Jake sanctions Brett and Pedro's relationship but also to the attendant question of *how*.

Paradoxically, the first stirring of sexuality in *The Sun Also Rises* is a moment of the *absence* of sexuality, a moment students often need guidance to understand. After Jake shares a drink with the prostitute Georgette, the two share a horse-cab to go to dinner. Georgette assumes that Jake's interest is sexual but finds her advance rebuffed: "She looked up to be kissed. She touched me with one hand and I put her hand away. 'Never mind.' 'What's the matter? You sick?'" (23). This touch, an understandable advance for a prostitute to make, is the reader's first clue to the nature of Jake's injury. Immediately following, Hemingway gives the cause of this injury: "She smiled and showed all her bad teeth, and we touched glasses. . . . 'It's a shame you're sick. We get on well. What's the matter with you, anyway?' 'I got hurt in the war,' I said. 'Oh, that dirty war'" (24). Hemingway focuses initially on the wound's immediate sexual effects. Georgette's comical understatement cements Jake's growing disdain for and boredom with her—though his injury is clearly a war wound in his groin (the place Georgette's "one hand" likely touched), even if Jake were capable of an active sexuality at this moment, it is clear that Georgette would not be the object of his desire. Jake is in good company with his wound, as well; not only did Hemingway himself receive a serious wound in the war—albeit to the knee, not the groin—but Jake's wound has a religious valence to it as well.[1] As H. R. Stoneback points out, "Saint Ignatius [of Loyola] was a soldier who received a serious groin wound from a cannonball in the siege of Pamplona in 1521 . . . the wound that led to his conversion" (45). Given Pamplona's centrality to the action of the novel, this connection takes on special importance. A few pages later, Hemingway introduces Brett, who arrives at the dancing club Jake and Georgette have gone to with an entourage of young men. This passage offers students an opportunity to practice close reading:

> Two taxis were coming down the steep street. They both stopped in front of the Bal. A crowd of young men, some in jerseys and some in their shirtsleeves, got out. I could see their hands and newly washed, wavy hair in the light from the door. The policeman standing by the door looked at me and smiled. They came in. As they went in, under the light I saw white hands, wavy hair, white faces, grimacing, gesturing, talking. With them was Brett. She looked very lovely and she was very much with them. (27–28)

Rather than naming the men with Brett specifically as homosexuals, Hemingway gives a precise series of descriptions, which sets them apart from the heterosexual men in Paris. The washed hands, wavy hair, and white faces are all qualities normally in the register of feminine sexual attractiveness, but because they belong to men, the inversion unsettles Jake: "I was very angry. Somehow they always made me angry" (28).

Students are often surprised at the end of this passage; why, they ask, should Jake be angry with these people? Part of the confusion is a sign of the times—the men don't automatically register as homosexuals for most students, and even when students do realize the nature of the group, they are still often confused at the seemingly disproportionate anger felt by Jake. To try to understand this moment, I encourage students to look very closely at the wording, which does not give a target of Jake's anger. While students assume he's angry at the homosexuals, persuasive arguments, like Stoneback's, can be made that Jake's anger takes not homosexuality as its object but sexuality as such.[2] In this way, Jake is angry at the group of men because they could have sex with Brett but don't, but he is also angry at himself for being unable to have the sexuality he desires. Jake's sexuality, therefore, cannot be reflective of his desire for Brett, and it's the tension between these two impulses that serves as one of the sources of Jake's anger.

The presentation of Jake's sexuality is further complicated by his triangular relationship with Brett and her lovers. After Brett and Cohn have gone to San Sebastian for a romantic tryst and returned, Jake is jealous of Cohn because, unlike the gay men at the Bal, Cohn was both able to have sex with Brett and, presumably, did so in San Sebastian. But the tryst effectively feminizes Cohn in Jake's eyes, especially after Brett arrives in Pamplona with her fiancé, Mike. Cohn pines for Brett, becoming very jealous of Mike and infuriated with their relationship. This feminization causes Jake's hatred of Cohn and so resembles more closely Jake's hatred of the gay men at the Bal. Jake reacts angrily toward any man he sees as compromising his own masculinity. But this hatred is not uncomplicated—Cohn, like the group of gay men, is subject to a detailed physical description from Jake earlier in the novel: "He was nice to watch on the tennis court, he had a good body, and he kept it in shape." Jake's opinion only changes "when he [Cohn] fell in love with Brett," suggesting that the pitiful, feminized Cohn is worthy of scorn (52). But it is precisely Jake's status as observer of Brett's relationships with other men and his inability to have sex with her that feminizes Jake himself. Jake's focus on the "white faces" of the homosexuals and the "good body" of Cohn suggests a sense of the homoerotic which, in the first instance, follows directly from a discussion of his wound.[3]

In my experience, students have been consistently well tuned to pick up these curious moments of homoeroticism, though they are occasionally loath to name it so when it comes from Jake. Often, they suggest that these moments only *appear* homoerotic because of Jake's injury—that it's unfair to see these moments as evidence of eroticism at all. The fishing scene, on the other hand, presents for students a clear suggestion of barely concealed eroticism that even Jake acknowledges consciously. When Bill joins Jake from New York, they head south early to Pamplona, and spend several days together fishing near Burguete. In the middle of this idyll, Bill confesses what he thinks of Jake: "'Listen. You're a hell of a good guy, and I'm fonder of you than anybody on earth. I couldn't tell you that in New York. It'd mean I was a faggot'" (121). In other words, Spain permits emotions, expressions, and actions that America, even cosmopolitan New York, prohibits. Homosexuality, then, is conduct centered, at least in part—because they are in Spain, Bill can make this admission to Jake without fear of reprisal. It is precisely because Bill is *not* a homosexual that he can safely say something that would *make him* a homosexual were the two in America. As Jake later remarks, "The things that happened could only have happened during a fiesta" (158). This claim, of course, is untrue; the sexual inversion in the novel has been happening all along, but Spain and the setting of the fiesta suddenly *license* the behavior. And, importantly, this fiesta, "the fiesta of San Fermin . . . is also a religious festival" (156).

That the festival is primarily religious is a fact that is lost on many of my students—they often see the bullfights as entertainment, and the sexual behavior a natural consequence of the liberal amounts of alcohol the characters imbibe. Students are frequently only aware of this festival in terms of the famous running of the bulls. It is helpful to explain that the novel, along with Hemingway's earlier newspaper articles for the *Toronto Star*, helped to introduce this continental European tradition to a North American audience.[4] Indeed, that Americans know about this festival at all is due in large part to the popularizing work Hemingway's writing performed. But in the face of the excitement of the bullfights, students overlook the religious origins of the festival. For many students, the praying Jake does seems incongruous and unnecessary. True, Jake has mentioned his Catholicism prior to the arrival in Pamplona, most notably in the scene with Georgette, when he suggests that the Church has a "good" solution for his difficulties, reconciling his wound with his desires, but it is not until this religious festival that Hemingway presents Jake's Catholicism in action. Immediately after checking in to the Hotel Montoya, Jake stops at the cathedral at the end of the street to pray. Later, after Brett and Pedro have begun their relationship, he prays with Brett in the chapel of San Fermin, the location where the fiesta officially begins, at Brett's request. They do not pray for very long before leaving the chapel: "'Don't know why I get so nervy in church,' Brett said. 'Never does me any good.' We walked along. 'I'm damned bad for a religious atmosphere,' Brett said. 'I've the wrong type of face'" (*Sun Also Rises* 212). Brett's prayer is unsuccessful inasmuch as she does not believe in the mechanism of prayer or in the possibility of her prayer being answered. Jake, by contrast, believes that his prayers have occasionally been answered, and though his spiritual commitment to Catholicism sometimes slips, he remains "pretty religious" inasmuch as his attention to particular rituals and sacraments remains acute (213).

Brett may claim to have "the wrong type of face" for religion, but it is simply because she has misunderstood the role religion plays in the fiesta, a misunderstanding shared by many students. Brett has precisely the right type of face for sexuality (or, more properly, for sex), a face with which she watches and is watched by the men surrounding her, principal among them Pedro Romero.[5] But this face also closely watches the bullfight. She watches Pedro attentively, not least because of her sexual attraction to him, and in so doing, Brett unwittingly finds herself in the most profoundly religious atmosphere of the novel—the bullfight—which she takes to be a *sexual* atmosphere. In fact, the bullfight is both. At this point, I like to guide my students through a brief history of the festival, stressing the importance of Saint Fermin of Amiens as the patron saint of Navarre and the festival's origins as a combination of a medieval commercial fair and the feast day of Saint Fermin. I also stress the religious significance of the bullfight as a continuation of prehistoric bull worship and sacrifice. Understanding the pagan religious valence to the bullfight often helps students better comprehend the reverence with which the bullfight is portrayed, and the religious significance attached to aficion.

On the final day of the fiesta, after Brett has prayed (unsuccessfully) in the chapel, she and Jake watch the procession of the matadors into the arena: "the three matadors walked out. Behind them came all the procession, opening out, all striding in step, all the capes furled, everybody with free arms swinging, and behind rode the picadors, their pics rising like lances" (216). The military imagery is unmistakable, but so too is the pageantry associated with a religious processional, and it recalls the start of the fiesta: "San Fermin was translated from one church to another. In the procession were all the dignitaries, civil and religious" (158–59). Once inside the arena, the third bull of the afternoon, killed by Pedro, "was named Bocanegra. . . . His ear was cut by popular acclamation and given to Pedro Romero, who, in turn, gave it to Brett, who wrapped it in a handkerchief belonging to myself" (202–3). Here Brett participates in a religious economy, assuming it to be a sexual one; however, the ear of Bocanegra she is given participates in a pre-Christian economy of the talisman, which would be later translated by Christianity into the veneration of relics. The saint, in this instance, is Pedro, a vanquisher of evil akin to Saint George and others. Indeed, after the fight, as the participants exit the arena, the quasi-religious processional becomes a recessional: "Romero turned and tried to get through the crowd. They were all around him trying to lift him and put him on their shoulders.... He did not want to be carried on people's shoulders. But they held him and lifted him.... They were lifting him and all running toward the gate" (225). This moment is merely a more animated mirror of the opening of the fiesta, when the statue of San Fermin was carried throughout Pamplona from church to church on people's shoulders. Pedro has become a kind of saint;[6] however, while he is being carried off to general acclaim by his adoring public, he "looked at us [Jake and Brett] apologetically" (225).

Pedro does not desire the acclaim of the public; he instead desires the acclaim of two people, Jake and Brett. Brett assumes that her relationship to Pedro is a sexual one, and she ignores the religious valences of their relationship. Jake, by contrast, assumes that his relationship to Pedro is a religious one, based primarily on the quasi-religious ceremonies of the bullfight. But when Jake first sees Pedro, calling him "the best-looking boy I have ever seen," he prefaces this comment by focusing his attention on the toreador attire: "His jacket hung over the back of a chair. They were just finishing winding his sash.... He wore a white linen shirt and the sword-handler finished his sash and stood up and stepped back" (166–67). The scene plays out not unlike the description of Cohn's body earlier in the novel. Students often find the first instance of Jake's erotic investment in another man hard to accept, but by this point in the novel such an investment seems more acceptable. This acceptance is most often due to the quasi-religious significance the bullfight has for Jake. Pedro's religious aura influences his sexual one—it is partly *because* of his bullfighting costume that Jake finds Pedro to be so good looking. The veneration of Pedro Romero, then, does not begin and end with his bullfighting prowess; it extends to his sexuality.

In this trio, both Jake and Brett are attracted, erotically, to Pedro Romero. Jake is in love with Brett, and has been for years, and Brett feels similarly about Jake. Finally, Pedro respects Jake and seeks his approval but is sexually attracted only to Brett. Eventually, Jake gives Brett and Pedro permission to initiate a sexual relationship; since he cannot satisfy his desire with either of them, he experiences a sexual relationship vicariously. This pivotal moment happens when the three of them are sharing drinks at a café. Brett has already confessed to Jake earlier that she's "mad about the Romero boy," and Jake has concurred, remarking again that "he's nice to look at" (187–88). Finally, as the three are talking at the table, Jake rises to leave: "I stood up. Romero rose, too. 'Sit down,' I said. 'I must go and find our friends and bring them here.' He looked at me. It was a final look to ask if it were understood. It was understood all right.... When I came back and looked in the café, twenty minutes later, Brett and Pedro Romero were gone" (190–91). My students have always been well aware of what is happening, though they often disagree as to its level of propriety. But, often, while they focus on the sexual aspect of this moment, they overlook the religious aspect. The look that Pedro gives Jake is crucial to the understanding of this scene. With this look, Pedro requests Jake's assent to the relationship, and Jake's instruction to sit, in addition to his silence after the look, gives the approval. Jake gives Brett to Pedro in this moment, but in introducing the two in the first place, he has also, in a sense, given Pedro to Brett, and he has done so in place of himself. In this way, Jake acts as a priestly figure—as one presiding over something akin to the sacrament of marriage. In this moment, Jake fuses the sexual and the religious, and his afición, crucially, ordains him to do so.

Students are rightly perplexed by Hemingway's brief definition of afición, often finding the explanation doesn't fully encompass all the different ways in which afición governs characters' behavior: Jake merely tells the readers "Afición means passion. An aficionado is one who is passionate about the bullfights" (136). When Jake arrives at the Hotel Montoya, its proprietor (Montoya) welcomes him gladly—Jake has stayed there before, and Montoya knows him to be a true aficionado like Montoya himself. It is this afición that prompts Montoya to introduce Jake to Pedro, and it is this shared afición that holds Jake up to a high standard of conduct, a standard he will eventually, at least in Montoya's mind, transgress. Montoya insists that Pedro should "stay with his own people," and avoid the influence of foreigners, people without afición, who "don't know what he's worth" (176). Montoya is suitably pleased when Jake suggests that Pedro not meet with an American ambassador, and this is why Jake's transgression of this code—when he sanctifies the sexual relationship of Brett and Pedro—makes him a pariah. Hemingway plays with the definition of afición as "passion," a passion in the religious sense, the quasi-religious code associated with the bullfighters and their admirers that Hemingway demonstrates throughout his descriptions of the fight. Of course, while we can usefully talk about passion in terms of religious faith, it may well be worth mentioning to students the definition of passion as suffering. Suffering, both sexual and emotional, is so central to the experience of the characters that this definition seems equally important.

Aficion, then, can be seen as a kind of spiritual vocation, and it is this vocation that Jake transgresses in his sanctification of Brett and Pedro's relationship. But if aficion means passion, then aficion also has a sexual component. Throughout the novel, Hemingway has fused the religious and the sexual, drawing the reader's attention to the "purity of line" of Pedro's technique, to the regalia that help make Pedro the "best-looking boy" Jake has ever seen, and to other moments of similar confusion. So, too, with aficion—Jake provides an extended description immediately following his initial definition:

> Somehow it was taken for granted that an American could not have aficion. He might simulate it or confuse it with excitement, but he could not really have it. When they saw that I had aficion, and there was no password, no set questions that could bring it out, rather it was a sort of oral spiritual examination with the questions always a little on the defensive and never apparent, there was this same embarrassed putting the hand on the shoulder, or a "Buen hombre." But nearly always there was the actual touching. It seemed as though they wanted to touch you to make it certain. (137)

Aficion functions here not unlike a "bringing out" of the closet, and it requires some form of bodily contact to ensure the other senses are undeceived. It is discovered with a system of questions, touches, smiles, and glances, and it belongs to a secret and select group of individuals. Jake comments on this secrecy in vivid terms:

> [Montoya] smiled again. He always smiled as though bull-fighting were a very special secret between the two of us; a rather shocking but really very deep secret that we knew about. He always smiled *as though there were something lewd about the secret* to outsiders, but that it was something that we understood. It would not do to expose it to people who would not understand. (136; emphasis mine)

Students have rarely failed to find these moments of touching and smiling curiously erotic. Indeed, this smile over the lewd secret recalls the scene very early in the novel with the group of homosexuals: "The policeman standing by the door looked at me and smiled" (28). This smile is also a smile of recognition, recognition of a lewd secret that "would not do to expose" to outsiders.

In recalling that earlier scene, Hemingway seems to suggest a parallel between the group of aficionados and the group of homosexuals. Both groups share a secret, a "lewd" secret that can, with the proper attention, be brought out into the open.[7]

It is in this way that aficion has a sexual component as well as a religious one, an idea students find both challenging and compelling. When Jake sanctifies the relationship of Brett and Pedro, he does so according to the dictates of aficion—he transgresses the religious nature of aficion, the nature represented by Montoya and his fetishization of the purity of the torero, but Jake remains faithful to the sexual nature of aficion. Montoya cannot see the relationship of aficion to sexuality—he can only see the religious aspect. On the other side of the divide Brett is equally blind to the religious aspects of her own sexuality and of the sexualities of those around her. Jake is the only character who recognizes and understands the fusion of sexuality and religion in the novel, and the only one who is able to translate one into the other. The transformation of the religious and the sexual, then, which culminates in the sanctification of the relationship between Brett and Pedro, is activated by the dual nature of aficion and Jake's successful negotiation of its inherent tension.

While this reading does not answer all of the questions students have asked about the novel, I've found that the notion of aficion as "passion," stressing both the sexual and the religious senses of the word, goes a long way to helping students see this loaded term in a new light. Where students are often inclined to treat aficion as mere bullfight jargon, defining this "passion" opens up new possibilities for the operations of desire in the text that otherwise remain mysterious. Above all, this emphasis helps students better understand their big question—why Jake would approve of the sexual relationship between Brett and Pedro—and goes some way to interpreting some of the fallout of this approval. The notion of the sexual component of aficion has been, in my experience with students, something of a revelation. Once I point out the language, which seems to contemporary readers so similar to the language of the closet, everything seems to fall into place. Suddenly, students find their earlier suspicions confirmed, and often relish the opportunity to explore other definitions of aficion to enhance their interpretations. Above all, this moment helps to bridge the gap between the nearly ninety years that separate us from the novel and, in so doing, helps students recognize a piece of the twenty-first century in Hemingway's Pamplona.

Notes

1. Teachers might also usefully turn to Jessie Weston, *From Ritual to Romance* (New York: Cosimo Classics, 2005). Weston's text, first published in 1920, was widely read among the expatriate circle to which Hemingway belonged, especially by T. S. Eliot, who credits Weston's readings of the Grail legend in his appendix to *The Waste Land*. Specifically, Weston's exegesis of the legend of the Fisher King is potentially important to a discussion of Jake's wound, inasmuch as it clearly connects the Fisher King's wound with a loss of virility. The sickened land in the legend, Weston argues, is a direct result of the wound the king receives for his sexual sin. Weston notes that in one version of the Grail legend "Joseph d'Arimathie... is the Fisher King; ensnared by the beauty of the daughter of the Pagan King of Norway, whom he has slain, he baptizes her, though she is still an unbeliever at heart, and makes her his wife, thus drawing the wrath of Heaven upon himself. God punishes him for his sin: 'His loins are stricken by this bane / From which he suffers lasting pain'" (22). Bringing Weston into the discussion gives Jake's wound a further, mythic significance as well as its religious significance.

2. Stoneback argues that Jake's evident homophobia in this moment is "conduct centered, and his [Hemingway's] main point is that Jake's anger is perfectly natural, since 'they' presumably could perform heterosexually but choose not to, while Jake physically desires and loves Brett but cannot consummate that love sexually" (46). It's unclear why Stoneback believes the aversion to the group to be "conduct centered," given that "grimacing, gesturing, talking" are the only actions (apart from, eventually, dancing) that they perform at the Bal, and these actions are certainly not the exclusive province of homosexuality. By "conduct centered," Stoneback suggests that Jake does not view homosexuality as a category of being inherent to one's identity, but rather is characterized by actions and behaviors only. Conduct-centered sexuality is opposed, therefore, to status-centered sexuality, in which one's sexuality is central to one's identity. These terms are usefully explained in Nan D. Hunter's essay "Life After *Hardwick*," in Lisa Duggan and Nan D. Hunter, *Sex Wars: Sexual Dissent and Political Culture* (New York: Routledge, 1995). Stoneback therefore argues that Jake's homophobia does not stem from a hatred of homosexuality as such, but rather its "refusal" to have the heterosexual intercourse he desires but cannot achieve due to his wound.

3. For further reading on masculinity, femininity, and the figure of Robert Cohn, see Jeremy Kaye's article "The 'Whine' of Jewish Manhood: Re-Reading Hemingway's Anti-Semitism, Reimagining Robert Cohn," *The Hemingway Review* 25.2 (2006): 44–60. This article explores the tension between Jake and Cohn, arguing that the "good body" of Cohn exemplifies hyper-masculinity and that this masculinity is tied intimately to questions of Jewish identity. Though the present essay focuses primarily on Catholicism and questions of sexuality, Kaye's article is useful for a broader discussion of religion in the novel.

4. See Ernest Hemingway, "Bull Fighting a Tragedy," *The Toronto Star Weekly*, 20 October 1923, in William White, ed., *By-line Ernest Hemingway: Selected Articles and Dispatches of Four Decades* (New York: Scribner's, 1967).

5. My reading here owes a great debt to the work of Jacques Lacan, specifically his work on the gaze in Alan Sheridan's translation of *The Seminar of Jacques Lacan, Book XI: The Four Fundamental Concepts of Psycho-Analysis* (New York: W. W. Norton, 1998). In this robust development of the concept of seeing and how it relates to desire, Lacan contends that when a subject looks at an object, the object is always already gazing back at the subject, thus producing a "split" between the eye and the gaze that is the mark of the Lacanian division of the subject itself. Instead of expecting students to dive into Lacan, however, I find that Laura Mulvey's work provides an excellent primer for how Brett is looking and being looked at; see Mulvey's "Visual Pleasure and Narrative Cinema," *Screen* 16.3 (1975): 6-18. Introducing students to the gaze through Mulvey's terms of scopophilia and identification with the cinematic male actor gazing at the female body helps them to better appreciate the interesting subversion of Brett's own gaze.

6. Pedro has also become, in the words of Kim Moreland, a knight. Moreland offers a reading of the sense of chivalry in *The Sun Also Rises* in her book *The Medievalist Impulse in American Literature: Twain, Adams, Fitzgerald, and Hemingway* (Charlottesville: UP of Virginia, 1996). Moreland's reading of the characters hinges upon an understanding of codes of chivalry and nobility that would pair well with a mythic reading of the novel using Jessie Weston's text. Moreland argues that Brett becomes a parody of the classic noble lady; she is surrounded by "knights" rather than remaining chaste and pure. Moreland's reading of Brett is less charitable than mine, but she is right to point out that Jake's war wound is not the only one in the novel: Brett, too, "has herself been wounded, psychologically and emotionally, by the war, which undermined any sense of permanence, certainty, and therefore commitment" (187). Moreland argues that Romero is the most successful of Brett's knightly courters because "the context of the bullfight offers him an appropriate locus in which to approximate the ideals of courtly and chivalric behavior" (187). While I take Moreland's point about Romero being the most successful suitor, I argue that he can be so only with Jake's blessing, a relationship in which Jake holds the sacramental power. And while Brett may not be able to remain sexually faithful, even to her most successful knight, she is most certainly faithful to sexuality itself.

7. In this reading, I am of course deeply indebted to the pioneering work of Eve Kosofsky Sedgwick and others, especially Sedgwick's *Epistemology of the Closet* (Berkeley: U of California P, 1990). In particular, one of Sedgwick's early definitions of the closet seems especially relevant: "'Closetedness' itself is a performance initiated as such by the speech act of a silence—not a particular silence, but a silence that accrues particularity by fits and starts, in relation to the discourse that surrounds and differentially constitutes it" (3). We can see how Montoya's aficion fits this bill well, since even Jake's supposed transgression of aficion is surrounded by a peculiar silence. Aficion, then, begins to inhabit a space by which it is recognized (by Montoya, primarily) in contradistinction to what it clearly is not. The silence of aficion's closet thus depends upon Jake's transgression for its very definition, just as the silence of the homosexual closet depends upon the act of "coming out" for its own retroactive definition.

Reading Hemingway Backwards

Teaching *A Farewell to Arms* in Light of *The Garden of Eden*

Carl P. Eby

"And you call me Catherine?.... Say, 'I've come back to Catherine in the night.'"
—Ernest Hemingway, *A Farewell to Arms*

"You call me Catherine always when you want. I'm always Catherine when you need her."
—Ernest Hemingway, *The Garden of Eden*

To teach gender and sexuality in the works of Ernest Hemingway, I suggest that we read Hemingway backwards. That is, instead of reading Hemingway chronologically, we do better by teaching Hemingway achronologically, in reverse order of composition and publication. After all, the reason we generally read authors chronologically is that we assume there is some pattern of development worth following—a thematic and stylistic continuity that can be followed as easily in reverse. What makes this strategy particularly appealing in the case of Ernest Hemingway is that as he grew older the structure and expression of his psychosexuality—what psychoanalyst Robert Stoller would call his "erotic scenario" (*Sexual Excitement* xi)—steadily became more pronounced.[1] That is, the major fantasies, anxieties, and signifiers of Hemingway's erotic scenario stay substantially identical, but they grow less subtle and more insistent in his later works. What is more fully censored and symbolized in the early fiction appears almost baldly, with little symbolization at all in Hemingway's late novels. Elsewhere I've explored this phenomenon at length and theorized why this is so—but in this essay I would like to focus instead on its implications for the classroom.[2] The more pronounced expression of psychosexual and gender issues in Hemingway's late fiction means that students can more easily pick up on the subtler expressions of Hemingway's erotic scenario in his earlier novels if they have first read and considered these issues in his later works—and no two Hemingway novels pair better together to demonstrate this than *The Garden of Eden* (1986) and *A Farewell to Arms* (1929).

It goes without saying that my classes are different every semester, and teaching issues of gender and sexuality and *A Farewell to Arms* in the way I suggest here doesn't always lead my students to the same place—but for want of a better example I would like to suggest where it leads *me*. It often leads my students there as well. I should also be clear that I don't organize my Hemingway seminars entirely achronologically, or "backwards." I'm interested in many issues in Hemingway's writing, not just issues of gender and sexuality, so I usually begin my classes with an introduction to reading Hemingway through a careful consideration of his early short stories. But I do teach Hemingway's novels achronologically, teaching *The Garden of Eden* before I teach *A Farewell to Arms* and all subsequent Hemingway novels. This pedagogical strategy makes my students closer readers—particularly when it comes to issues of gender and sexuality in Hemingway's works. Moreover, I think this approach to gender and sexuality, which can easily be adapted to courses where there is room for only two works by Hemingway, can lead us to a new and richer understanding of *A Farewell to Arms*.[3]

When I introduce students to *The Garden of Eden* in my graduate or undergraduate seminars devoted to Hemingway, it should go without saying as well that we consider the novel from multiple angles and consider questions of gender and sexuality from several perspectives.[4] For the purposes of this essay, however, I want to focus on how I teach those aspects of Hemingway's psychosexuality that I consider at length in my book *Hemingway's Fetishism*—namely a psychoanalytic approach to issues of fetishism, transvestism, narcissism, ego splitting, trauma, dissociation, merger, castration anxiety, gender anxiety, male homophobia, and a fascination with lesbianism. These issues lie close to the surface in *The Garden of Eden*, so their rough outlines aren't too difficult for students to identify. I usually begin this part of our discussion by asking some fairly obvious questions about the book:

- Why all of the focus on haircuts?
- How *specifically* are haircuts used in the book?
- How can a haircut transform Catherine into "Peter" (17), a "boy" (15), or a "girl and a boy both" (192)?
- How can the identical haircut on David transform him into a girl named Catherine?
- How might these games with hair be linked to the obsession with mirrors, twinning, and the merger of Catherine and David?
- How does the obsession with hair function as a nodal point for gender fantasies and anxieties in the book?

From here, aided by a bit of lecture in my undergraduate courses and in my graduate courses by some essays and passages from Sigmund Freud, D. W. Winnicott, and Robert Stoller, we arrive, more or less, at a reading of Hemingway's fetishism much like the one I offer in my book.[5] That argument is elaborate, but a thumbnail sketch will have to suffice: I read Hemingway's obsession with hair as a classic erotic fetish—a tool for disavowing sexual difference—which explains both why it can transform Catherine into the "boy-girl" "Peter" and why it can be worn transvestically by David (particularly in front of the mirror, where subject becomes object) to engineer his transformation into "Catherine."[6] (Fetishism and transvestism are really different logical moments within a unified psychology, and a different name for *transvestism* is *fetishistic cross-dressing*.)[7] This psychology both emerges from and reinforces a bisexual rift in the fetishist's ego, and the fetish retains the magical qualities of the childhood comfort object (what Winnicott calls the *transitional object*) both to disavow difference between the self and the other and to ward off loss and depression.[8] Perhaps most importantly, the fetish allows the fetishist to turn trauma into triumph, converting the very actions and objects that threatened him as a child into the prerequisites of adult fulfillment.

When we move from our reading of *The Garden of Eden* to *A Farewell to Arms*, I ask students to look for similarities between the erotic and psychological dimensions of the two books—and they quickly note the glaringly obvious: both novels tell tragic tales of intense loves for somewhat "crazy" Catherines. After reading *The Garden of Eden*, in which Catherine Bourne's haircuts are unbearably exciting and make anything possible in bed—transforming her into a "boy" named "Peter," or into a "girl and a boy both," and transforming David, through their identity with his own haircut, into a "girl" named "Catherine" (50)—it's difficult to read Catherine Barkley's visit to the coiffeur and

Frederic's obvious excitement watching her in the three mirrors there, in *A Farewell to Arms,* as a mere trip to the barber:

> Catherine was still in the hair-dresser's shop. The woman was waving her hair. I sat in the little booth and watched. It was exciting to watch and Catherine smiled and talked to me and my voice was a little thick from being excited. The tongs made a pleasant clicking sound and I could see Catherine in three mirrors and it was pleasant and warm in the booth. Then the woman put up Catherine's hair, and Catherine looked in the mirror and changed it a little, taking out and putting in pins; then stood up. "I'm sorry to have taken such a long time."
> "Monsieur was very interested. Were you not, monsieur?" The woman smiled.
> "Yes," I said.
> We went out and up the street. It was cold and wintery and the wind was blowing. "Oh, darling, I love you so," I said.[9] (292–93)

These echoes of *The Garden of Eden* are all the more pronounced when this trip to the barber shop is followed a few pages later by Catherine Barkley's suggestion, "Darling, why don't you let your hair grow? . . . [A]nd I could cut mine and we'd be just alike only one of us blonde and one of us dark. . . . Then we'd both be alike. Oh, darling, I want you so much I want to be you too" (*Farewell* 299). This use of the fetish as a tool to facilitate twinning and merger, of course, sounds uncannily like something out of *The Garden of Eden,* where the desire for merger is so pronounced that Catherine Bourne tells her identically coifed husband, "Now you're me, you're you so much better,"[10] as does the passage a few pages later when Catherine Barkley speaks of cutting her hair after "young Catherine" is born as a "surprise" and to be a "new and different girl" for Frederic (304). And when Frederic asks Catherine, "What do you want to do? Ruin me?" Her reply, "Yes, I want to ruin you," and Frederic's rejoinder, "Good, . . . that's what I want too" (305) can only take on new meaning in light of Catherine Bourne's playful but prophetic promise to "destroy" David with a tonsorial surprise (*Eden* 5).

But when we push beyond these obvious similarities—the fetishization of hair, fantasies of identical haircuts, a fascination with twinning, mirrors, and merger—reading *A Farewell to Arms* in light of *The Garden of Eden* inspires students to read carefully to make more subtle discoveries. For instance, with a little help, students usually call attention to a similar sort of dissociation when Frederic Henry and David Bourne misrecognize their own images in the mirror:

"So that's how it is," he said to himself. "You've done that to your hair and had it cut the same as your girl's and how do you feel?" He asked the mirror. "How do you feel? Say it."

"You like it," he said.

He looked in the mirror and it was someone else he saw but it was less strange now. (*Eden* 75)

I could not shadow-box in front of the narrow long mirror at first because it looked so strange to see a man with a beard boxing.

—or—

I looked in the glass and saw myself looking like a fake doctor with a beard. (*Farewell* 311, 319)

Catherine Barkley's desire "to do something really sinful" with Frederic (*Farewell* 153), expressed as she combs her hair before the mirror, often reminds students of Catherine Bourne's question after cutting her hair and switching genders with her husband, "You don't think I'm wicked?"[11] (*Eden* 16). And students sometimes note a similarity between Catherine Barkley's suggestion to Frederic, "Wouldn't you like to go on a trip somewhere by yourself darling, and be with men and ski?" (*Farewell* 297) and Marita's pronouncement to David Bourne, "You've been over-run with girls. I'm going to see you have your men friends" (*Eden* 224). Sometimes students discover the similarity between Catherine Barkley's skin, which Frederic describes as "smooth as piano keys" (*Farewell* 114), and David's declaration to Catherine Bourne, "You're just like ivory. That's how I always think. You're smooth as ivory too" (*Eden* 154). (We of course note in our reading of *Eden* that "Ivory" was Ernest's longest-running nickname for his older sister, Marcelline, with whom Ernest's mother raised him "as much like twins as possible" throughout his earliest years.)[12] Even after reading passages from the *Eden* manuscript in which Marita and Barbara Sheldon both speak of having erections, many students quite reasonably still balk at Freud's assertion that the fetish functions as an imaginary substitute "female phallus" ("Fetishism" 152); yet these same students sometimes note with incredulous wonder how Catherine Barkley enters *A Farewell to Arms* with attention both to her beautiful hair and to her "thin rattan stick like a toy riding-crop, bound in leather," an object which used to belong to her first love (18).[13] With a little help from the *Eden* manuscript, students note that both Frederic and David have war wounds, and they can compare the disavowal of homoeroticism in Frederic's relation with Rinaldi with Nick Sheldon's worries about looking like a "bloody sodomite" when he grows his hair out to match Barbara's.[14] And while Frederic Henry, unlike David Bourne, never swaps genders to "become" Catherine, he responds to Catherine's claim that

"We're the same one" with "At night we are" (299), and when Catherine gets pregnant, it's Frederic (thanks to jaundice), not Catherine, who comes down with morning sickness. This list of similarities between the two novels is far from complete, but suffice it to say that almost the entire psychosexual content of *The Garden of Eden* can be found in *A Farewell to Arms*, only expressed more subtly—that is, with a greater degree of condensation, displacement, and symbolization.

Yet noting these similarities only gets us so far. True, generating a list of this sort can teach students something about the durability of Hemingway's erotic scenario, and it can help them to appreciate how subtly and pervasively these issues are expressed throughout Hemingway's work—something students are far more willing to accept when they've first seen these same fantasies, anxieties, and symbols expressed in a less subtle form. And yet whatever these similarities, it's clear that, even within this psychosexual dimension, *The Garden of Eden* and *A Farewell to Arms* are hardly the same book. To more fully appreciate this difference, I challenge my students to move beyond a mere catalog of phenomena and toward an actual reading of this dimension of *A Farewell to Arms*. This move of course takes different readers different places, so here I can offer only my own interpretation.

It seems to me that, on this level (and only on this level), *A Farewell to Arms* is a book about the onset of Hemingway's fetishism and the birth of "Catherine" as the split-off other-sex half of his ego. Certainly, as generations of critics have noted, the book takes a Frederic who "did not love Catherine Barkley" and who had no idea of loving her—who thought of his relationship with her as "a game, like bridge, in which you said things instead of playing cards" (30)—and transforms him into someone "crazy in love" with her (92). What effects this sudden change? And it is *very* sudden. It isn't anything that Catherine does. That's clear. Isn't it Frederic's response to his wounding? Although rooted in childhood, fetishism generally manifests itself in young adulthood after a trauma interpreted as a severe castration threat—and given characters such as Jake Barnes, it's hardly a stretch to assert that this was the case for Hemingway. (Freud advised anyone who doubted the existence of the castration complex to study fetishism.)[15] More to the point, directly before Catherine arrives at the hospital in Milan—directly before Frederic falls "crazy in love with her"—Frederic asks for a haircut and almost gets his throat cut by a barber who mistakes him for an Austrian—"'Ho, ho, ho,' the porter laughed. 'He was funny. One move from you . . . And he would have—' he drew his forefinger across his throat." As the porter walks out, Frederic hears someone coming down the hall: "I looked toward the door. It was Catherine Barkley. . . . I thought I had never seen anyone so beautiful. . . . When I saw her I was in love with her. Everything turned over inside of me" (*Farewell* 91). Something has changed in Frederic—and perhaps it's only a new sense of his own mortality—but I think it's something more.

Frederic's out of body experience when he is wounded—"I felt myself rush bodily out of myself and out and out and out and all of the time bodily in the wind. I went out swiftly, all of myself. . . . Then I floated, and instead of going on I felt myself slide back" (54)—is a common experience in severe trauma called *peritraumatic dissociation*. It involves a splitting of the ego and is associated with such aftereffects as the sort of misrecognition or dissociation experienced by Frederic in front of the mirror. "Looking in the glass," watching Catherine brush her hair in the mirror, Frederic thinks, "I looked strange to myself in . . . civilian clothes" (258)—but I don't think clothes are the issue, for later, while shadowboxing in front of the mirror, Frederic experiences the same dissociation, and then again in the hospital, where he feels like "a fake doctor with a beard" (319). Here is the effect of the splitting of the ego. But whereas peritraumatic dissociation always involves an element of ego splitting, we're seeing the effect of an ego that split along a preexisting bisexual line of fissure—and the ego we're talking about isn't just Frederic's, it's Hemingway's.

Fetishism both responds to and exacerbates a bisexual rift in the ego.[16] If Hemingway, like Frederic, experienced peritraumatic dissociation when he was wounded at Fossalta di Piave in 1918—and there's good reason to think that this was so—it's reasonable to think that his ego split along a line of fissure that was already there.[17] Thus "Catherine," as the split-off other-sex half of Hemingway's ego, would be coeval with his adult fetishism, and *A Farewell to Arms* would memorialize her "birth." This is the Catherine who Hemingway reveals in his 1947 letters when he dyes his hair bright red and calls himself Catherine.[18] This is the Catherine of "the new names department," when Hemingway signed himself "Katherin Ernest Hemingway" in his wife's 1953 African Journal (Eby, *Hemingway's Fetishism* 176–80). This is the inspiration for Catherine Bourne in *The Garden of Eden*. To misappropriate a sentence Hemingway wrote on a stray sheet in the *Moveable Feast* manuscript when he was considering naming *two* of *The Garden of Eden's* characters "Catherine,"—it applies as well to Catherine Barkley and Catherine Bourne—he had called both characters "Catherine," he explains, "because I have the most pleasant name"[19]

The coeval birth at Fossalta of Hemingway's fetishism and "Catherine" as the split-off other-sex half of Hemingway's ego, reimagined through the wounding of Frederic, at least partly explains why Frederic falls so suddenly in love right after his wounding. This reading links love and war in the novel—suggesting how matching haircuts might offer an idyllic escape from the ravages of the front—and it explains something of Catherine's dreamlike quality. It helps us to understand why Catherine and Frederic want to "be" each other—for on some level, as emblems of two halves of a divided ego, they already *are*. It makes sense of Frederic's "morning sickness," his obsession with hair, his misrecognition in the mirror, and his homophobic anxiety about Rinaldi. (Since the fetish helps the fetishist to disavow gender difference, he half-suspects himself of harboring homosexual desires which he feels compelled to disavow.)[20] True, this interpretation offers only a very partial reading of gender and sexuality in *A Farewell to Arms*, much less of the entire novel, yet its explanatory power to link together so many disparate elements of gender and sexuality in Hemingway's novel makes it an approach worthy of consideration. Even for readers who resist my psychoanalytic approach, the parallels between *The Garden of Eden* and *A Farewell to Arms* are so overwhelming and raise issues of gender and sexuality of such importance, issues that are so much clearer in the latter novel, that it only makes sense to flip chronology and read these two novels "backwards."

Notes

1. Stoller uses the term "erotic scenario" in his book *Sexual Excitement: Dynamics of Erotic Life* to describe the fantasy narratives embedded in such manifestations as daydreams, choice of pornography, object choice, or styles of intercourse (London: Karnac Books, 1986). My use of this term is conditioned by my argument—made at great length in my book *Hemingway's Fetishism: Psychoanalysis and the Mirror of Manhood* (Albany: State U of New York P, 1999)—that Hemingway was a fetishist. For a fetish is, as Stoller explains in *Observing the Erotic Imagination*, "a story masquerading as an object" (155), and fetishism manifests itself through a sort of ritual theater as "the production of a scenario, for which characters—in the form of people, parts of people, and nonhuman (including inanimate) objects—are cast" (31). Stoller's line of thought here owes much to the work of Joyce McDougall.

2. See Carl Eby, "'He Felt the Change So That It Hurt Him All Through': Sodomy and Transvestic Hallucination in Late Hemingway," *The Hemingway Review* 25.1 (2005): 77–95. Building upon the argument I made in *Hemingway's Fetishism*, this essay explains that "transvestism exists on a continuum between two poles, corresponding to the relative strengths of the two halves of a bisexually riven ego, and functions quite differently at each pole. At one pole . . . we find fetishists, such as Hemingway, who merely make occasional forays into transvestic behavior; at the other pole we find those men who have become what Stoller calls 'secondary transsexuals' (*Presentations* 20–21)" (Eby, "He Felt the Change," 90). In *Presentations of Gender*, Stoller distinguishes between male "primary

transsexuals"—men who have always known that their biological sex assignment was a mistake and for whom cross-dressing has never been sexually arousing—and male "secondary transsexuals"—men who once engaged in fetishistic cross-dressing, where cross-dressing was a turn-on, but who have now assumed a female identity in which cross-dressing is no longer sexually arousing (New Haven, CT: Yale UP, 1992). I have argued that "[w]hile Hemingway may have been well toward the masculine and fetishistic end of this transvestic continuum, it needs to be noted that all transvestites move along this continuum throughout their lives—some very little and some a great deal—and always in the direction of the more feminine pole. (Thus the not too uncommon septuagenarian who seeks sex reassignment.) The reason for this, I think, ... lies in the splitting of the ego, which as Freud observed, never 'heals' but rather 'increases as time goes on' [Sigmund Freud, "The Splitting of the Ego in the Defensive Process," *The Standard Edition of the Complete Psychoanalytic Works of Sigmund Freud*. Trans. James Stratchey. Vol 23. (London: Hogarth, 1964), 276]. As this splitting increases, the split-off other-sex half of the ego is able to assert itself more fully" (Eby, "He Felt the Change" 90). The widening split in the ego, with its strengthening of the opposite-sex half of the ego, leads to a greater acceptance of transvestic fantasies. This accounts, I argue, for the more pronounced expression of sexual fantasy in Hemingway's work as he aged. In another essay I also suggest why the split-off other-sex half of the ego may have less access to the sort of symbolization, displacement, condensation, and overdetermination that tends to mask unconscious content in narrative ("'Who Is the Destructive Type': Re-Reading Literary Jealousy and Destruction in *The Garden of Eden*, *The Hemingway Review*, 33.2 [2014]: 100–101). It would follow that as this half of Hemingway's ego grew in strength, the erotic scenario in his texts would gradually grow less opaque. I should add a note here about terminology. The language of Stoller's distinction between "primary" and "secondary" transsexuals may strike some readers as outdated or politically suspect, but the distinction itself is genuine and important, and it is obscured by the broader umbrella term *transgender*.

3. Although *A Farewell to Arms* and *The Garden of Eden* were composed decades apart, there *is* an interesting temporal link between the two works. *The Garden of Eden* has strong autobiographical roots in Hemingway's honeymoon with Pauline Pfeiffer at Le Grau du Roi in 1927. *A Farewell to Arms* was written in 1928.

4. For instance, we consider issues of gender and sexuality in the novel in relation to culture and history, biography, semiotics, queer theory, and Butlerian performativity, relying upon the work of such critics as Spilka, Comley and Scholes, Moddelmog, and Strychacz (See Moddelmog's Selected Bibliography in the Appendix of this volume). We also consider the novel in relation to eco-criticism, post-colonial theory, textual theory, debates about authorship, and what the novel suggests about the process of composition.

5. We read Freud's short essays "Fetishism" (1963) and "Splitting of the Ego in the Defensive Process" (1964) [*The Standard Edition of the Complete Psychoanalytic Works of Sigmund Freud* Vols. 21 and 23, (London: Hogarth), 147–158; 271–278] and D. W. Winnicott's "Transitional Objects and Transitional Phenomena." [*International Journal of Psycho-Analysis* 34 part 2 (1953), 89–97.] I rely heavily upon the first two chapters of Stoller's *Observing the Erotic Imagination*, but I find it easier to expose students to this indirectly through the final chapter of *Hemingway's Fetishism*.

6. In a fragment from the *Eden* manuscript, David thinks "I'd never known anyone named Peter that wasn't a prick." See the *Garden of Eden* manuscripts at the John F. Kennedy Library in Boston, item 422, miscellaneous notes and fragments. (Subsequent references to these manuscripts will be cited using the following system of abbreviation: JFKL/EH 422.1 followed by folder number, chapter number when there is more than one chapter in a folder, and page number. All passages from the manuscript cited in this essay have previously appeared in print.)

7. The GLAAD Media Reference Guide prefers the term *cross-dressing* to *transvestism*, and I try to honor that in my daily speech and in most classroom conversations, but in my writing about Hemingway I use the older term from the world of psychoanalysis, *transvestism*, because the term *cross-dressing* tends to obscure something vital in Hemingway. People generally imagine the crucial act of *cross-dressing* to be a wearing of the clothing of the opposite sex, but while this is often enough the case, this can also be very misleading. The issue isn't the clothing at all but rather what the clothing means for the person wearing it—and the item worn doesn't need to be clothing at all. The transvestic act (i.e., the act of fetishistic cross-dressing) hinges upon the wearing of a fetish object (often in front of a mirror) to negotiate a cross-gender identification. This fetish object might be a pair of pantyhose or shoes (and often such fetishes expand to include a complete set of clothes), but the object could as easily be, in the case of a hair fetishist, a haircut. Hemingway never to my knowledge wore women's clothes—although his wife, Mary, did talk him out of piercing his ears (Eby, *Hemingway's Fetishism* 178–79)—but when he dyed his hair red in 1947 (Eby, *Hemingway's Fetishism* 199–204), and shaved his head in 1953 (Eby, *Hemingway's Fetishism* 174–79), in each instance calling himself "Catherine," he was wearing his fetish to negotiate a cross-gender identification. We can call this *cross-dressing*, but *transvestism* seems to be less confusing. I am, however, careful to discuss with my students how to speak respectfully and supportively about transgender issues. Here the GLAAD Media Reference Guide is an excellent tool.

8. A classic transitional object would be something like a child's special blanket. Warm and soft and endowed with bodily odors, it is a sort of mother substitute, functioning as a comfort object and a bridge, both joining and separating the child to and from the mother's body as the child separates and individuates and begins to explore the world. As the child develops a relatively stable ego, the need for this object gradually diminishes. In the case of the pre-fetishist, an unstable ego, body image, and gender identity make this sort of transitional thinking more difficult to relinquish. When questions of sameness and difference become gendered for the male pre-fetishist, the fetish inherits the core qualities of the transitional object. See Phyllis Greenacre, *Emotional Growth: Psychoanalytic Studies of the Gifted and a Great Variety of Other Individuals*. 2 Vols. (New York: International Universities P, 1971).

9. In *The Garden of Eden*, when Barbara and Nick Sheldon, like the Bournes, get identical haircuts, it not only excites them, it excites their barber so much that his hands are shaking. Following the haircuts, Nick and Barbara run home to make love, but no amount of lovemaking can kill the excitement (JFKL/EH 422.1 3.15.).

10. JFKL/EH 4221. 25.35.

11. An even better comparison would be Barbara Sheldon's entreaty from the *Garden of Eden* manuscript, "Let's think of something fun to do that we've never done that will be secret and wicked" (JFKL/EH 422.1 3.1). Needless to say, this is a plea for identical haircuts with her husband. As Robert Stoller explains, "a desire to sin" (even if sin is a purely imaginary construct) is a constituent quality of fetishism and transvestism (*Observing* 7).

12. See Marcelline Hemingway Sanford's personal account of this pseudo-twinning, *At the Hemingways: A Family Portrait* (Boston: Little, Brown, 1962), 61–62; 109–111, or see Kenneth S. Lynn's biography *Hemingway* (New York: Simon and Schuster, 1987), 39–43.

13. For instance Barbara Sheldon describes Catherine to David, "You know no man ever looked at her that didn't have an erection. I don't know what women have but whatever it is I have it" (JFKL/EH 422.1 5.5.7). Marita likewise asserts that Théophile Gautier's cross-dressing novel *Mademoiselle de Maupin* gave her an erection (JFKL/EH 422.1 36.22).

14. JFKL/EH 422.2 39.5.

15. See Freud, "Fetishism," 155.

16. Here, I am relying not only on Freud but on subsequent psychoanalysts such as Winnicott and Greenacre.

17. See Allen Josephs's essay "Hemingway's Out of Body Experience," *The Hemingway Review* 2.2 (1983), 11–17.

18. See Eby, *Hemingway's Fetishism*, 200–204.

19. JFKL/EH 123.

20. It is important to remember that in psychoanalytic usage a "disavowal" implies a divided attitude structured around the split in the ego. It blends both an acknowledgment and denial and is best summed up by Octave Mannoni's formula "Je sais bien, mais quand même" [I know well, but all the same] in *Clefs pour l'imaginaire ou l'autre scène* (Paris: Editions du Seuil, 1969) *passim*. This in turn can help us to see why Catherine must be a little "crazy." While the fetishist holds two incompatible attitudes toward fantasy and reality (for instance, concerning the existence of sexual difference) structured by the logic of disavowal and the split in his ego, the split-off other-sex half of the ego (i.e., "Catherine") holds an attitude that in isolation is psychotic. That is, it completely denies the reality principle in deference to fantasy.

Economic Power and the Female Expatriate Consumer Artist in *The Garden of Eden*

Catherine R. Mintler

The Hemingway myth has remained engrained in the cultural narrative of the American male writer, despite nearly three decades of critical insights that have revealed this iconic, hyperbolic masculine image to be a façade constructed by Hemingway and encouraged by generations of readers and critics. Those familiar with outdated readings of Hemingway's work might be surprised to find *The Garden of Eden* on a gender and women's studies syllabus. However, recent Hemingway criticism, influenced by previously unpublished letters and the unpublished manuscript of *Garden*, has uncovered beneath the myth a male writer who constructed complex women characters, who was interested in gender fluidity, and whose public identity obscured unconventional views about gender and sexuality. How we teach Hemingway must catch up with these critical insights.

Courses that once included Hemingway as the misogynistic male writer whom his female contemporaries were writing *against* might instead read him as an unanticipated ally since he tackles issues addressed by women writers commonly read in gender and women's studies classes. *The Garden of Eden*, which I teach in advanced women's studies seminars, echoes concerns shared by women writers who challenged gender essentialism and documented the struggles of women artists. *Garden*'s female protagonist, Catherine Bourne, represents the precarious position of women who resisted object status in masculine exchange economies like marriage; its plot interrogates her treatment as an expatriate woman artist who, denied other means of aesthetic expression, refigures the conventional, often stereotyped, gender role of the female consumer to the extent that fashionable consumption—the purchase and display of sartorial fashion and beauty products—becomes the media for making art.[1] The narrative giving her husband's perspective shows how misogyny, fear of the feminine, and repression of women's desire and artistic production—recurrent subjects in women's literature—oppress women and the woman artist. The novel also provides examples of terminology and theories commonly introduced in gender and women's studies, such as gender role reversal, sartorial fetishism, and nonbinary gender identity.

As a male writer addressing these concerns, Hemingway offers an insider's critical insight into why and how male-dominated institutions, represented by male authority figures like husbands, oppressed women as sexual objects and thwarted their artistic ambitions. The feminist reading that follows—which performs the close reading, contextual framing, and analysis we invite students to practice in class discussions and essays—argues that *The Garden of Eden* further examines the conflict between masculine and feminine exchange economies first hinted at in *The Sun Also Rises*. In *The Garden of Eden* Hemingway exposes the insincerity and hypocrisy of men and male-dominated social institutions that purported to offer women financial empowerment and creative opportunities, only to turn against and oppress them as women and as artists. That complex women like Catherine fail or die is not evidence of Hemingway's misogyny—a reading common in second wave feminism—but of misogyny endemic in Western culture and society.

The greatest innovation of Hemingway's late work was his creation of a complex woman protagonist: the economically empowered expatriate consumer artist Catherine Bourne in *The Garden of Eden* (1986). Upon its publication, both critics and novelists regarded Catherine as a "major achievement," noting that "There ha[d] not before been a female character who so dominates a Hemingway narrative. Catherine in fact may be the most impressive of any woman character in Hemingway's work."[2] Recent scholarship about Hemingway's fetishism and interest in androgyny contends that the hyper-masculinity responsible for the Hemingway myth masked a more complex view of gender, and that his later work, *Garden* in particular, worked out his gender anxieties.[3] This reading of Catherine supports arguments that Hemingway admired strong women and concurs with scholarship identifying feminist modes of thinking indebted to feminine influence in his life and work.[4]

Hemingway's experience as a male writer privileged by the male-dominated literary marketplace, and his knowledge of how economics differently affected men and women, help cast Catherine as a sympathetic woman artist who uses economic empowerment, sartorial and tonsorial fetishism, and experiments in gender role reversal to produce art. Her artwork is a form of what feminist criticism calls writing on the body: she refashions commoditized femininity and the commodified body, and then stages gender experiments in public and private. Her subversive performance art unhinges the connection between sexual dimorphism and the gender binary, and further disrupts gender and sexuality in the role reversals she orchestrates during lovemaking, where she performs as a boy and David becomes her girl. Her artistic authority extends to the honeymoon story, which she narrates and David transcribes. Catherine is the heroine of a female *Künstlerroman* buried in the published novel beneath the male *Künstlerroman*.[5] Perhaps as a result of its heavy editing, the published novel undermines the female *Künstlerroman*, showing how "the male *Künstlerroman* does not tell the woman artist's story," and instead silences it (O'Brien 354). Catherine's endeavors to become an artist are thwarted by the male-dominated literary marketplace—the fictional literary marketplace that encourages and rewards David's writing and the real one responsible for *Garden*'s posthumous publication. Making Catherine an artist who struggles to create suggests that Hemingway recognized the importance of feminine artistic production and criticized economic exchange systems that undermined women's art.

The concerns of *Garden*'s female *Künstlerroman* narrative echo twentieth-century feminist writing about the plight of women writers. Without economic means to finance artistic production, Catherine couldn't benefit from the financial independence that Hemingway's contemporary, Virginia Woolf, claimed women needed to produce art. In giving Catherine an inheritance, Hemingway seems to agree with Woolf's claim in *A Room of One's Own* (1929) that, "a woman must have money and a room of her own if she is to write" (4). As was Woolf's experience, Catherine's inheritance frees her to produce art; Catherine's economic autonomy ensures that neither she nor David needs to earn a living from regular paid work. Unlike Woolf and her protagonist in *Room*, Catherine never has a room of her own.[6] As if to compensate, Hemingway transforms private and public settings—bedrooms, museums, bars, barbershops—into temporary studio space for the production, exhibition, and performance of Catherine's art. A Rodin sculpture in a museum provides her with the artistic inspiration that ignites her desire to transgress gender roles.[7] She then purchases fashionable commodities and services that assist her writing on the body and performance art. Hemingway differs from Woolf only in adding feminine consumer identity and fashionable consumption to the financial independence required for female artistic production.

Similar to the woman writers Woolf examines in *Room*, Catherine discovers her art isn't valued in a literary marketplace governed by exchange economies where men control women's circulation. Hemingway complicates Woolf's economically empowered woman artist by having Catherine's marriage to a male writer echo the competition between early twentieth-century men and women writers. The silenced female *Künstlerroman* in *Garden* anticipates the critique of misogyny, sexism, and fear of the feminine that Sandra Gilbert and Susan Gubar explore in *No Man's Land: The Place of the Woman Writer in the Twentieth Century*. In *Volume II: Sexchanges* (1989), they argue that for Hemingway—as for other early twentieth-century male writers—gender subversions like transvestism were "evoked to maintain or reassert a fixed social order" (363). However, *Garden*'s female *Künstlerroman* narrative opposes the published novel's silencing of the female artist, revealing Hemingway's critique of a fixed social order that undermines women's art. In Catherine, Hemingway creates a twentieth-century heir for Gilbert and Gubar's madwoman writer. In *Garden*, Hemingway takes the metaphorical madwoman artist out of her domestic attic prison, relocates her in circumstances where she temporarily influences male writing and produces art, and shows the consequences she pays for being a woman artist in a world that supports male artistic production. Much as it did the nineteenth-century madwoman writer, repressed artistic production drives Catherine mad.[8] This narrative strategy demonstrates how women who are denied access to benefits conferred upon male writers pay for attempting to create art outside of exchange systems that privilege men. Like Woolf, Hemingway champions an economically empowered, androgynous woman artist who produces art; like Gilbert and Gubar, he impugns the treatment women artists received in a male-dominated literary marketplace that thwarted their artistic endeavors.

Both the unpublished manuscript of *Garden* and the novel posthumously published in 1986 contain evidence of Hemingway's interest in feminine influence upon male artistic production and its importance in disrupting master narratives that govern artistic production and modern gender identity. The specific issues he explores that pertain to gender and women's studies—gender role reversal, feminine influence upon masculine writing, and female artistic production—occur within masculine economies of exchange that suppress female empowerment and thwart subversive gender performance. Even though the published novel excluded material from the manuscript that supports a reading of the plight of the economically empowered female consumer artist, the radically truncated, published version still echoes Hemingway's critique of the institutionalized sexism and misogyny that undermine female artistic production.

Hemingway's first examination of the plight of strong, economically empowered women in masculine economies of exchange occurred in *The Sun Also Rises* (1926), which foreshadows issues involving gender and sexuality he explicates in *The Garden of Eden*. Though Catherine has been read as a composite of wealthy expatriate women Hemingway knew with varying degrees of intimacy—Lady Duff Twysden, Zelda Fitzgerald, and his wives Pauline Pfeiffer and Martha Gellhorn—she is more the heir of fictional expatriates in *Sun*.[9] She is not Hemingway's first character to be strongly connected with money and consumerism. One precursor is the financially preoccupied expatriate writer Jake Barnes. Jacob Michael Leland suggests that using money to construct a façade of masculinity enables consumerism to replace sexual potency: for Jake Barnes in *Sun*, money and the commodities it buys replace sex, while consumer identity replaces sexual identity. Consuming becomes part of an "expatriate performance" in which Barnes "receives what he sets out to purchase—the appearance, if the not performance, of masculine sexual agency" (42–43). Unlike Jake, Catherine doesn't need to work to earn money, she doesn't need to keep track of expenses, and she doesn't need to consume to compensate for sexual dysfunction. Catherine consumes and dresses in menswear and gets men's haircuts to blur and transgress gender norms that govern masculine and feminine appearance—the very same gender norms that enable Jake to appear as a sexually functional, virile, and masculine man. Catherine doesn't create a façade of gender or sexual normalness, but challenges sex and gender norms that prevent women from controlling their sexuality and creating art. Her economic independence and transgressive gender performances also connect her to Brett Ashley. Both are economically empowered female expatriates who blur gender boundaries in ways that challenge norms governing feminine appearance, female sexual desire and expression, and traditional women's roles. They also both pay for these sexual and sartorial transgressions. Brett's financial independence, androgynous dress, rebellious sexual behavior, and promiscuity, when combined with Jake's use of spending to construct a façade of sexual virility, provide the genesis of Catherine Bourne in the later novel.

When interpreted through a feminist lens and connected to its literary precursors, *The Garden of Eden* recounts the tragic fate of the economically empowered woman artist. In the novel's female *Künstlerroman* narrative, Catherine's consumption, sartorial transvestism, and gender role reversal experiments merge to challenge masculine economies of exchange in marriage and the literary marketplace. Where they merge—and perhaps why they do—is rooted in the differing systems of exchange within which and outside of which Catherine tries to work. I agree with feminist readings of *Garden* that interpret Catherine's art as a form of *écriture féminine* that rejects the male economies' "emphasis upon return, exchange, repayment, and debt," while espousing instead female economies that include "unrestricted, unlimited expenditure, expecting nothing in return"[10] (Willingham 55–56). In *Garden*, Hemingway exemplifies the feminine gift economy of exchange in which women's art flourishes. Catherine constructs a feminine gift economy in which she "gives more, with no assurance that she'll get back even some unexpected profit from what she puts out" (Cixous 893). She frequently gives in excess without seeking remuneration for her expenditure; moreover, her expenditures are motivated by generosity, not return. Her experiments are intended to please David, and she strongly desires that her artistic endeavors involve mutual collaboration and participation. For example, she envisions their collaboration on the honeymoon narrative as a gift they share, not a saleable commodity, when she exclaims, "I'm so proud of it already and we won't have any copies for sale and none for reviewers and then there'll never be clippings and you'll never be self-conscious and we'll have it just for us" (77–78). However, Catherine's participation in an economy that, as Cixous explains, "dispenses gifts freely," only temporarily subverts masculine exchange economies that control her circulation as woman and wife and fail to recognize her as an artist (Willingham 56).

The existence of both exchange economies in *Garden* suggests that what critics have labeled as Catherine and David's artistic competition is, in fact, conflict between two different systems of exchange. Jacqueline Vaughn Brogan suggests that, as male and female artist figures in *Garden*, Catherine and David develop competing artistic and economically motivated jealousies, explaining further that "if Catherine is jealous of David's writing (and particularly of the good reviews his writing receives) and utterly indifferent of his writing's making money, David is completely jealous of Catherine's having the money in their relationship and particularly desires that his writing become commercially successful" (238). In Brogan's view, David and Catherine compete over who possesses economic power. However, interpreting their artistic and marital tensions as personal competition produces a reductive understanding of how Hemingway viewed gender and economics at work in the novel. David and Catherine create from within different exchange systems. David is motivated by a masculine economy of exchange, the market economy that circulates different forms of money, or capital—cultural, symbolic and, most importantly, economic capital. Catherine participates in Cixous's feminine gift economy of exchange motivated by generous expenditure, doesn't seek her gifts' return, and doesn't value artistic production in competitive or pecuniary terms.

The symbols of the masculine exchange economy in which David circulates are royalty checks and newspaper clippings from his publisher. Catherine recognizes their negative effect on David's self-worth as a writer and their marriage when she asks, "'How can we be us and have the things we have and do what we do and you be this that's in the clippings? . . . They're terrible . . . they could destroy you if you thought about them or believed them . . . you don't think I married you because you are what they say you are in those clippings, do you?'" (24). This scene reveals David's economic competitiveness and artistic insecurity and Catherine's worry about his obsession with economic value; it warns writers working within masculine exchange economies about the consequences of obsessive overreliance on symbolic capital, like book reviews. When the conversation turns to her mail, which contains inheritance checks, Catherine insists they live off of her money, which she calls *their* money. Her wish to participate in a gift economy isn't premised upon competition or pecuniary investment and return, but by her desire that David value artistic production rather than art as commodity. Her wish for them to collaboratively write the honeymoon narrative shows that her artistic endeavors aren't in competition with David's identity as a writer.

Unfortunately, Catherine needs to remind David that participation in a feminine gift economy makes his writing possible, asking "Isn't it lucky Heiress and I are rich so you'll never have anything to worry about?" (122). When he abandons their collaborative honeymoon narrative to write his Africa stories—a metaphorical returning of her check un-cashed that rejects her artistic identity—Catherine again reminds him where the money that allows him to write comes from. She seeks recognition—*credit,* if you will—for financially supporting his artistic production. As she explains to Marita, "I've only tried to make it economically possible for him to do the best work of which he is capable" (156), and later to David and Marita, "I knew it would be so humiliating if the money ran out and you had to borrow and I hadn't fixed up anything nor signed anything" (163). When she burns his clippings and the notebooks containing his Africa stories, the only symbols of his economic value as a writer, Catherine destroys his commodified writing identity and value in the literary marketplace. While this might be interpreted as competitive vengeance, it is her attempt to prevent David from becoming reabsorbed into a masculine economy of exchange that makes him paranoid about his work's exchange value.[11] In economically empowering Catherine with independent wealth, Hemingway enabled her to opt out of masculine exchange economies and choose a system that invited both collaborative and female artistic production. She can afford to enter the feminine gift economy, and for a short time her participation and generous expenditure invite David to join and collaborate with her. However, like fictional Hemingway heroines before her, Catherine must pay. When participating in a gift economy that allows her to pay with generous expenditure fails to sustain the conditions Catherine needs to produce art, she pays in consequences instead.

Much of Hemingway's fiction illustrates the different ways that men and women pay. In *The Sun Also Rises* (1926), Jake Barnes, acting as Hemingway's spokesperson, shares his observation of how women like Brett Ashley pay for gender and sexual transgression. Barnes's epiphany is that women pay differently than men pay: "I thought I had paid for everything. Not like the woman pays and pays and pays. No idea of retributions or punishments. Just exchange of values. You gave up something and got something else" (152). Jake contrasts men's paying in terms of costs and benefits with women's paying in costs and consequences. How a woman "pays and pays and pays" as a form of "retribution or punishment" is quite different from how men pay through suffering but are compensated by an "exchange of values" that involves their "giv[ing] up something and [getting] something" (152). In *The Garden of Eden*, Hemingway unveils how masculine exchange economies that take advantage of female generosity make women pay for attempting to create art, revealing how women pay and who makes them pay. Catherine has already paid by being born a woman and thus is denied the same access men have to artistic production. She pays when she provides economic support so David can write, and she pays when she consumes sartorial fashion and beauty products to produce art. However, she also pays in consequences. To revise Barnes's epiphany: the woman artist "pays and pays and *pays*" (emphasis mine). A superficial reading of *Garden* might misconstrue Catherine's paying as simply mirroring the subordinate female position in marriage hierarchy that casts women in roles deferential to men. This is certainly a traditional way that a woman *pays* for becoming a wife; however, in *Garden* Catherine pays for rejecting this role.

Economic empowerment enables Catherine to pay so she and David can produce art. She begins paying in consequences when David becomes obsessed with his economic value and jealous of her generous expenditure and her trespass into the male world of artistic production. Catherine engages in generous expenditures that free them from work and financial worry and provide opportunities for collaborative artistic production, while David engages in competitive accounting to increase his economic status and value in their marriage. David obsessively tallies his earnings, establishing a pecuniary competition intended to undermine the gift economy of Catherine's generosity. His clippings represent bills of paper money, and the envelope that contains them becomes his metaphorical wallet. He resents that Catherine's inheritance checks designate her the economic provider in their marriage. David produces art to make money; Catherine shares her independent income so they can both produce art. After Catherine burns his clippings, David acknowledges how Catherine will pay in consequences financially when he tells Marita: "You just stay around and help me not kill her.... She's going to pay me for the stories so that I won't lose anything ... She's going to pay me double the appraisal price" (231).[12] Hemingway shows here a male artist deciding how a woman must pay in consequences when the gift economy she creates from within competes with exchange economies that privilege male artistic production and value male writing as publishable commodity.

David makes Catherine pay with other consequences as well; as a result, her efforts to transform marriage—by participating in a feminine gift economy that balances gender and power relations and by writing a collaborative honeymoon narrative that establishes egalitarian spaces where male and female artists can cocreate and live as equals—ultimately fail. Her anticipation of this failure may be the reason she "strongly advocates using her money to perpetuate the honeymoon, for its end will halt the narrative which she is creating," and finds for David a substitute wife (Willingham 55). Additionally, Catherine "not only wishes to support David, but also lavishes him with gifts such as the 'Dent edition' of the Hudson text he so desires." He is not capable of similar generosity. While he initially buys into the androgynous sartorial gender experiments and sexual role reversals that Catherine uses to transform their bodies into sculptural and performance art, he ultimately rejects them. Initially allowing Catherine to support him financially and enjoying the role playing that sexually excites him, he feels threatened when she refashions herself as his androgynous double, stages theatrical scenarios that cast him in a subordinate sexual role, and assigns him the role of amanuensis to transcribe the honeymoon narrative.

We don't know whether Hemingway intended to cast the female artist as rebel against or victim of masculine economies of exchange. In both published and manuscript versions of *The Garden of Eden*, Catherine pays in consequences only after disrupting the masculine exchange economy and male *Künstlerroman* narrative. David's refusal to further participate in and write the honeymoon narrative thwarts her artistic production. This denial drives her mad, as "it is the women who pay the price of madness for transgression, and as we have seen, transgression consists not only of sexual acts, but also of the women's attempts at creativity" (Comley, "Hemingway" 292). Like her madwomen in the attic ancestors, the modern madwoman is sexually and artistically repressed.[13] David exchanges one heiress wife for another, negating the gift economy his first wife's generous expenditure created to support his writing, and returns to the masculine code represented by the Africa stories.

When Tom Jenks edited *The Garden of Eden* to end with the male *Künstlerroman* narrative, he banished Hemingway's Lilith, the female artist, from Eden, and replaced her with a more conventional and submissive Eve, thereby preserving both the patriarchal prelapsarian Eden myth and the Hemingway myth constructed by "the popular, commodified Hemingway and his work" (Moddelmog, *Reading Desire* 59). He modeled how masculine exchange systems prohibit feminine writing from entering public circulation, enacting the very gendered politics Hemingway interrogates in the manuscript and that still come through in the published novel. The female *Künstlerroman* sections of the novel show that Hemingway's "treatment of Catherine provides insights into the struggles of the female artist. . . . [whose] suffering and assumed decent into madness relate directly to her debilitating insecurities in the face of the patriarchal dominance of the arts" (Willingham 47).[14] Teaching such readings of *The Garden of Eden,* which has contributed greatly to my own evolving understanding of Hemingway's views of gender and economics, helps students understand Hemingway's complex views about the construction and expression of gender and sexuality and illuminates the misogyny and fear male authors felt toward their female contemporaries. Similar to his women contemporaries and feminist critics writing after *Garden*'s posthumous publication, Hemingway championed the woman artist in a society that denigrated female artistic production. His work should not be read or taught as complicit with the social and sexual prohibitions that repressed and silenced women and women artists but rather as critical of them.

Notes

1. The creation of the modern female consumer as a stereotypically feminine gender role arguably begins with the 1883 publication of *Au Bonheur des Dames* (*The Ladies' Paradise*), Emile Zola's novel about the first nineteenth-century French department stores and the women who worked and shopped in them.

2. Mark Spilka quotes from E. L. Doctorow's review of *The Garden of Eden. Hemingway's Quarrel with Androgyny* (Lincoln: U of Nebraska P, 1990).

3. See the essay by Carl Eby in the present volume as well as his important and groundbreaking analysis of gender identity and gender politics in Hemingway's major works, *Hemingway's Fetishism: Psychoanalysis and the Mirror of Manhood* (Albany: State U of New York P, 1999). Eby's analysis reads Hemingway filtered through personal correspondence describing his tonsorial fetishes and desire to perform gendered role reversal.

4. Spilka notes that "the great change, the important and startling change, was in Hemingway himself, in his late attempt to come to terms once more with his own androgynous nature" (*Hemingway's Quarrel* 2). Specifically in relation to feminine influence upon the male writer, which Spilka views as an important theme in *The Garden of Eden*, he adds that "what seems instructive is the degree to which he listened to and learned from the devilish and adoring muses within himself—learned, that is, about what a woman is and suffers and, less consistently, about his own severe dependencies and evasive strengths—and so left us with this lumbering elephant of a book for future hunting" (13). In terms of understanding how Hemingway viewed women, Spilka reveals the following "self-revelation . . . that his emotional dependency on his wives and mistresses, his androgynous complicity with their several obsessions with hair, skin, dress, gender, and lesbian attachments, is what makes for his strength as a creative writer" (294). For an approach to teaching Hemingway and women writers, see Sara Kosbia's essay in this volume. For an alternative point of view suggesting that Hemingway's fraught relationship with his mother—herself a talented painter and singer—may have had "consequences" that were "paradoxical and far-reaching," see Kenneth S. Lynn's controversial biography *Hemingway* (Cambridge, MA: Harvard UP, 1995), 38.

5. A *Künstlerroman* is a subgenre of fiction, usually a novel that chronicles an artist's development. While mostly thought to follow the artistic development of male protagonists, as in James Joyce's *A Portrait of the Artist as a Young Man* (1916), the *Künstlerroman* traces the artistic development of women as well, such as in Kate Chopin's *The Awakening* (1899) and Radclyffe Hall's *The Well of Loneliness* (1928). The development of the female artist in the *Künstlerroman* narratives of *Awakening* and *Well*, much like that in *Garden*, illustrates the importance of being liberated from the restrictive gender and sexual norms of female artistic production.

6. Both parts of this equation are important: Woolf argues that women must possess both an independent income and a room of their own in order to write. Catherine Bourne's inheritance provides financial freedom; however, she never has her own space. After marrying her, David has access to both money and a private, usually locked room in each hotel they live in.

7. Catherine experiments with tonsorial and sartorial appearance and persuades David to engage in role reversals during sex after being inspired by the famous Rodin sculpture "Damned Women," which draws on a story from Ovid's *Metamorphoses*. Rodin's sculpture captures the moment when, as a man and a woman embrace during lovemaking, the man changes into a woman. This gender transformation is reflected in the androgynous rendering of the figure that is male. (See Spilka, *Hemingway's Quarrel*.) Eby points out in *Hemingway's Fetishism* that Hemingway preferred his wives and lovers to wear their

hair boyishly short; he would recommend to his wife, Mary, what color she should dye her hair, and, on occasion, dyed it for her. Hemingway even dyed his own hair and, in a letter to Mary, describes his new hair color: "red as a French polished copper pot, or a newly minted penny" (Eby, 203). In the same letter, Hemingway writes, "So now I am just as red headed as you would like your girl Catherine to be and don't give a damn about it at all." The letter continues to discuss hair as a fetish object.

8. Gilbert and Gubar discuss a genealogy of repressed women artists in the nineteenth century in *The Madwoman in the Attic: The Woman Writer and the Nineteenth-Century Literary Imagination* (New Haven, CT: Yale UP, 1979).

9. In "Hemingway's Barbershop Quintet: The Garden of Eden Manuscript," *Novel: A Forum on Fiction* 21.1 (1987), Mark Spilka offers his account of the women Hemingway used to construct Catherine's character: "she most obviously combines Pauline's possessive and controlling use of money, Mary's resentment of her own infertility and perhaps also of her gender, Zelda's artistic rivalry with Scott and her ultimately vengeful hostility, and Jane Mason's suicidal recklessness and emotional instability. Like Hadley, who once lost a suitcase containing her husband's early manuscripts, and who may have resented them, as Jeffrey Meyer asserts, for keeping her and Ernest apart, Catherine is jealous and resentful of David's African tales" (51).

10. In "Hemingway's The Garden of Eden: Writing with the Body," *The Hemingway Review* 12.2 (1993): 55–56, Kathy Willingham convincingly argues that Catherine is a version of the female artist who writes with her body to create art and "prefigures many contemporary theories concerning l'ecriture feminine as articulated in particular by Helene Cixous" (46). Willingham notes the significance of Catherine's generous gift expenditure in her development as an artist, contrasting participation in a female gift economy to that of male gift economies. Feminine writing involves expressing the feminine outside of the boundaries of patriarchal structures (logic and language being two examples) and exchange economies through the body. Catherine performs a version of feminine writing when she re-sculpts her gender by dressing in men's clothes, cuts her hair to mirror David's appearance, and assumes the dominant, male role in sex. Cixous's theory of *écriture féminine,* writing on, through, or with the body, which is not necessarily limited to writers or artists who are women, is explored in Hélène Cixous's "The Laugh of the Medusa," trans. Keith Cohen and Paul Cohen, *Signs* 1.4 (1976).

11. In a brilliant use of foreshadowing, Hemingway forecasts Catherine's destruction of David's clippings and Africa stories when she dyes her hair ash-blond. In French, the term for ashes is *cendres. Cendre* also refers to fashionable hair dye color in the early twentieth century that resembled the color of ashes.

12. Though Catherine is ultimately forced to put a price tag on David's artistic production, she is nevertheless empowered. As David notes, "The doubling of the appraisal . . . makes [her payment] generous and gives her pleasure" (231).

13. See Sandra Gilbert and Susan Gubar, *The Madwoman in the Attic: The Woman Writer and the Nineteenth-Century Literary Imagination* (New Haven, CT: Yale UP, 1979).

14. Rose Marie Burwell notes in "Hemingway's Garden of Eden: Resistance of Things Past and Protecting the Masculine" *Texas Studies in Literature and Language* 35.2 (1993) that "Catherine's actions seem not so much madness as healthy anger" (204–5).

Part Three

Hemingway and Women

Hemingway and the Modern Woman

Brett Ashley and the Flapper Tradition

Crystal Gorham Doss

Traditionally, the scholarly focus on women in Ernest Hemingway's works has been on how male characters react to "modern" women but not on the struggles of the female characters as worthy of consideration in and of themselves.[1] Hemingway's modern women are expected by his male characters to be adventurous, to drink heavily, and to desire a modern life free from domesticity. Students may read Brett Ashley of *The Sun Also Rises* (1926) as liberated because she is single, travels, and is free of marriage and family. Likewise, in "The Snows of Kilimanjaro" (1936), students may read Helen as liberated because she drinks, hunts, and is independently wealthy. The struggle of female characters to define themselves against oppositional stereotypes—*either* as single, modern women *or* as traditional wives and mothers—is often overlooked.

I typically teach Hemingway within the context of an American literature survey course (1865 to present), which is required for majors but also serves as an elective for non-majors. I often find that students bring assumptions to their reading of Hemingway's work that are based on Hemingway's public persona and the reception of his work. Because *Sun* and "The Snows of Kilimanjaro" invite autobiographical interpretations, students assume that narrators and characters are voicing Hemingway's opinions on gender roles. Thus, students often oversimplify the text and focus on Hemingway's narrator's sexist attitudes or on male characters and their development. In other words, because Hemingway is best known for his strong male characters—he even titled one of his short story collections *Men Without Women* (1927)—students tend to overlook the complexity of Hemingway's modern women. In addition, students often don't have much knowledge of women's history in the early part of the twentieth century. They may have heard of flappers, but students often don't understand the flapper beyond the iconic fashion trends she inspired; nor do students tend to understand the flapper's relationship to her predecessors.

My objective is for students to develop a more nuanced understanding of femininity in Hemingway's work and to see Hemingway's modern women as the complex characters they are. This objective also aligns with course and program objectives that ask students to situate texts in cultural and/or historical contexts and to understand issues of diversity as they shape literary and cultural production. Students also fulfill other outcomes geared toward writing analytical arguments. In addition to participating in formative assessments, like in-class writing and blogs, students demonstrate their increased skills in these areas on summative assessments, like final project wikis. Students might trace a key concept, like femininity, through multiple literary texts over time, incorporating both historical and cultural multimedia artifacts into a literary analysis of writers throughout the late nineteenth century and through the twentieth century. In so doing, they see how a writer like Hemingway fits into the larger literary tradition that includes contributions by and about women.

In the essay that follows, I will explain the theoretical basis for my reading of Hemingway's modern women and offer an analysis of two commonly taught Hemingway texts—*The Sun Also Rises* and "The Snows of Kilimanjaro." Rather than viewing Hemingway's modern women characters simply as being free of the constraints of the domestic—itself a narrow view of proscriptive turn-of-the-century gender roles—this approach asks students to explore Hemingway's modern women characters as engaged in a struggle with various models of femininity.

In order to understand Hemingway's women, we must first acknowledge their predecessors. In her work on nineteenth-century literature by and about women, Lauren Berlant argues that women's sentimental literature is not only a literary genre but also a medium that circulates norms for gender roles, genres of being and becoming. Berlant argues that "To call an identity like a sexual identity a genre is to think about it as something repeated, detailed, and stretched while retaining its intelligibility ... it is a structure of conventional expectation that people rely on to provide certain kinds of affective intensities and assurances" (4). Berlant argues that women's sentimental literature and the genres of femininity therein provide a framework for becoming *somebody* and negotiating a range of relationships. Hemingway's work demonstrates how women use models of femininity, or "genres" of femininity as Berlant calls them, to work out how to be *somebody*. These genres of femininity also carry with them ethical and moral norms, which are especially important to reading *The Sun Also Rises* and Hemingway's short fiction of the 1920s and 1930s.

Fig. 1. Examples of visual rhetoric, such as this now-iconic illustration by Charles Dana Gibson of the eponymous "Gibson Girl," introduce students to the different genres of womanhood familiar to late nineteenth- and early-twentieth-century audiences. In the public domain and available on Wikimedia Commons, the image is readily accessible to students and instructors.

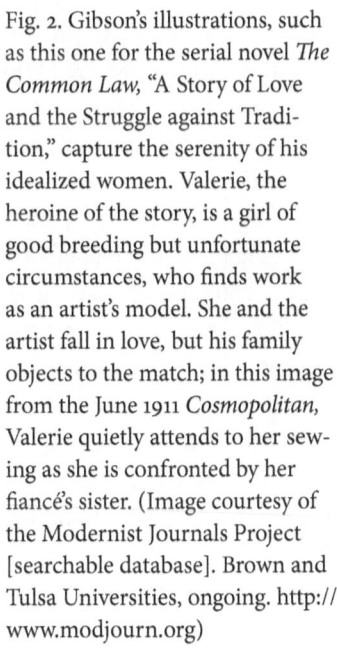

Fig. 2. Gibson's illustrations, such as this one for the serial novel *The Common Law,* "A Story of Love and the Struggle against Tradition," capture the serenity of his idealized women. Valerie, the heroine of the story, is a girl of good breeding but unfortunate circumstances, who finds work as an artist's model. She and the artist fall in love, but his family objects to the match; in this image from the June 1911 *Cosmopolitan,* Valerie quietly attends to her sewing as she is confronted by her fiancé's sister. (Image courtesy of the Modernist Journals Project [searchable database]. Brown and Tulsa Universities, ongoing. http://www.modjourn.org)

Through brief lectures, readings, and multimedia presentations, I ask students to consider femininity as a genre with moral and ethical dimensions, so they are able to move past traditional readings of Hemingway's female characters as one-dimensional foils that aid in the development of male characters.

The genres of femininity dominant before World War I closely align womanhood and femininity with domesticity. In a survey course, I introduce these genres of femininity early in the semester and discuss them as growing out of the Victorian image of the angel of the house, who is transformed at the turn of the century into the "modern" Gibson Girl. Because the early twentieth-century Gibson Girl was an image circulated through advertisements in mass media publications—including *Scribner's Magazine,* the in-house publication of Hemingway's own future publisher—images of the Gibson Girl and women who look like her are widely available through Google Images, Wikimedia Commons, and the Library of Congress website. I share these images with my students to introduce the Gibson Girl, who is devoted to her family and obeys her husband, though she is more modern than her Victorian counterpart because she is more engaged in public life, sports, and so forth. (See figures 1 and 2.) Despite some modernization, the Gibson Girl remained "the manikin" on which her husband "hung the symbols of his prosperity" (Yellis 53). While the respectable man of the early twentieth century was a breadwinner who derived his sense of purpose and fulfillment from the home, his wife, too, "was . . . responsible for the 'good name' of her household, living testimony to its economic as well as its moral respectability; this was her job. . . . to be her husband's 'prized possession' was her career" (Yellis 53).

The genres dominant after World War I are the New Woman and her more extreme counterpart, the flapper. (See figures 3 and 4.) Unlike the Gibson Girl, the flapper is single and works outside of the home; she desires fun and public amusements. Flappers are unconcerned with domesticity as either a place or state of being. As Kenneth Yellis notes, "The flapper could hardly have been a more thorough repudiation of the Gibson Girl if that had been her intent, as, in a sense, it was" (45). In addition to her lack of domesticity, the flapper differed from her counterpart in her consumption of alcohol. The Gibson Girl may have drunk at home as part of a social function—wine at dinner, for instance—but the flapper drank "more flagrantly and more self-consciously" and "challenged the model of pure and pious American womanhood on which the temperance movement was based" (Murdock 5). Because she was a respectable young woman engaging in activities that were previously thought disreputable, such as smoking in public and drinking with men, the flapper

Fig. 3. "The Flapper" by Frank Xavier Leyendecker (1922) offers a whimsical interpretation implying that the flapper is an exotic other species.

was a shocking and controversial figure. To give students a more in-depth understanding of the flapper, I not only share images but also ask students to read brief opinion pieces or social commentary from the 1920s to get a sense of the extent to which women's roles were changing and the intense public anxiety these changing roles created. Examples can be found in databases such as *American Periodicals Online*.

When students better understand these genres of femininity, they are able to engage the complexity of Hemingway's female characters. If students understand how radically different the modern woman is from her predecessors and how much controversy she sparked, they will have an easier time understanding the importance of Hemingway's depiction of modern femininity. In an

Fig 4. With bobbed hair, bare shoulders, and a cigarette, the figure on the cover of the March 1922 *Smart Set* depicts a quintessential flapper. The self-consciously clever magazine was co-edited by H. L. Mencken, a critic for whom Hemingway harbored a particularly vitriolic antipathy. (Image courtesy of the Modernist Journals Project [searchable database]. Brown and Tulsa Universities, ongoing. http://www.modjourn.org)

American literature survey course, I assign texts like "The Yellow Wallpaper" (1892) by Charlotte Perkins Gilman or "The Story of an Hour" (1894) by Kate Chopin in the opening weeks of the semester, and we discuss these texts in relation to arguments about "domestic industry" (Gillman 8). Later we put the Hemingway text in dialogue with short fiction by Katherine Anne Porter or Dorothy Parker.[2] Such juxtapositions allow students to see clearly the changing expectations for different genres of femininity. In order to establish these connections and contexts, gender roles are addressed in our discussions of every text throughout the semester. In addition, I periodically ask students to answer to the following questions in response to in-class writing prompts or blog entries: What are the norms against which women's behavior and appearance are measured? How do female characters both conform to and push back against these norms? Because these are recurring question in discussion and writing assignments throughout the term, I know students have put much time and effort into thinking about shifting norms for femininity by the time we get to Hemingway at mid-semester.

Likewise, students may find it useful to see images of the Gibson Girl and flappers. Students can look at the photographs and images and see the difference in dress and comportment, which can give them a way to think about physical manifestations of these different genres. The Gibson Girl is physically bound by corsets and hampered by long skirts, while the flapper's uncorseted dress allows for freedom of movement. Both genres of femininity are sexualized, but they are sexualized in different ways. Gerald Leinwald explains, "As eroticism shifted from the breasts (Gibson Girl) to the limbs (Flapper), the latter's costume also heralded a shift from women as wives and homemakers to competitors of men in business. Flappers' fashion made it possible for women to move around in the world of business. . . . The dress and grooming of the flapper . . . was efficient for work in an office and for businesslike activities with male and female peers" (175). It may also be useful to read short essays or opinion pieces like "Fears For Modern Woman: Dr. Crafts Predicts End Of Double Standard Of Morality" (*New York Times*, 1921) or "Plea for Old-Time Girls" (Gallatin). With these texts, I also pair reference sources that provide an overview of debates about women's status, like that in *Modernism: Keywords* (Cuddy-Keane, Hammond, and Peat).

Located at the intersection of these two oppositional stereotypes are Hemingway's female characters. I encourage students to consider that flappers and other genres of modern femininity, though not domestic, are hardly liberated, and Hemingway demonstrates the limits of defining the modern genres of femininity through compulsory "fun." Rena Sanderson argues that "what had seemed like liberation became prescription. Women were not just free to be modern—they were expected to be modern" ("Women" 146). Hemingway's characterization of modern women exposes asymmetrical relations of power and states of domination that must be negotiated but cannot be transcended. The issue then is not how the modern woman is "free" from the limitations of domesticity and sentimentality but how she negotiates changing norms of a modern femininity.

Hemingway's female characters tend to fall neatly into genres. However, regardless of their genre of femininity, these female characters actively engage in ethical negotiations between traditional and modern femininity. In *The Sun Also Rises*, Frances Clyne has a domestic, yet economic, model of ethics—she has paid for Robert Cohn, so he belongs to her. (Georgette, as a sex worker, operates on a similar economic model.) Frances Clyne passive-aggressively rebukes Cohn across five pages of the novel, hardly allowing him to get a word in (53–58). She chatters endlessly, though cheerfully, about how Cohn has done her wrong and forces Jake to be her audience. Frances invokes feminine qualities subversively to assert her claim to modernity. Frances feigns devotion and obedience to Cohn while simultaneously emphasizing her status as breadwinner. Frances "was very forceful" (13). She is well aware that Cohn is replacing her with another woman, and she is not going away quietly, especially after she has supported him, financially and otherwise, in his career: "It's my own fault, all right. Perfectly my own fault. When I made you get rid of your little secretary on the magazine I ought to have known you'd get rid of me the same way" (56). Frances desires a traditional, domestic life with Cohn but also behaves in modern ways, acting as a breadwinner and aggressively pursuing Cohn.

On the train to the Basque country to go fishing, Jake and Bill encounter a family from Montana. Jake and Bill discuss fishing and drinking with the husband and wife. Like Frances, Mother, the Montana woman on the train with her husband and son, also represents the ethics of domesticity. Her husband points out that if he took a "jug" or beer on any of his fishing trips, his wife would think it was "hell and damnation." However, she is quick to respond that she voted "against prohibition to please him" but "like[s] a little beer in the house." That her husband calls her Mother illustrates her position in the family. Mother is characterized by Jake as an asexual hayseed with a "comfortable lap" (92). She lacks all of the sophistication of expatriate women like Brett and Frances. Nevertheless, Mother is making complex ethical negotiations between two oppositional genres of femininity. On the one hand, Mother enacts her domestic duties by attempting to maintain the moral and religious standard of the domestic sphere by connecting drinking to "hell and damnation," and she votes against Prohibition to please her husband.[3] On the other hand, she, too, likes having a beer, and she did *vote*, both of which point to her modernity. (Students may need to be reminded that American women had just gained the right to vote in 1920 with the ratification of the Nineteenth Amendment to Constitution.) Like Frances, whose forcefulness is complicated by rhetorical questions, self-deprecation, and forced cheerfulness, Mother's seeming inconsistency in relation to drinking speaks to the complexities of her negotiations of modern womanhood. Both Mother and Frances are bound by contradictory genres of femininity, and both characters are trying to simultaneously be both modern and traditional.

In the short story "The Snows of Kilimanjaro," Harry, a writer, is dying of gangrene while on an African safari with his rich companion Helen. Like the female characters of *The Sun Also Rises*, Helen makes similar negotiations. Helen is adventurous, self-sufficient and "love[s] anything that [is] exciting." Helen is clearly a modern woman: "She had a great talent and appreciation for the bed, . . . she read enormously, liked to ride and shoot and, certainly, she drank too much" (45). Both Robert Cohn and Harry depend upon women for security. Like Frances Clyne, Helen is the breadwinner and provider and is expected to be modern, yet Helen constantly downplays her modernity to fit herself within the confines of the genre of traditional womanhood. Helen takes on a nurturing role: doting on Harry, feeding him, getting him medical care as best she can, offering to read to him. In response to Harry's viciousness, Helen says, "You don't have to destroy me. Do you? I'm only a middle-aged woman who loves you and wants to do what you want to do" (46). Helen pushes back against Harry's characterizations of her as "rich bitch" by refusing to be the rich bitch. Harry tries again and again to force Helen into that genre, but she refuses to be positioned in that way. Traditional genres of femininity limit women's freedom by aligning femininity and womanhood so closely with domesticity. More modern types of femininity do not represent freedom from such an alignment but instead come with their own restrictions and limitations. So while modern modes of femininity can be used to complicate and expand traditional genres of femininity, the reverse is also true. In the case of both Helen and Frances, traditional womanhood is not a weakness to overcome or bondage from which to be freed. Rather the genre of traditional womanhood is used as a tactic against the different set of pressures brought to bear by more modern types of womanhood.

In *The Resisting Reader*, Judith Fetterley concluded that in *A Farewell to Arms* "the only good woman is a dead woman, and even then there are questions" (71). However, Hemingway's female characters are not static; they negotiate the limits of and contradictions of multiple models of womanhood while simultaneously using those models for their own ends. In *The Sun Also Rises*, Brett Ashley's negotiation of the genres of femininity differs from that of Helen or Frances, for Brett largely refuses the traditional genres of femininity and embraces more modern genres of womanhood, with all of their allures and dangers. One thing students can see through an examination of characters like Brett is that modern genres of womanhood don't necessarily offer unrestricted freedom. Though Brett refuses more traditional feminine genres, she is still measured by them and, thus, must negotiate and reckon with them. Brett's ethics, or ways of being, are based on not being a "bitch" (188). The bitch ethics are reactionary and lack foresight; they are guided by compulsion and the judgment of others, not self-control. Repeatedly, but most notably when she is about to run off with Romero, Brett asserts that she has "never been able to help anything" (187). Throughout the novel, Brett will not control herself in any area—she is promiscuous and nearly always drunk—and doesn't perceive her lack of control as morally problematic. She knows seducing Romero is wrong but does it anyway because she wants to do it: "I don't say it's right. It is right though for me. God knows, I've never felt such a bitch" (188). Her ethics are grounded in how she exists for others, how others perceive and judge her actions after the fact.

Brett's ethics are not constituted solely by acting on compulsion, for that would not be ethics at all. Brett's ethics assume, indeed, require the judgment of others. This objectification is part of Brett's strangeness; she is a force in the novel, a spectacle of New Womanhood, dancing and drinking. As Philip McGowan argues, "Brett is a conspicuous figure throughout because her Otherness is continually brought into view by Jake's narration" (90). In the same way that Jake must always foreground Cohn's Jewishness, he (and all other male characters) must always foreground Brett's difference. Cohn watches her dance at the *bal musette* and later comes to San Sebastian where she is staying with Mike and "just *looked* at her" (*Sun* 147). The count watches her dance at Zelli's. When the group arrives in Pamplona, Brett's walking down the street is a spectacle: "The woman standing in the door of the wine-shop looked at us as we passed. She called to some one [sic] in the house and three girls came to the window and stared. They were staring at Brett" (142). During the fiesta's opening parade, "some dancers formed a circle around Brett and started to dance. ... Brett wanted to dance but they did not want her to. They wanted her as an image to dance around" (159). On the final day of the fiesta, Brett will not go into the Paseo de Sarasate because she does not want to be stared at.

Brett is always an object for others, and though McGowan argues that this objectification undermines her transgressive potential, I would argue that, while she may be objectified, she is an object that resists categorization largely because she refuses to participate in traditional genres of femininity. Brett is strange and transgressive in several ways: She drinks, a lot. She experiments with her gender by manipulating her appearance, wearing her hair short, "like a boy's," but also wearing clothes that reveal "curves like the hull of a racing yacht" (30). She is not in, nor does she seem to desire, a sexually monogamous relationship. She has interracial/ethnic sexual relationships with Cohn, Romero, and the drummer at Zelli's. She has friendships with gay men, the men at the *bal musette* and Count Mippipopolous. She has affairs with two younger men, Cohn and Romero. She is simultaneously in the process of getting divorced and engaged to be married. She is a survivor of domestic violence.

While Brett mentions many reasons for leaving Romero—he wouldn't accept her boyish hair, he wanted to marry her, she was "bad for him"—the reason that she repeats most often is that she doesn't want to be a bitch. She tells Jake, "I'm not going to be one of these bitches that ruins children. . . . I won't be one of those bitches" (246–47). Again, in her conversation Brett is compulsive: Before she and Jake leave the room at the Hotel Montana, Brett tells Jake repeatedly that she does not ever want to discuss the Romero incident again. Later, at the bar, Jake attempts to oblige her, but she keeps bringing the conversation back to Romero. She tells Jake, "You know it makes one feel rather good deciding not to be a bitch. . . . It's sort of what we have instead of God" (249).

Ethics for Brett are not ending compulsion or controlling desire or obeying God. For Brett, not being a bitch and not settling into the roles laid out for her are what guides her behavior. Ultimately, Brett's ethics are a reflection of her being-for-others (not wanting to appear to them as a bitch) but at the same time a resistance to categorization. In Jake's world, there are only bitches; there is the temptress bitch who will manipulate a man sexually or the nagging wife bitch who will simply castrate a man with masculine domesticity. By not being a bitch, Brett is transgressive in her ethics and resists easy categorization.

Modernist texts offer multiple, fragmented, and incomplete points of view, yet, in my experience, especially when reading Hemingway's deceptively clean prose, students apply realist reading strategies to modernist texts.[4] As a result, they see one character's point of view as the point of view of the author. Recently, a student asserted in a discussion board post that "Harry [of

"Snows"] is Hemingway." When students understand that one character does not serve as Hemingway's mouthpiece, students are better able to examine the complexities of how Hemingway explores gender roles, and, conversely, when they recognize that complexity, they are less apt to limit their interpretations of the works to conclusions supported by Hemingway's own biography.

When we focus on manhood as the dominant theme of texts such as *The Sun Also Rises*, students miss how male characters' reactions shape and are shaped by genres of femininity. For example, when we ask students to consider how Hemingway offers multiple points of view on the relationship between gender roles and morality, they can move beyond seeing Jake Barnes as offering Hemingway's definitive view of how to be an ethical man. With this way of reading, students are able to move beyond the limits of the Ernest Hemingway "code" hero, or at least begin thinking of Hemingway's "code" as broader than Philip Young and subsequent scholars defined it.[5] In terms of the "code hero" tradition, this may mean redefining the code to include the dynamic women characters who push the code's boundaries as they have been defined.[6] Rather than seeing female characters as part of Barnes's moral development, students who explore genres of femininity are asked to consider how Hemingway juxtaposes multiple points of view in order to ask readers to consider the limitations of Barnes's viewpoint.

In our class discussions, from the very beginning of the semester, I foreground issues of gender and how characters simultaneously conform to and resist these norms. I also contextualize these discussions with images of iconic genres of femininity, like the Gibson Girl and the flapper, so, by the time we get to Hemingway, I am able to anticipate and address some of the misconceptions that students have about his characters. This approach not only allows students to develop a more complex and sophisticated view of Hemingway's female characters but it also helps them better understand him as a modernist writer and a key figure in the American literature survey.

Notes

1. Ellen Lansky argues that, in *The Sun Also Rises*, Jake works throughout the novel to care for Brett, which involves drinking with her, protecting her from the negative effects of her drinking, and guarding her from outside influence. This, according to Lansky, gives Jake "the illusion that [he has] power and control over Brett" (208). Mark Spilka explores Hemingway's "secret and continuing dependence on women" as it puts in jeopardy his reputation for rugged masculinity, the "myth of mystical camaraderie" ("Importance" 202, 203). Thomas Strychacz argues that rather than Hemingway's representing manhood

as being something that one has or doesn't have, Hemingway represents manhood as a process, a process which he terms "manhood fashioning" (*Hemingway's Theaters*).

2. For further suggestions on pairing Hemingway with women writers, see Sara Kosiba's essay in this collection.

3. Mother's voting is representative of anxieties about women's suffrage, especially in terms of how women would vote in relation to their husbands. Suffrage opponents argued this point in two ways. Some argued that women should not get the vote because they would vote only as their husbands did, while others argued that women should not get the vote because they would vote against their husbands. Women's role in temperance reform was often linked to women's suffrage by suffrage opponents. See Nancy Burkhalter, "Women's Magazines and the Suffrage Movement: Did They Help." *Journal Of American Culture* 19.2 (1996): 13. *Academic Search Complete*.

4. Philip Weinstein argues that modernist fiction cannot be understood in realist terms (plot, linear time, coherent subjects with projects), and that we need a different model to understand it. According to Weinstein, the realist text seeks to know (and knowing is possible because the texts contain discernible plots, linear time, and so forth), while the modernist text seeks to unknow. Weinstein argues, "In realism the facts of the case emerge in time, earlier misassessments get revised, the subject's viable social orientation comes—however painfully—into focus" (187). This speaks not only to how characters and plots proceed but also to the task of readers of realist fiction. The judgment required by realist fiction requires "a fantasy of detachment, completion and innocence" (187). Modernist fiction rejects "the fatuity... of a judgment-centered stance towards its materials.... These novels refuse... to grant their protagonists the ever more accurate judgments of their world that constitute maturation" (188). See Philip Weinstein, *Unknowing: The Work of Modernist Fiction* (Ithaca, NY: Cornell UP, 2005).

5. Young's "code" hero interpretation of Hemingway dominated Hemingway criticism for years. See Philip Young, *Ernest Hemingway: A Reconsideration*. Revised Edition (University Park: Penn State UP, 1966).

6. For more on reading Hemingway's female characters as code heroes and redefining the code to include women, see Sandra Whipple Spanier, "Catherine Barkley and the Hemingway Code: Ritual and Survival," in *Modern Critical Interpretations: A Farewell to Arms*, ed. Harold Bloom (New York: Chelsea House, 1987): 131–148, and essays in Lawrence R. Broer and Gloria Holland, eds. *Hemingway and Women: Female Critics and the Female Voice* (Tuscaloosa: U of Alabama P, 2002).

Men Without Women?

Can Hemingway and Women Writers Coexist in the Classroom?

Sara Kosiba

Works by Ernest Hemingway already appear alongside those of women writers in classrooms around the country. However, these works are often used in isolated or limited ways. A Hemingway short story like "A Clean Well-Lighted Place" may be included in a basic literature anthology as an exemplar for discussing tone and style (as it is in one of my composition textbooks) alongside a story by Kate Chopin, like "The Storm," exemplifying setting (e.g., Kennedy and Gioia). Or, in surveys of the American novel or courses on literary modernism, Hemingway's story collection *In Our Time* (1925) or novels like *The Sun Also Rises* (1926) are used alongside texts by writers such as Willa Cather or Djuna Barnes. While there are advantages to examining the stylistic modes of the time period or the recurring or similar themes present in different stories, each text is often examined individually, without considering any direct engagement on the part of the authors in terms of craft, dialogue, or shared interest. Additionally, the lingering association of Hemingway as a misogynistic, hunting, fishing, overtly masculine drunkard continues to pose challenges for students when viewing the author alongside his female contemporaries. Too many individuals still associate Hemingway with these exaggerated masculine images in popular culture rather than with more accurate information, and movies like HBO's *Hemingway & Gellhorn* (2012) and Woody Allen's *Midnight in Paris* (2011) do little to dispel those images.

One way to fix these problems, both the problem of merging Hemingway's writing and career more smoothly with those of women writers and the problem of fighting the popular misconceptions, is for teachers and scholars to gain a broader awareness of Hemingway's associations with many of his female literary contemporaries. Surprisingly, there has been little scholarship in this area, although recent years have shown a rising interest in the topic. One of the most noteworthy essays contrasting Hemingway with some of his female contemporaries is Rena Sanderson's "Hemingway's Literary Sisters: The Author through the Eyes of Women Writers." Sanderson notes that Hemingway's relationship with Gertrude Stein has been rather well established, and she astutely observes that "relatively little has been said, however, about Hemingway's relationship with other women writers" (276). Her examination of the careers of Dorothy Parker, Lillian Hellman, and Martha Gellhorn (whom Hemingway married in 1940) in relation to Hemingway is insightful, but Sanderson focuses mainly on the antagonistic dynamic between the women and Hemingway. She primarily reinforces the gender binary in the relationships, concluding, "It has not been noted sufficiently, however, that Hemingway typically responded to women competitors as *women*" (292). This comment augments the prevalent concern of many scholars who tend to focus on the public antagonism between Hemingway and fellow writers, both male and female.[1] Whether critiquing his male counterparts by assessing their manhood or asserting sexual domination over female competitors, Hemingway could be antagonistic or engage in gender stereotyping with both sexes equally. Therefore, Sanderson's assessment regarding Hemingway's gendered competitive responses is not unique to women, and such an argument often limits a reader's interactions with or opinion of the text.

Rather than examining gender issues and stereotypes alone, teachers and learners should focus on a shared emphasis on quality and craft when considering Hemingway's relationships with women writers, as most of the agreements and disagreements between the writers were based on criteria associated with craftsmanship. Hemingway was an unflinching critic when he felt fellow writers were not performing at their highest potential, yet he was quick to praise when he felt the work was of high quality. Evidence shows, from letters, essays, and other sources, that the writers Hemingway knew and associated with expressed the same observations regarding his work in return. Therefore, examining Hemingway and women writers as first and foremost *writers*, and incorporating discussions of gender in a secondary fashion, allows us to see these relationships and these comments in their truest light. Gender plays a role for these writers in terms of their sense of identity and in terms of the issues they often focus on, but their dedication to craft comes first. This primary focus on writing has been noted by several of Hemingway's female contemporaries. For example, Dawn Powell, in a letter to biographer Carlos Baker regarding her memories of

Hemingway, noted, "I believe he was instrumental in Max Perkins' initial interest in my writing, tho we were both bored by book-blah-blah-blah feeling that the great thing was in *doing* it and then flying into play or nonsense, becoming another person, in fact, after the work was done" (Kosiba and Page 156).[2] By focusing on craft first, a reader observes the true substance that Hemingway and his female contemporaries were dedicated to creating in their work.

War and Literature

Interesting pairings can be made between Hemingway and women writers in courses on war writing, particularly regarding the Spanish Civil War. While Hemingway's reputation as a war reporter has been well established in the popular imagination, the war reporting of many women writers has been viewed more tangentially. Evidence of this tangential status appears even in a useful text like *Teaching Representations of the Spanish Civil War* (2007), edited by Noël Valis. While Valis's collection provides detailed summaries of the timeline of the conflict and helpful contextual essays, American women journalists only receive passing mention throughout the book.[3] Collections like this do little to illuminate that male and female correspondents often experienced the Spanish Civil War side by side. Hemingway biographer Michael Reynolds described, "Living in a city bombarded, their hotel rooms within walking distance of the front lines, these writers became an informal brotherhood for whom this war was the initiation" (*The 1930s* 264). This sentiment of a brotherhood (and sisterhood, considering the presence of many female journalists) and the significance of being an eyewitness to circumstances that would shape the world war to come appear in the writing of both men and women who reported on the conflict.

Many talented women viewed the dynamics of the Spanish Civil War firsthand as Hemingway did. Writers such as Martha Gellhorn, Lillian Hellman, Dorothy Parker, Virginia Cowles, and Josephine Herbst employed similarly creative tactics and narrative styles to report on what they saw and sought to invoke similar reactions among readers. Work by these authors creates a great opportunity for students to read about the conflict from more than one point of view, as male and female writers may focus on different aspects of the conflict. For example, Giovanna Dell'Orto notes the contrast in details between Hemingway's writing and that of Martha Gellhorn: "Gellhorn's gaze covered the little incongruities of immense suffering and reflected a sense of extreme moral urgency. Her style, modern and impressionistic like Hemingway's, is coupled with a passion for victims of war to produce an unrelenting assault on the wickedness of suffering" (306).

Finding textual examples for comparison in the classroom is a relatively easy task. Hemingway's Spanish Civil War reporting for the North American Newspaper Alliance is readily accessible in *By-Line: Ernest Hemingway* (1967), edited by William White, and the spring 1988 issue of *The Hemingway Review*, accessible via a library subscription to EBSCO online databases. Many of Gellhorn's articles can be found in the paperback collection *The Face of War*, and a few of Dorothy Parker's articles are available online or in collections such as *The Portable Dorothy Parker*.[4] Josephine Herbst's memoir, *The Starched Blue Sky of Spain*, is currently out of print, but the collection is still widely available through used book retailers.[5] In all of these cases, if students were not able to purchase the collections in their entirety, it would be easy for an instructor to scan the material and make it available within the bounds of fair use via a handout or PDF file.

One simple activity would be for an instructor to assign a Spanish Civil War article by Hemingway alongside one by a writer such as Gellhorn, Parker, or Herbst and ask students to note the similarities or differences. For example, Hemingway describes the countryside as he chronicles his arrival in Spain in "The First Glimpses of War" (reprinted in *By-Line Ernest Hemingway*):

> Flying low down the coast toward Alicante, along white beaches, past gray-castled towns or with the sea curling against rocky headlands, there was no sign of war. Trains were moving, cattle were plowing the fields, fishing boats were setting out and factory chimneys were belching smoke.
>
> Then, above Tarragona, all the passengers were crowded over on the landside of the ship, watching through the narrow windows the careened hulk of a freighter, visibly damaged by shellfire, which had driven ashore to beach her cargo. (257)

Herbst spends most of her essay "The Starched Blue Sky of Spain" talking about the people in Spain and describing the countryside as well. In one of her first ventures near the front, Herbst describes:

> Looked at from the top, the view was beautiful. You could see the town hall and the church of Murata, and you could see olive orchards and vineyards spreading softly along the hills toward the valley. The ground where there were no trees was harsh and brutally rocky. A man plowing in the distance was steering his

plow as if it were a boat avoiding obstacles at bay. The view in the other direction toward the front lines was wavery ground; many of the olive trees looked as if they had been split open with an ax. The inside pulp was pinkish and blue, with the look of quivering flesh. Blackened twigs lay scattered around the trunks. The ground itself had little plowed up runnels that burst now and then into star-shaped pockets. (142–43)

Both authors highlight the seeming normality in contrast to the scars and signs of war. Similarities like these speak to a shared experience and observation that transcend gender differences. These war correspondents are equally impacted by the incongruities within the countryside and the stark lines between beauty and brutality. These writers also make a shared effort to put the reader into the experience through their narrative strategies. Their efforts are consistent with the primary focus in war writing: "to achieve believability through an *ethos* (the Aristotelian term for persuasive appeal located in character) based on *autopsy* or firsthand experience" (McLoughlin 48).

Another useful activity would be to have students contrast how the different points of view represented in the articles potentially impact a reader. In many of his articles about the war, Hemingway brings first-person narration to the experience, providing readers with an eyewitness account: "Yesterday I watched an attack against these positions where government tanks, working like deadly, intelligent beetles, destroyed machine gun posts in the thick underbrush while government artillery shelled the buildings and Insurgent trenches" (*By-Line* 260). What Hemingway does just as effectively at times, in order to bring readers into the experience, is employ the rarer second-person narration, as he does in the dispatch "A New Kind of War." Hemingway writes:

> In the morning, before your call comes from the desk, the roaring burst of a high explosive shell wakes you and you go to the window and look out to see a man, his head down, his coat collar up, sprinting desperately across the paved square. There is the acrid smell of high explosive you hoped you'd never smell again, and, in a bathrobe and bedroom slippers, you hurry down the marble stairs and almost into a middle-aged woman, wounded in the abdomen, who is being helped into the hotel entrance by two men in blue workmen's smocks. (*By-Line* 262)

For students who have never entered a theater of war, this is an effective way to present the real effects and human costs of military conflict, particularly among noncombatants; for students who are veterans recently returned from

Iraq or Afghanistan, the pieces can provide them with a way to verbalize or contextualize the abstraction of their own experience.

Known for her wit, Parker deviates from her traditional humor in her coverage of the Spanish Civil War and also employs some interesting rhetorical points of view. In "Soldiers of the Republic," available through the online archives of *The New Yorker*, a reader can feel the impact that meeting six soldiers in a random café in Valencia had on Parker:

> They told about how they had not heard from their families for more than a year. They did not tell it gallantly or whimsically or stoically. They told it as if— Well, look. You have been in the trenches, fighting, for a year. You have heard nothing of your wife and your children. They do not know if you are dead or alive or blinded. You do not know where they are, or if they are. You must talk to somebody. That is the way they told about it. (106)

Through Parker's words, a reader feels as though he or she is sitting at the table with Parker in the café listening to the stories firsthand. For students, this point of view becomes a way to empathize or understand a conflict that happened decades ago. Hemingway showed respect for this essay as this piece by Parker was one of only two pieces by women he selected for *Men at War: The Best War Stories of All Time* (1942).

Modern American Writers

While it is entirely common for male and female writers to appear alongside each other in a modern American writers course today, there are still times when authors appear on syllabi because instructors feel the responsibility to be suitably representative and diverse in their selections. In creating a syllabus, instructors could elicit new insights and contrasts by encouraging deeper consideration of the interaction between the authors themselves and not just their gendered contributions to the time period in question. Sandra M. Gilbert notes that many contemporary feminist critics are engaged in an "excavation and reevaluation of not just of individual women writers, not just of a female tradition, but of an intricate female and male history reimagined to factor in an overlooked but powerfully influential female-male dialectic. In such revisionary historicizing, the 'mainstream'/male stream canon appears as new and different as the formerly subaqueous female canon does" ("Finding Atlantis" 42). In essence, through careful syllabus choices, the dialectic (and actual dialogue between writers) can not only recover forgotten or underappreciated women writers but also provide new insights into the work of critically established writers like Hemingway.

One writer whom Hemingway expressed a great deal of respect for but who has been rather ignored by students and scholars is Dawn Powell. Powell's satirical writing style, particularly in her later novels, differs from Hemingway's realism, but the two writers, both Midwesterners who left that past behind to experience bigger places, admired each other's work, particularly when each felt his or her friend was writing well. The two writers form an interesting contrast in that they met only a few times in person but corresponded for many years and maintained a familiarity with the other writer's career. In an 8 October 1942 letter from Hemingway to Maxwell Perkins (Hemingway and Powell's mutual editor at Scribner's), the author compliments Powell's latest book, *A Time to Be Born,* and comments, despite noting some inconsistency in her work, that "she is certainly the best woman writing and truly one of the best people writing."[6]

In a course on modern American literature, instructors could pair a novel such as Hemingway's *The Sun Also Rises* (1926) alongside Powell's *Turn, Magic Wheel* (1936) and have students, either in discussion or through written assignments, contrast the way the two authors approach characterization. Characters in both novels experience a similar sense of disillusionment or lack of focus. While Hemingway's novel captures the ennui of the "lost generation" of the 1920s, Powell's novel explores the lingering displacement of urbanites a decade later. The characters from the two novels are divided by an ocean and face different circumstances, but many of them are caught up in the same perpetual human search for meaning and understanding in life. For example, characters in both novels address the struggles of love. In Hemingway's novel, Brett Ashley describes her struggles with finding happiness by stating that love is "hell on earth" (35). In Powell's novel, Effie and Marian Callingham, first and second wife, respectively, of character Andrew Callingham, mourn the loss of his love to yet another woman: "the two of them helping each other to stand before the storm, the hurricane, that was Andy's love and Andy's love withdrawn" (487). While Hemingway's Jake Barnes and Powell's Dennis Orphen are decidedly different characters, the friends and festivities they surround themselves with and the observations of surrealism they make are comparable and speak to a common sense of displacement in the world.[7] For students, the value would lie in realizing that two authors, regardless of gendered differences, were both focused on a shared worldview. Both books speak to the desires of human beings and the various obstacles, both those self-fabricated and those of fate, that intervene and shape human lives.

The American Short Story

Examples from the short fiction of Ernest Hemingway are often standard in any discussion of the American short story, and this ubiquity can provide an easy opportunity to contrast the stylistic and thematic concerns between his work and that of female writers. One potential comparison is to have students examine a short story by Eudora Welty alongside one by Hemingway. Their work is not often placed side by side in the classroom, despite the fact that both authors were contemporaries, are often anthologized, and collections of their short fiction are widely available.

One of the easiest forms of contrast between the two writers is found in their sense of place. Welty is almost always classified as a regional writer, while Hemingway's work is often viewed more broadly. Those distinctions, however, are imposed by teachers and critics and not by the writers themselves. An interesting starting point for a class discussion of Welty and Hemingway would be to have students create their own definition of the importance of place in American literature and then compare those comments to Welty's widely reprinted essay "Place in Fiction" to see where they may agree or disagree with her philosophy. She even addresses a Hemingway story in her discussion:

> The response to place has the added intensity that comes with the place's not being native or taken for granted but found, chosen; thereby is the rest more heavily repudiated. It is the response of the aficionado; the response, too, is adopted. The title "A Clean Well Lighted Place" is just what the human being is not, for Hemingway, and perhaps it is the epitome of what man would like to find in his fellow man but never has yet, says the author, and never is going to. (131–32)

This discussion would open the door for students to better examine what *place* means, as both Hemingway and Welty often describe very particular locales in their work, and to discuss how the two writers may be invoking the concept in similar or different ways.

While setting and location are significant in analyzing stories, what students are often far less observant of is a writer's craft, particularly the depiction of characters. Both Welty and Hemingway are adept at incorporating elements of the grotesque into their characters. To use this as a focus of classroom discussion, instructors might have students read the introductory chapter of "The Book of the Grotesque" from Sherwood Anderson's *Winesburg, Ohio* (1919) or a definition of the grotesque from a reference text such as *The Bedford Glossary of Critical and Literary Terms*, (3rd edition 2008) edited by Ross Murfin and Supryia M. Ray. After a discussion of how the term is defined, students could then apply their understanding to a discussion of stories such as Welty's widely anthologized piece, "Petrified Man," first published in *A Curtain of Green* (1941), and Hemingway's "The Light of the World," first published in his collection *Winner Take Nothing* (1933).

Welty's "Petrified Man" contains several characters who are exaggerated and extreme in their behavior. Leota, with her gossipy nature, dyed hair, bright red fingernails, and cigarette, and working in the entirely lavender salon, is the epitome of hairdresser stereotypes. The story's irony—that Leota fails to see her own extremes but is shocked and amazed by the petrified man at the freak show who "*looks* just *terrible*" (22)—establishes a strange yet revealing juxtaposition where, as Sarah Gleeson-White notes, "violence and beauty are intriguingly entangled" (50). As Émilie Walezak observes about the cast of characters at the train station in Hemingway's "The Light of the World":

> The cook's characteristic feature is his clean white hands. Peroxide comes to be named after the color of her hair. Alice is in turn an amount of flesh, a face, and a voice. Such focus on particular body parts that the text, as in a close-up, seems to enlarge so much that the cook becomes a pair of hands and Peroxide a hair color, makes the characters into grotesque figures, again undermining the so-called realism of Hemingway's text. (par. 20)

Each of these characters becomes an exaggerated representation of a larger "truth" or idea that they claim to embody.

The irony in both of these stories forces readers to question how we may characterize ourselves and how we may appear to others. For students, this is an observation that can be particularly tailored to the world around them by extending the discussion to portrayals of beauty in advertising or the double standards often apparent in politics and media.

While Hemingway's behavior toward some of his female contemporaries makes the "misogynist" labels understandable, broader reassessment of the relationships allows for more options in representing both genders in literature syllabi. Karen Kilcup, a noted editor of an anthology of women writers, reflected regarding the use of anthologies to teach or introduce writers that "academics *and* 'general readers'—still need particularist connections, with ample apparatuses and critical work to frame those collections; at the same time, we need comprehensive accounts of how particularist traditions mesh (or conflict) with one another"(319). Therefore, gender distinctions can be important in helping us better understand what motivates or characterizes aspects of a writer's identity and craft, but to make that the sole consideration or to place that classification above the idea of craft itself fails to capture the attitudes of the writers—that they were colleagues.

Yes, Hemingway and women writers can coexist in the classroom, and they should coexist in the same way they did as they were writing: as individuals dedicated to the creation of significant prose and to capturing the social, cultural, and historical elements of their time.

Notes

1. Hemingway's legendary male writer rivals have included F. Scott Fitzgerald, John Dos Passos, and many others. In one infamous example, Hemingway took umbrage at a comment by fellow writer Max Eastman, which he felt questioned his masculinity and, as the *New York Times* reported, "he bared his chest to Mr. Eastman and asked him to look at the hair and say whether it was false. He persuaded Mr. Eastman to bare his chest and commented on its comparatively hairless condition." ("Hemingway Slaps Eastman in the Face," *New York Times*, 14 August 1937.)

2. See also Sara Kosiba, "Dawn Powell: Hemingway's 'Favorite Living Writer,'" *The Hemingway Review* 29.2 (2010): 46–60.

3. As an example of the diminished status of female American journalists in Valis's collection, just among those mentioned in this essay, Martha Gellhorn is only mentioned in the Resources section under "Biography, Memoirs, and Testimonies" for her collection *The Face of War* and in the Works Cited; Dorothy Parker merits only two brief mentions in the chapter dedicated to teaching the film *The Spanish Earth*; and Josephine Herbst receives only one passing mention as her name is included in a group of "notable personalities" (148). No work by any of these women appears in any of the sample syllabi included in the volume, despite their eyewitness accounts.

4. Paperback reprints of Gellhorn's *The Face of War* (New York: Atlantic Monthly, 1994) and *The Portable Dorothy Parker* (New York: Penguin, 2006) are available from a number of mainstream book retailers.

5. Josephine Herbst, *The Starched Blue Sky of Spain and Other Memoirs* (New York: HarperCollins, 1992). The title essay is the primary Spanish Civil War narrative in this collection.

6. Ernest Hemingway to Maxwell Perkins, 8 October 1942, Charles Scribner's Sons Archive, Princeton University Library, Princeton, NJ.

7. For example, some of the Pamplona party scenes Jake experiences in *The Sun Also Rises* are comparable to the bar crawl Dennis goes through on pages 500–18 in *Turn, Magic Wheel*. In addition, there is a shared sense of surrealism, as evidenced by Jake's comment about everything appearing "new and changed" (196) and Dennis's comment that "the whole thing was a dream" (421).

Katie and the Pink Highlighter

Teaching Post-"Hemingway" Hemingway

Hilary Kovar Justice

Prologue

It is a truth universally acknowledged that the author is dead, but rumors of the author's death are never more exaggerated than in Ernest Hemingway's case. In Hemingway's own theoretically prescient analysis of the author question in *Death in the Afternoon* (1932), the author is but an apostrophic grotesque with which an inept audience ("Old Lady") so encumbers a text that she can't see the words for the author's name. Eighty years after *Death in the Afternoon*, fifty after Roland Barthes's "The Death of the Author," a still- and yet-vocal faction of academics—those most deeply invested in burying Hemingway—remains paradoxically and equally invested in refusing to let "Hemingway" die. Not Hemingway-the-person nor Hemingway-the-writer; the effigy they resurrect to re-ignite is scare-quotes "Hemingway," a socially-constructed symbolic embodiment of mid-twentieth-century American misogynistic, homophobic masculinity.[1]

Well, scapegoats serve a function.

I come to bury "Hemingway," not to praise him.

Act I: The Question

There is a question asked of female Hemingway scholars in nearly every professional Q & A:

> "How do you, as a woman, justify working on Hemingway?"

This question is emphatically not the one Jim Hinkle asked Linda Patterson Miller in 1986: "So, what is it you do when you, as a woman, 'read' Hemingway?" (Miller 7). Hinkle's question concerned reading *practice;* the Question in its current form asks nothing so professional, subtle, or at all, really. Whatever it appears to be asking, at its core it's a thinly veiled rhetorical dismissal of one's choice of reading *material.*

In October, 2011, a few minutes before we were due on stage for a Q & A as part of the University of Idaho's Hemingway Festival, Susan Beegel, then editor of *The Hemingway Review,* turned to me and said, "You know we're going to get the Question."

I didn't have to ask which one. "You're *kidding.* Still?"

"Still." She paused. "And you know, Hil, after all this time, I still don't have a good answer."

No more should she. No more should anyone; it's a ridiculous question. The problems with "as a woman" and "justify" are obvious; they reek of Johnson's dog and Kafka's trial.[2] Even so, someone will ask, half the room will nod, and attempts at polite deflection only result in the Question repeating with McCarthy-esque monotony.

There is something about "Hemingway" that demands the Question, some melancholy burden that women unwittingly assume when they have the audacity to open *A Farewell to Arms* (1929).

What a successful mess the mid-twentieth-century media machine made of the construction of a symbol of masculinity that, like all symbols, eventually carries more popular truth than whatever made it interesting to begin with. As a journalist, Hemingway was without question complicit in the construction of his hyper-masculine image. But as with all complicity, there was something he needed from it—celebrity was integral to his livelihood (and an expensive livelihood it was)—and something he despised about it (and sometimes his hostility was overt, his irony too subtle). He doubtless hoped that his writing might overcome the ephemeral quality of popular media if only by outlasting it; in his Nobel Prize acceptance speech, he mentions facing "eternity, or the lack of it, each day" ("Nobel Prize" 196).

What has the Question to do with teaching Hemingway? One word: "justify." As recently as the mid-1980s, the canon wars prohibited female scholars from teaching Hemingway at all (Miller 7).

Surely those days are over. Surely.

Yet within the last year, I've been informed, "Hemingway isn't an appropriate topic for graduate study."

I cannot lift a single, sardonic eyebrow. I look completely comical when I try.

The Question is but one variation of an attack that has no identity, no particulars—only teeth. And it's strange. A gender studies colleague tells me she gets less flak for teaching Stephanie Meyer's popular teenage-vampire series *Twilight* than I do for teaching Hemingway, and wonders why, in a post-Theory world, the Question even exists.

Why, indeed.

The problem, of course, is "Hemingway."

But what does "Hemingway" mean, exactly?

The English language has some peculiar idiosyncrasies when it comes to conflating author and work. The collective noun for an author's works is often the author's name. "I study Shakespeare." "I study Austen." "I study Morrison." To study "Author-name" is not (necessarily) to study the person; the works are a given. So when I, as an academic, say, "I study Hemingway," I don't mean the man/myth; in Hemingway studies I might say, "the Text," after Nancy Comley and Robert Scholes—the cultural matrix of which Hemingway is the center (x).

But Hemingway scholars don't enjoy the presumption of critical integrity; the Question labels one the academic equivalent of the tabloid paparazzi. The Inquisitor deploys selective amnesia regarding Barthes; the Question-as-utterance implies *a priori* that Hemingway scholars require re-education. Clearly, their choice of topic is the only thing noteworthy in their scholarship.

Fascistic questions are flagrantly unprofessional, but armed rebellion isn't good manners either, so as Susan and I stood on the sidewalk in Idaho, groping for good answers to a bad question, I wondered what I could possibly say that an entire generation of scholars hadn't already said—and why the Question persisted.

Interlude: The Accidental Hemingway Scholar

Unlike Linda Patterson Miller, whose essay "In Love With Papa" answered the Question eloquently in 1999 (and it should have ended there), I began my study of Hemingway not out of love but prosaically: I switched disciplines mid-education. As an early 1980s music major, I'd missed the canon wars. Musicologists didn't have to "justify" studying Bach; playing Beethoven "as a woman" held only physical meaning: the later piano sonatas require overt upper-body strength. And the pertinence of gender to critical work in the humanities was a total mystery to me.

With utter ignorance regarding the canon wars and the difference between gender and sex, I began my English master's program assuming I should choose courses with authors' names in the title, one of which was "Hemingway's Short Fiction through the Manuscripts."

This choice shanghaied my life.

I had no preconceptions of Hemingway other than that he'd had a beard. My response to seeing my first photocopied Hemingway manuscript was neither goosebumps nor revulsion, just "He writes like a girl." I've since heard "writes like a girl" echoed by high school sophomores and college seniors. His handwriting is open, loopy, and easy to read once your eyes adjust to the fact that Xs are periods, Os and As often indistinguishable, and when the writing was flowing a T might be crossed a half a word late.

Visual impressions aside, two things matter here. One is that I had no more investment in the concept of "Hemingway"—the man, the myth, the scapegoat—than I did in the number of Bach's children (twenty) or in the fact that Schubert died of syphilis. That man or myth could be relevant to art never crossed my mind. The other is that the professor was Paul Smith, of whose acclaimed status in Hemingway studies I was equally, blessedly ignorant. Had I known he was considered by many to be the world expert on Hemingway's short fiction, I might not have been as fast on the draw, not quite as cheeky, and our "discussions" might not have devolved into fierce, cheerful shouting matches.

"You're wrong! You're wrong! You're wrong!" he shouted after my presentation on "Hills Like White Elephants," pounding the table to punctuate each "wrong!"

"Prove it!" I shot back.

"*I CAN'T!*" he yelled, his arms flung open.

We both burst out laughing, and a career was born.

My pedagogical style is the opposite of his—probably for the best, these days—but my Hemingway class exists because of him. (I inherited his course materials, a box left in a closet at Trinity College. The department chair phoned, asking, "Looks like stuff from the Hemingway course. Want it?" Yes, please.)

After a master's in Hemingway Illyria, though, the first tendrils of the Question—the would-be elegy by which my work and Hemingway's are both made smaller—slithered into my world, but my image of Hemingway studies will always be Paul Smith with his arms flung open, tossing the syllabus and dedicating the next class meeting to proving my reading wrong.

When he couldn't, he said, "Go to the Kennedy and look at the originals. You can't base an argument on a photocopy. If it's still worth anything, publish it."

So when I heard, "Studying Hemingway is professional suicide" (Distinguished Professor, 1999), I didn't listen.

"Hemingway? I thought we killed him already" (Famous Gender Studies Scholar, same year).
"Prove it," I muttered.

Act II: Katie and the Pink Highlighter

My teaching copy of *The Sun Also Rises* has no cover. I ripped it off in the first graduate class I ever taught when confronted with the student version of the Question: "I hate Hemingway."
"He hates women." A female graduate student.
"Your evidence?"
"He describes her as a boy."
"And that indicates hatred?"
"Yes."
"How?"
Silence.
"Well, if so, how do you account for the fact that she has curves two sentences later?"
She glared at the page, saying nothing.
"'Her hair was brushed back like a boy's. She started all that. She was built with curves like the hull of a racing yacht' [30]. Yachts connote money, leisure, and power. She's a trendsetter. She has tremendous power. Where in there do you locate misogyny?"
Silence.
"Read the full passage."
"No."
I responded by ripping the cover off and instructing students to do the same. Some complied; many were horrified.
"If you can't read past the single word 'Hemingway' on the cover, rip it off; get past it; pretend Louise Erdrich wrote it—do whatever you have to, but read *every* word. Not just the ones that reify received prejudices."
I don't know if I'd play that moment the same way now; I may never get the chance. After all, "Hemingway isn't an appropriate topic for graduate study."
And Brutus is an honorable man.
Sometimes "I hate Hemingway" plays out differently. Sometimes it's innocent of the self-conscious performativity that often underlies the Question (or at least some of the nodding) on the more even playing field of academic Q & As or even a graduate seminar. "I hate Hemingway" is admirably Hemingway-esque

in its brevity; it's a stance I've since found I can work with, for therein lies not only the problem with the Question but also the best answer I've come up with so far.

I hastily sketched that answer for Susan that evening in Idaho and shared it in full later, when—alas, poor Yorick—we got the Question that, like the author it scapegoats, refuses to die. My answer is the story of Katie and the Pink Highlighter, which likewise hinges on that problematic word, "Hemingway."

At the end of our English studies major at Illinois State University, undergraduates take any one of a number of capstone senior seminar courses the topic of which is at the discretion of the professor. In an ideal world, students would select a section according to their interests, and some manage to, but other curricular requirements often make for schedule constraints, and sometimes these constraints chafe.

Which is what happened to Katie, which is not her real name, about two years after I ripped the cover off *The Sun Also Rises*.

On the first day of class, Katie was in no mood to ask the Question. She entered the classroom in as high a dudgeon and in as foul a mood as I have ever seen a student, thumping her bag on the desk, slouching in her chair, crossing her arms, her posture shouting, "The universe hates me, and boy howdy, it's mutual."

I begin every class meeting by taking attendance, asking each student how he or she is doing, but in Katie's case, that much was self-evident. Instead, I just said, "Dare I ask?"

"I. HATE. HEMINGWAY."

Well, okay, then. "Can I ask why?"

"He hated women."

"That could be an excellent reason to hate someone. . . ."

"And he was drunk all the time."

"Hmmm. Perhaps more pitiable than loathsome, but I take your point."

"And I don't want to take this section for my senior experience but I *have to* because of the *stupid English Ed requirements and I don't have a choice.*"

"I hate when that happens. I ended up in the scariest class I ever took because I needed a course that began with a certain number, and it was the only one that fit."

She glared at me through her hair. "And?"

"Uh . . . I passed."

"I want to do more than pass; I want to *learn*. And this class is going to *fuck* my GPA."

"Are you planning to blow it off?"

"I *told* you. I hate Hemingway."

"Because he was a drunken misogynistic bastard, and probably a homophobic racist, to boot."

"*Yes.*"

"Katie, there is absolutely no reason why you can't earn an A in this class."

"But . . . but I hate Hemingway."

"And?"

She paused, then ventured, "You know, you're not supposed to be cool right now. You're supposed to be pissed off."

I shrugged. "I've heard worse."

Another glance through her hair. "From a student?"

"From a distinguished professor in my grad department: 'To study Hemingway is to commit professional suicide.'"

She waited.

"From the trendiest, scariest, possibly smartest person in that department—who, incidentally, was a feminist scholar: 'I thought we killed him already.'"

"*I'm* a feminist."

"So am I."

Silence. "Then how—" Having recovered her manners, she couldn't finish.

"How can I, as a feminist, justify studying Hemingway?"

"I guess, yeah."

"I've never found a single thing in any of his works that proves he hated women."

"He kills them all."

"One or two. *Islands in the Stream;* Catherine in *A Farewell to Arms.*"

"Yes, but he kills *her* in *childbirth.*"

"That happened pretty frequently back then."

"Well, he treats them badly."

"His female characters?"

"Yes." (She didn't say "duh," but you could hear it.)

"How boring would a story be if nothing bad ever happened?"

She said nothing.

"He didn't go easy on his male characters either. And he did win a Nobel Prize for literature. And although, no, he wasn't the world's greatest husband, I think—no, I *know* he's a really good writer. And there *is* a difference."

Her look accused me of betraying the Sisterhood. "Good because of a Nobel Prize?"

"Good because I've been studying his works for about ten years, I have really high standards, and I'm not bored yet."

Nothing.

"Tell you what. Buy a highlighter and save it for one specific purpose: to highlight every single instance of Hemingway's misogyny—not his characters'; his—and we'll talk about it in class. Okay?"

"His."

"Right."

"So it's like, when a Faulkner character uses the N-word, it doesn't mean Faulkner thought that word was a good thing. It means the character's an asshole."

"Exactly like."

She considered this. "What do I do when I find it?"

(An echo from 1994: *You're wrong! You're wrong! You're wrong!*)

"You find it, we stop everything until we hash it out to your satisfaction. I can't change the syllabus now, and I don't want to. But you can bring the whole class to a screeching halt, and if I'm wrong, I'll admit it"—(*I CAN'T!*)—"and I'll help you shout it to the heavens." (*Publish it.*)

"Deal."

Next class:

"Katie?"

"Here." She waved the highlighter. It was pink. "I'm *empowered*."

I laughed; I couldn't help it. "Pink?! What kind of color is *pink* for a feminist?"

She grinned. "Reclamation. Or irony. Your choice."

For sixteen weeks, she was as cheerfully ruthless as Paul Smith had been. We began each day with the Pink Report:

"Katie? Any pink?"

"Not yet." Fierce smile. "Still looking, though."

Finally, the last class of the semester came.

"Katie?"

"Hey."

"How are you today?"

"Fine." A cheeky smile. (After reading "Hills Like White Elephants," the class had outlawed the word "fine.")

"Brat. Do you mean fine in the Hemingway sense, or fine-good?"

"Fine-good, except . . ." She looked around the room. "For sale: pink highlighter. Never used."

Act III: Teaching Post-"Hemingway" Hemingway

That was seven years ago (2006); in the last year or so, I've begun to hear rumors of the death of the Question.

In the fall of 2011, during the first day's discussion of "Out of Season," the conversation (in which all names are changed) ended like this:

Brian: I am so missing something here.

Amy: [*nodding emphatically*]

Someone else: Duh; it's Hemingway. Of course we are.

When I walked in for the second day's discussion of the story, I found Amy at the board writing a very long list; Brian waved me to a student chair. "We got this, Dr. J."

They outlined a reading of "Out of Season" that began with Brian's theory that what they'd been missing was Peduzzi's sexuality: "The young gentleman's jumpiness—the whole end of the story—makes total sense if Peduzzi's gay."

Amy, whose talent for detailed research rivals that of any student I've ever taught, had combed the story for evidence, starting with the meaning of Peduzzi's name ("It's a diminutive of 'foot'"), moving to 1920s slang for homosexuality and images of Max Beerbohm's cartoons ("They all have tiny feet; Beerbohm, who's mentioned randomly in the story, was homosexual; why include that reference at all?"), and ending deftly with a now-archaic ballroom dance instruction role in which older, more experienced men taught younger ones how to lead. Then Brian, using Amy's evidence and the lens of sexuality, took us through the story from beginning to end, concluding with "And the young gentleman is ambivalent—see, here he says, 'I may not be going. Very probably not.'—and although Hemingway's always *ambiguous*, he's *never* ambivalent. So maybe it's a moral judgment when a character is. Hemingway respects the wife; her moral stance is clear; he doesn't seem to respect the young gentleman at all."

I raised my hand. Everyone laughed.

Brian: Yes, Dr. J.?

Me: Is it necessary that Peduzzi actually be homosexual, or does your reading work if the young gentleman merely thinks Peduzzi is?

Brian: Because of all the issues with mistranslation, you mean? Like "Tochter" and "Geld"?

Amy: And we all know what "geld" means in English.

I nodded. "Maybe the social cues aren't translating either."

Another student added, "Like Stefan and Fabio on [the reality TV show]

Top Chef. Americans thought they were gay, but they just laughed: 'No; we're European.'"

"So," I offered, "perhaps the young gentleman misreads culturally specific expressions of homo-sociality for homosexuality. 'Caro' doesn't translate neatly; literally it means 'Dear,' which in English means both 'expensive' and 'Hey, baby,' but in Italian it's ... hm ... more like 'Buddy.' There's value in friendship, and nouns have gendered endings in Italian."

Brian and Amy allowed that this variant reading was possible and the linguistic evidence pretty good, but, finally, they preferred their reading of actuality over cultural mistranslation.

Me: Because it offers certainty in the face of ambiguity?

"Well ..." Brian glanced at Amy, and she shrugged, so he continued. "Doesn't all Hemingway make us want that?" He thought for a moment. "Either way, the young gentleman fails. Peduzzi may smell like manure on the outside, but the young gentleman reeks on the inside, where it counts."

Granted, being told "We got this, Dr. J." is exceptional. But the next semester, walking into a different class to begin the discussion of "Ten Indians," amid the pre-attendance chatter I heard a student tell another, "I can't not read this as a postcolonial story."

"I know, right?" she replied. "And Prudence Mitchell—feminist hero!"

Me: Feminist hero?

Student: Yeah, it's awesome—she has sex with whomever she wants to just because she wants to. I mean, if that had been rape, Dr. Adams would've known and done something, right? Because in "Indian Camp" he used "lady" where Uncle George used "Damn squaw bitch"? (68).

Me: Go on.

Student: And it's July Fourth—Independence Day—and she's definitely enacting her independence, sort of in a literal "screw the white man" way! And you've told us if we find a dirty pun in the deep structure of a Hemingway story, we're onto something.

This was not the first time I'd heard, "Prudence Mitchell, feminist hero" from my students. The story's celebration of her agency is indeed a plausible reading; Hemingway's sympathies in the short fiction almost always lie with the female characters.

When I teach back-to-back sections of this class, the sections nearly always disagree, arguing with equal conviction that Uncle George of "Indian Camp" *must* and *can't* be the father of the baby. So when a student in the other section (code name: Jenny) said, "I have a reading of the Native American female characters in 'Indian Camp' and 'Ten Indians,'" I wasn't expecting this:

> Jenny: They're the only characters who are allowed to express their feelings—the mother bites Uncle George (who totally deserves it); Prudence chooses a sexual partner; the white males can't express emotions—they get tangled in and silenced by social codes; these women can and do, with their voice or body. They're *held* down, both of them, literally "beneath" the white man's cultural oppression, yet they have rage, pain, desire, and they express it. Despite oppression, they have expression—a freedom the white men don't have. Isn't that *cool?*

The Question simply doesn't occur to these undergraduates, and I wonder if the stranglehold of scare quotes "Hemingway" (a mid-twentieth-century relic) is finally losing its grip on the text. Whatever my current students bring to the text, it's not that dusty souvenir.

Epilogue: The Death of the Author Question

In 2006, a reporter from *The Chronicle of Higher Education* asked me the Question by any other name: why I thought so many newer voices in Hemingway Studies, including my own, were female. I countered by naming several established female scholars, but, pressed, proffered that things were perhaps getting easier.
"How?"
"Perhaps it's easier to forgive a grandparent than a parent."
In the seven years since Katie, there's been at least the beginning of a generational shift. To my current undergraduates, the word "Hemingway" holds no more authority over their reading than their great-grandparents hold over their fashion choices. Hemingway is one among many dead white male writers whose works are nonetheless worth reading; to argue that "he" should not be read because he is eternally a relic of his culture and time seems nonsensical to them. In their perception, he is a closer contemporary to Edgar Allan Poe and Harriet Beecher Stowe than to themselves. Not blinded by the "Hemingway" on the book cover, students note instead how very subtly he navigated issues of gender, sexuality, and race in ways they read as transgressive, progressive, and—their highest compliment—"relatable." As problematic as that word sounds to my ears, if students are rejecting generational authority, the generation they're rejecting isn't Hemingway's, but ours.

They can see that the Question finally isn't a question at all; it's a performative statement: "You shouldn't like Hemingway."

Predictably, they rebel.

The challenge to me in my current (and I hope everyone's future) classroom isn't to convince a group of protesting students to read Hemingway "for" issues of gender and sexuality; thanks to shifting hegemonic terrain on questions of equality and justice, my students are already there. Each generation will meet the writing on its own terms; perhaps the academy will eventually release the word "Hemingway" from its reductive scare quotes and celebrate the subtlety of the writer's craft on questions of gender, sexuality, and everything. Time may yet effect the death of the scapegoat lurking behind "How do you, as a woman, justify...?"; it's the writing that ultimately courts eternity. However "betrayed" readers may feel by the man (Miller 4), as long as they wonder, "How does Hemingway get words to do that?" we can feel quite sure that he will never die.

Notes

1. Michael Pollan provides an excellent example of scare-quotes "Hemingway" in *The Omnivore's Delimma: A Natural History of Four Meals* (New York: Penguin, 2006), uncritically invoking Hemingway as one of "those hard-bitten, big-bearded American wilderness writers who still pine for the Pleistocene" (336).

2. Samuel Johnson famously compared women preachers to dogs walking on their hind legs, concluding, "It is not done well; but you are surprised to find it done at all." Quoted in James Boswell, *Life of Samuel Johnson,* LLD. Vol. I (Chicago: Brittanica, 1954), 132. Franz Kafka's novella, *Der Prozess* (engl. *The Trial;* Berlin: Verlag die Schmiede, 1925), tells the story of a man who suddenly finds himself being tried by unnamed prosecutors for an unstated crime.

Appendixes

Teaching Materials

Drawing from a wide range of experiences, the contributors to this volume have shared below a selection of teaching materials that demonstrate how instructors might approach teaching Hemingway and gender. The in-class activities, essay prompts, and syllabi are representative of the approaches described in the preceding essays, and they are adaptable enough to work for students from high school through graduate school and in literature, gender studies, and general education courses.

Appendix A

Discussion Questions and In-Class Activities

Adapted from Crystal Gorham Doss

Doss uses these questions to generate class discussion about "The Snows of Kilimanjaro," but they can serve as in-class writing prompts as well. They can also be reworked to generate discussion of characters in other Hemingway works, such as "The Three Day Blow," "Hills Like White Elephants," and *The Garden of Eden*, to name just a few.

1. How do social class and gender roles intersect in "The Snows of Kilimanjaro"?
2. What are the complications of Harry's being a "kept man"? How does Helen's wealth affect her relationship with Harry?
3. In what ways is Harry sentimental? How does he reject sentimentality? How do you explain this conflict?
4. Is Helen objectified? If so, by whom: Harry or Hemingway? How so?
5. Do you consider Helen a round character? A strong woman? Why does she tolerate Harry's verbal abuse?

Adapted from Joseph Fruscione

The writing prompts, prewriting exercises, and reflection prompt below illustrate a process approach to writing about gender in "Cat in the Rain." Across several class meetings, Fruscione allows students to develop their thesis statements in response to questions they generate themselves while receiving feedback from the professor at each stage in the process.

Purpose:
1. To understand the story's subtle and complex portrayals of gender roles by performing the characters' interaction out loud
2. To understand how this story's portrayals of masculinity and femininity function in the larger work, *In Our Time*
3. To relate the construction of gender in *In Our Time* to that in our other course readings (e.g., *Cane* and *The Awakening*)
4. To establish an original interpretation that you expand upon and research in your writing

Practice:
Read the story aloud in threes (man, woman, narrator/Italians) and emphasize or "perform" the characters' tones and ways of speaking to make a case for one interpretation as most sympathetic. Consider also what might not be on the page but is still "there" in the conversation—such as a pause, sigh, *sotto* line, dismissive eye roll, and the like. For instance, if the woman is unsympathetic to you, try to give her words a self-pitying and/or shallow intonation. If you see the husband as cold and selfish, try to speak his dialogue accordingly. If you feel Hemingway is trying to sway interpretation through his narrator, make his words reflect this bias.

Discussion Questions:
1. How (and why) does Hemingway portray their marital . . . Happiness? Ennui? Tension? Disconnect?
2. How do the bullfighting vignettes bookending this story complicate our reading of it?
3. What is the significance of the story's expatriation theme and multilingual dialogue?
4. How and why are this story's themes, symbolism (e.g., cat, hair), and style (e.g., repetition) echoed in other *In Our Time* texts?

Think especially about how to present the following moments:

Opening paragraph (91)
"'Si, si, Signora, brutto tempo. It's very bad weather'" (92).
"'I like it the way it is.' 'I get so tired of it,' she said. 'I get so tired of looking like a boy'" (93).
"'And I want to eat at a table with my own silver and I want candles. And I want it to be spring and I want to brush my hair out in front of a mirror and I want a kitty and I want some new clothes.' 'Oh, shut up and get something to read,' George said. He was reading again" (94).

Prewriting I:
Sample "Why" question
This sample "why" question—used as a model for the questions the students write themselves to formulate research topics and thesis statements—is part of the pre-writing exercise students conduct as they generate paper topics. Students then formulate their own questions and read them aloud to the class, pointing out what is arguable and researchable about them. The instructor guides the students to self-correct if they slip into "what" mode:

How and why does Hemingway accurately reflect, yet subtly challenge, ideas of womanhood in post-WWI America in *In Our Time*? In "Cat in the Rain," for example, how and why does Hemingway draw the characters' expectations of marriage from period constructions, as seen in advertisements and media pieces? Why, moreover, does Hemingway challenge such limited gender constructs in this and other stories from *In Our Time*?

Prewriting II:
The instructor demonstrates both positive ("example") and negative ("anti-example") model thesis statements in class, reading each example below aloud. The students then analyze the wording, intended argument, and ideas of each in order to articulate why the first example introduces a viable essay topic (argument) and why the second does not (observation). The length of the examples is kept roughly the same in order to demonstrate that word count has little to do with the quality of the work.

Example: Hemingway's 1925 work *In Our Time* successfully reflects modernist-era ideas of womanhood, while complicating notions of marriage and motherhood in such stories as "Indian Camp" and "Cat in the Rain." *In Our Time*'s diverse portrayal of gender roles—Indian and European mothers, American wives and husbands—shows Hemingway using characters ranging from passive to progressive in order to critique binary gender constructions. Studies of modernist-era gender by Janet Lyon and Bonnie Kime Scott, along with period advertisements from *Vanity Fair*, can contextualize *In Our Time* and deepen Hemingway's simultaneous reflection of or challenge to 1920s womanhood.

Anti-example: Hemingway's 1925 work *In Our Time* depicts ideas of womanhood from the modernist era in "Indian Camp" and "Cat in the Rain." Whether his characters are single women, wives, or mothers, Hemingway portrays different kinds of European American women in the post-WWI period. Some women are in unhappy marriages or romantic relationships, and others give birth under tense circumstances. At the time, gender roles and expectations were undergoing drastic changes from the nineteenth century, as several scholarly works and contemporary advertisements from the time *In Our Time* was written show.

Reflection:
Assigned in-class when students submit the final draft of their essays and written on the verso of the submission.

When and how did you start this paper? What (if any) prewriting do you do? Did you reread "Cat in the Rain" and/or the other works your paper focuses on? If so, how did this help you? If not, why not?

Considering that a challenge is good at the college level, what about this assignment challenged you as writer and researcher? What, for example, was constructively challenging about writing on Hemingway and Toomer meaningfully, but *without* following a basic comparison-contrast approach? What was new about this approach, and how did it make you a better writer?

Why do I want you to find and then use scholarly works not directly related to your topic in your research-based assignments? How can you find sources that, for instance, historicize *and* contextualize post-WWI gender roles? What can this variety do for your argument and approach to "Cat in the Rain" and other works?

Adapted from Sarah B. Hardy

Hardy's note to her students introduces them to the week's reading. (The four weeks preceding "Hemingway week" were devoted to Chekhov, Joyce, Kafka and Bowen.) Hardy uses students' online posts to bookend class discussion. First they respond to the reading and then, after the class meeting, reflect upon the issues raised in class. Excerpts from student postings in response to this assignment appear in Hardy's essay in this volume.

Short story scholars:

It's time for us to read Hemingway. And it's very hard for me to choose which stories should be our focus. I really like them all! However, here is a plan. We will pick our way through, following the order Hemingway set up in the collection [*The Fifth Column and the First Forty-Nine Stories* (1938)]:

Day 1:
"The Short Happy Life of Francis Macomber"
"The Snows of Kilimanjaro"
"Indian Camp"
"The End of Something"

Day 2:
"Big Two-Hearted River: Part I"
"Big Two-Hearted River: Part II"
"Hills Like White Elephants"

Day 3:
"A Pursuit Race"
"A Clean, Well-lighted Place"
"Fathers and Sons"

Feel free to read around in the collection, though, and take a few minutes to look at some of the italicized chapter divisions [from *In Our Time*]. If you have read other Hemingway stories in the past, you might want to remind yourself of them and be ready to bring them into discussion. Don't forget to post on Blackboard. I look forward to talking to you about these stories. See you in class.

Online Discussion:
By Sunday night you should have begun your reading for Monday in time to log on and make a "first response" contribution to the week's forum. I will keep track of who is present in this space and who is not, and I will use your responses to get ready for Monday's class. Absence from these discussions will affect your final grade. But your informal contributions will not be graded, so this is a place to ask questions and try out ideas.

Applied Response:
Every Wednesday you will need to make another posting to the discussion forum. This response will focus on an idea that came up in class on Monday or Tuesday and apply to a story from that week's author [*Note: the class met Mondays, Tuesdays, and Thursdays*]. These are due in the discussion forum by 10 p.m. on Wednesdays. This is a fairly informal assignment, but it should be a well-written and informed idea or question about the text. Start with a quotation from one of the stories we are reading and develop a brief but insightful idea about that quotation. We will be using these to generate and sharpen class discussion; they will also serve as a check on your engagement with the reading. You will receive a paper grade for your combined online postings. I will let you know how you are doing midway through the semester.

Adapted from Catherine R. Mintler

Mintler asks her students to generate their own discussion questions for course readings in order to earn participation credit. A "good" discussion question, she notes in her assignment sheet, will invite participation and possibly even differing points of view; it will be thought-provoking and engage readers. It will not be limited to one answer, nor be answered in only one way; moreover, it should not be limited to a "so, how do you feel about this?" question that draws readers away from the text. Students are directed to consider how to answer their own questions, perhaps in a Response Paper.

Below is a sample of real student-generated discussion questions for *The Garden of Eden* written in response to this assignment:

1. What similarities are there in David's story of hunting the elephant in his youth and in his married life, and how is his past relevant to his present?
2. What is the significance of Catherine's cutting her hair and her constant attempt to become more like a boy; what triggered this behavior?
3. How does the use of alcohol affect the relationships of the characters? Is there any significance in the amount or types of drinks they consume?
4. There is a mirror that comes into the story time and time again that is often a topic of conversation. What purpose does it serve or did the author intend for it to serve?
5. Why the title "Garden of Eden?" How does this novel compare to the biblical story of the Garden of Eden? Are there similarities?
6. Despite the initial happiness the girl [Marita] brings to Catherine and David's life there are many instances that foreshadow an ultimate outcome, an outcome that obviously will leave one, if not all of them, unhappy because of jealousy. This comes to fruition after Catherine finds out that David and the girl have slept together. What exchanges throughout the book demonstrate not only Catherine's jealousy, but also the girl's and David's? Could it have been possible for the three of them to have lived happily ever after?
7. Throughout the novel Catherine enjoyed testing limits and pushing David, as exemplified in this quotation: "you aren't very hard to corrupt, and you're an awful lot of fun to corrupt." What does she mean by saying "corrupt"? Where in the novel are examples that show this corrupting taking place? Does she act alone in corrupting David? Does [Marita] contribute as well?
8. In the novel David wakes every morning to work on his stories. Although the stories seem out of place, they not only give the reader background

about David's past, but also help to lead him to the future. What effect does his writing have not only on himself, but also on those around him? Why does Catherine seem so jealous of the critics? Does David's writing bear any resemblance to Hemingway's writing?

Adapted from Debra A. Moddelmog

Moddelmog describes an in-class activity that compels the students to make interpretive decisions that, in turn, lead to investigations of the text they might not otherwise have considered.

Students act out one of the more dramatic conversations between a male-female couple in Hemingway's work. Ask them to play the scene in different ways that suggest stereotypical femininity and masculinity vs. more complex demeanors. For example, in the scene in "Hills Like White Elephants" where Jig tells the man to please stop talking, have the student play her, first, as growing more and more hysterical and then repeat the scene but by playing Jig as growing more and more serious and resolved. Or for the final scene of *The Sun Also Rises*, ask the student who plays Jake to respond to Brett as if he were still hopeful and then play him as if he were supremely skeptical. In every case have the other class members provide evidence to support the strength of one version over the other (or to offer another version). Other possibilities: any part of the conversation between the man and woman in "The Sea Change"; the scene where Catherine Barkley tells Frederic Henry, "I want what you want. There isn't any me any more. Just what you want" (105–06) or a later scene in which she claims to want him so much that she wants to be him too (299–300); or the conversation between Marjorie and Nick in "The End of Something."

Adapted from Douglas Sheldon

Sheldon designed this series of writing prompts for use in the ESL classroom following an assignment to read Hemingway's "A Very Short Story" for homework outside of class. It will likely make up three or more 50-minute class sessions. The assignment could also be adapted for first-language speakers of English or for use with other stories as well. Discussion of current events (i.e. the 2015 Supreme Court ruling legalizing same-sex marriage) may also prove relevant here, especially in ESL or introductory-level courses.

Part I: Solo Work/Freewriting
Think of your understanding of marriage: What does it mean to be engaged? What roles do the parties in the relationship play in this decision? Do your ideas of marriage differ from those you see in "A Very Short Story"? Spend some time freewriting in response to these questions (and don't worry about revision right now).

Part II: Small Group Work/Prewriting
Working with a partner or in a group of three (at least one person in your group should not share your home language) swap papers and read each other's responses to Part I. In your group, discuss the similarities and differences of your responses. Discuss how these responses compare to the relationship described in "A Very Short Story." Take notes and record any questions your group has.

Part III: Group Work/Drafting and Revision
Working with your partner(s) from Part II, review the section on thesis statements in *Subjects and Strategies* [or a relevant Composition handbook/textbook] and consider this line from "A Very Short Story": "They felt as though they were married, but they wanted everyone to know about it and to make it so they could not lose it." Develop a thesis statement and introductory paragraph for an essay considering *why* the couple wants to be married, *what* their attitude about marriage is, and *how* these desires and attitudes bring about the ultimate failure of the relationship. Working together, revise your work and be prepared to present your working thesis and a draft of your introductory paragraph and/or outline to the class at our next meeting.

Adapted from Joshua Weiss

This group research activity makes the religious festival of San Fermín the centerpiece of the class's understanding of *The Sun Also Rises*. Putting the festival (instead of the characters) at the center of the investigations opens students up to the possibilities of understanding the relationships between Jake, Brett, and Pedro through the festival, rather than seeing the festival as a mere backdrop for the emotional drama. Weiss notes that, individually, the groups unearth some interesting facts about their topics, but when the groups come together to present their findings in class, students are able to better understand how intimately connected all of these seemingly diverse elements really are. Weiss notes that the emphasis on a religious understanding helps students approach the idea of aficion with a new understanding, particularly when reminded of the religious context of the word "passion," which translates to an understanding of the "passion" circulating among the three main characters.

Research Topics:
1. San Fermín: saint's life, veneration, canonization
2. Chupinazo and Riau-Riau: opening ceremony of the festival and ceremonial dancing, including political connotations
3. Procession of San Fermín: *gigantes y cabezudos* (large heads) and the *jota* (dance)
4. Encierro: running of the bulls, with emphasis on ritual prayers and singing (familiar to students and always a popular selection)
5. Corrida: the bullfight, particularly ritualistic elements understood in a religious context (sacrifice, bull worship, and tripartite structure)

Adapted from Belinda Wheeler

The in-class activity described in Wheeler's essay in this volume is part of her American Literature Since 1870 course. The Hemingway lesson comes in at Week 5, and Wheeler notes that she leaves the reading assignment off the syllabus so that students come to the class without preconceived notions about Hemingway or the short story, either their own or from Wikipedia or "homework help" resources like Shmoop. This lesson plan works for other authors whose short stories appeared in mass market "slicks" as well.

Course Overview:
We will read and study works of poetry, fiction, and nonfiction prose, by men and women of diverse backgrounds and interests. Our objective will be to study the many voices that constitute what we call American literature, addressing questions such as How do the gender, race, and class of writers and readers affect the creation and reception of a literary text? What constitutes a literary canon? What does *American* mean? What role has literature played in the cultural and historical story of what the United States is today?

Student Learning Outcomes:
After completing this course students should be able to do the following:
- Demonstrate a critical understanding of the specific authors and texts covered in the course.
- Understand the significant ideas and important social conditions of each period and be able to relate that to an author's position on a given subject.
- Analyze the geographical, cultural, economic, and social influences on the development of American literature from 1870 to today.
- Show how contemporary literary forms have evolved from earlier forms.
- Express ideas and perform analysis in clear, concise, logical, and persuasive writing.
- Articulate ideas clearly through relevant contributions to class discussion and in response to the ideas of other students.

In-Class Activity:
- Invite students to come forward to examine the September 1936 issue of *Cosmopolitan* magazine, experiencing the materiality of the original document; invite observations on the texture of the pages, color and contrast of the ink, size of the page, etc. Story title and author name are obscured.

- Invite students to examine the content of the issue, including paratextual elements like advertisements
- Place the September 1936 issue of *Cosmopolitan* on the classroom's document camera, still obscuring the story's title and author's name
- Read the story during class time
- Lead discussion about the magazine's audience and its purpose
- Lead discussion of the story's themes and how they are in conversation with the magazine's ads and other content
- Reveal authorship and discuss how knowing the author's identity affects the way we interpret the story. How does Hemingway portray Margot? How does that portrayal fit with the way *Cosmopolitan* presents women to its audience? How does this experience of reading differ from that of our other reading [*Bedford Anthology of American Literature Volume Two: 1865 to the Present*]?

Appendix B

Essay Prompts

Adapted from Crystal Gorham Doss

Doss notes that the scholarly focus on women in Ernest Hemingway's works has often been on how male characters react to "modern" women but not on the struggles of the female characters as worthy of consideration in and of themselves. This essay prompt gets students thinking about how Hemingway's women navigate the problems of modernity. Doss originally devised this essay prompt to assess the students' ability to engage with themes of "The Snows of Kilimanjaro," but it can be used as a prompt to discuss other works by Hemingway as well, and it is sufficiently open-ended as to allow students to agree or disagree with Broer and Holland's claim.

1. In their Introduction to the collection *Hemingway and Women*, Lawrence R. Broer and Gloria Holland write that "gender was Hemingway's constant concern, and [. . .] his female characters are drawn with complexity and individuality equal to Hemingway's males" (ix). Based on your reading of Helen in "The Snows of Kilimanjaro," how would you position yourself in this scholarly debate about Hemingway's female characters? Use textual examples to support your answer.

Adapted from Sara Kosiba

In her essay in this volume Kosiba stresses the importance of reading Hemingway intertextually with the women who were his contemporaries. The prompt assesses the students' ability to consider three masters of the American short story in conversation with one another: Sherwood Anderson, Ernest Hemingway, and Eudora Welty.

In "The Book of the Grotesque," which opens his 1919 collection *Winesburg, Ohio*, Sherwood Anderson writes:

> [. . .] in the beginning when the world was young there were a great many thoughts but no such thing as a truth. Man made the truths himself and each truth was a composite of a great many vague thoughts. All about in the world were the truths and they were all beautiful. [. . .] There was the truth of virginity and the truth of passion, the truth of wealth and of poverty, of thrift and of profligacy, of carefulness and abandon. Hundreds and hundreds were the truths and they were all beautiful. And then the people came along. Each as he appeared snatched up one of the truths and some who were quite strong snatched up a dozen of them. It was the truths that made the people grotesques. The old man had quite an elaborate theory concerning the matter. It was his notion that the moment one of the people took one of the truths to himself, called it his truth, and tried to live his life by it, he became a grotesque and the truth he embraced became a falsehood.

Anderson's description highlights the often malleable nature of "truth" and the subjective nature of how we determine standards by which to live our lives. Using Anderson's description as a guide, look at the characters in Eudora Welty's "The Petrified Man" and Ernest Hemingway's "The Light of the World." What truths do these characters live by? What elements of the story give us that impression or show us the characters' truths? What, if any, similarities can you find between the truths the characters live by and the ideas or truths that govern our lives today? Support your answer with evidence from the texts.

Adapted from Catherine R. Mintler

The list of topics below are suggestions for the final project in Mintler's Women and Literature course that culminates in either a research-based, analytical paper of 7–8 pages (undergraduates) or 10–12 pages (graduate students) OR a research-based creative project in an alternative form. Mintler notes that the creative projects should offer an interpretation of a major theme, include secondary research and a bibliography, and represent work equivalent to the page count of the traditional academic essay assignment. Students will present their final projects to the class during the final exam period.

Essay Prompts:
1. Explore "sex" and/or "gender" patterns in several readings, using secondary sources as needed to support your interpretation. You cannot just mention that patterns exist in these works, or simply say what the patterns are; rather you must analyze and discuss what meanings arise from them. In other words, have something to suggest or argue about a specific use of patterning.
2. Compare and contrast how women's sexuality or sexual desire is treated in two different major course texts.
3. Apply Adrienne Rich's idea of the "lesbian continuum" to 1–2 major course texts/characters.
4. Discuss any readings as emblematic of what Hélène Cixous calls "feminine writing."
5. Discuss Biblical allusions in 1–2 readings; explain how they further a discussion of sex and gender.
6. Offer an analysis of "compulsory heterosexuality" in 1–2 course texts, and apply several tenets of Rich's essay to support a specific reading of women's oppression or a proposal for their sexual liberation through your understanding of the "lesbian continuum."
7. Analyze how male identity is constructed in 1–3 texts. You should offer a specific way of looking at how male characters are presented in these texts and use textual references to interpret or explain the possible meanings behind those representations.

Creative Prompts:
1. Construct a dialogue between several authors/characters we have read. You need to create the reason for their meeting and write dialogue in the style of the author and/or persona of the character.

2. Construct an interview between yourself as interviewer and one/several authors or characters from different course readings. You need to create good interview questions and believable answers. The characters should speak as they do in the novels (including any dialects or slang). You will create the reason for the interview, as well as introduce yourself as interviewer and describe your interviewees. This project may be entirely written, or written and filmed or performed.
3. Rewrite one or several scenes from the point of view of a character whose thoughts we do not have access to, such as Robin Vote, Jody Starks, Teacake, Marita, Catherine Bourne, Madame Reisz or Madame Ratignolle, Leonce Pontellier, Bertha Coutts, or Richard Dalloway. Or, you can choose to rewrite a scene from one novel in another author's style.
4. Artists may elect to paint, draw, or illustrate a character, issue, or scene; or construct an installation or multi-media collage to represent how gender/sexuality are presented in a particular novel.
5. Rewrite in another format—such as a play, a long poem, a script, or a graphic novel—the narrative or part of the plot of a novel we have read. You must demonstrate an understanding of the genre you choose.
6. Students who are foodies, chefs, or dieticians or otherwise interested in restaurants or food culture can create a menu or cookbook for a particular novel. Dishes on your menu—appetizers, main courses, and desserts—should include a brief rationale that relates the menu to the novel and course themes. (Examples could include Provençal French cuisine for Hemingway or Cajun for Chopin).

Adapted from Debra A. Moddelmog

Moddelmog makes the task of the state-of-the-field or bibliographic essay accessible (and fun!) for undergraduates and beginning graduate students with the assignments below, some of which contain a creative or interactive element. Suitably narrow in scope and targeted in their purpose, the assignments ask the students to understand and weigh in on the ongoing scholarly conversation on gender and sexuality in Hemingway's life and work.

1. Engage students in some of the critical debates regarding how to read gender and sexuality in Hemingway's work by setting up a "case study" in which students read a Hemingway story or novel about which critics have taken different, often conflicting, views about the meaning of gender and/or sexuality in the work. Ask students to write about these different views in an essay, arguing for (1) the strength of one view over the other; (2) a brand-new interpretation; and/or (3) a historicized recognition of how societal understanding of gender and sexuality has changed over time. Or divide them into two or more groups that will, after careful study of a particular critic's argument, present that argument in class and then engage with the other group/s in a debate about the story.

Possible case studies:
"Up in Michigan"
1. Nancy Comley and Robert Scholes, "Reading 'Up in Michigan,'" *New Essays on Hemingway's Short Fiction*, ed. Paul Smith (Cambridge: Cambridge UP, 1998), 19–45.
2. Marylyn A. Lupton, "The Seduction of Jim Gilmore," *The Hemingway Review* 15.1 (1995): 1–9.
3. Lisa Tyler, "Ernest Hemingway's Date Rape Story: Sexual Trauma in 'Up in Michigan,'" *The Hemingway Review* 13.2 (1994): 1–11.

"The Sea Change"
1. Julie Hough, "Hemingway's 'The Sea Change': An Embracing of Reality," *Odyssey: A Journal of the Humanities* 2.2 (1978): 16–18.
2. J. F. Kobler, "Hemingway's 'The Sea Change': A Sympathetic View of Homosexuality," *Arizona Quarterly* 26 (1970): 318–24.
3. Erik Nakjavani, "The Rest Is Silence: A Psychoanalytic Study of Hemingway's Theory of Omission and Its Adaptation of 'The Sea Change,'" *North Dakota Quarterly* 65.3 (1998): 145–73. (Only the first four pages are relevant)

4. Lisa Tyler, "'I'd Rather Not Hear': Women and Men in Conversation in 'Cat in the Rain' and 'The Sea Change,'" *Hemingway and Women: Female Critics and the Female Voice*, ed. Lawrence R. Broer and Gloria Holland (Tuscaloosa: U of Alabama P, 2002), 70–80.

2. Engage students in a performance of the history of criticism about some of Hemingway's female protagonists by asking them to read differing interpretations of these women and then act out key scenes where these women appear, performing these characters according to the interpretations offered by different critics. Conclude the exercise by asking how such disparate understandings of these women could be offered and which version seems to align best with the evidence of the text.

Here are some sources for critical interpretations of various female characters that might present students with differing understandings of their behavior and motives:

Catherine Barkley, *A Farewell to Arms*
1. Judith Fetterley, "*A Farewell to Arms:* Hemingway's 'Resentful Cryptogram,'" in *The Resisting Reader: A Feminist Approach to American Fiction* (Bloomington: Indiana UP, 1978), 46–71.
2. Sandra Whipple Spanier, "Hemingway's Unknown Soldier: Catherine Barkley, the Critics, and the Great War," in *New Essays on* A Farewell to Arms, ed. Scott Donaldson (Cambridge: Cambridge UP, 1990), 75–108.
3. Joyce Wexler, "E.R.A. for Ernest Hemingway: A Feminist Defense of *A Farewell to Arms*," *Georgia Review* 35.1 (1981): 111–23.

Catherine Bourne, *The Garden of Eden*
1. Theodore Solotaroff, "Sexual Identity in *A Farewell to Arms*," *The Hemingway Review* 9.1 (1989): 2–17 (the first few pages are about Catherine Bourne).
2. Kathy G. Willingham, "Hemingway's *The Garden of Eden:* Writing with the Body," *The Hemingway Review* 12.2 (1993): 46–61.
3. Sarah Wood Anderson, "Hemingway's Feminine Madness in *The Garden of Eden,*" *Readings of Trauma, Madness, and the Body*, ed. Sarah Wood Anderson (New York: Palgrave Macmillan, 2012), 74–84.

Brett Ashley, *The Sun Also Rises*
1. Wendy Martin, "Brett Ashley as New Woman in *The Sun Also Rises*," in *Ernest*

Hemingway's The Sun Also Rises: A Casebook, ed. Linda Wagner-Martin (Oxford: Oxford UP, 2002), 46–62.
2. Kathy G. Willingham, "The Sun Hasn't Set Yet: Brett Ashley and the Code Hero Debate," in *Hemingway and Women: Female Critics and the Female Voice,* ed. Lawrence R. Broer and Gloria Holland (Tuscaloosa: U of Alabama P, 2002), 43–58.
3. Leslie Fiedler, *Love and Death in the American Novel* (New York: Stein and Day, 1960).

3. Assign some historical reading on homosexuality and transsexuality in the U.S., Great Britain, and other parts of Europe during the 20th century and ask students to use that background to provide a fuller understanding of how to interpret one of Hemingway's characters or stories in which homosexuality or gender transition is either prominently featured or implied.

Selected Historical Sources:
Julian Carter, "On Mother Love: History, Queer Theory, and Non-Lesbian Identity," *Journal of the History of Sexuality* 14.1–2 (2005): 107–38.
George Chauncey, *Gay New York: Gender, Urban Culture, and the Making of the Gay Male World, 1890–1940* (New York: Basic Books, 1994).
Laura Doan, *Fashioning Sapphism: The Origins of a Modern English Lesbian Culture* (New York: Columbia UP, 2001).
Laura Doan, *Disturbing Practices: History, Sexuality, and Women's Experience of War* (Chicago: U of Chicago P, 2013).
Lisa Duggan, *Sapphic Slashers: Sex, Violence, and American Modernity* (Durham, NC: Duke UP, 2000).
Henry Minton, *Departing from Deviance: A History of Homosexual Rights and Emancipatory Science in America* (Chicago: U of Chicago P, 2001).
Siobhan Somerville, *Queering the Color Line: Race and the Invention of Homosexuality in American Culture* (Durham, NC: Duke UP, 2000).
Marc Stein, *Rethinking the Gay and Lesbian Movement* (New York: Routledge, 2012).
Susan Stryker, *Transgender History* (Berkeley: Seal Press, 2008).
Jennifer Terry, *An American Obsession: Science, Medicine, and Homosexuality in American Society* (Chicago: U of Chicago P, 1999).

Possible Hemingway stories and characters: "Mr. and Mrs. Elliot," "Mother of a Queen," "A Simple Enquiry," "The Sea Change," "A Lack of Passion," Helen

Ferguson (*A Farewell to Arms*), Rinaldi (*A Farewell to Arms*), Jake Barnes (*The Sun Also Rises*), Pilar (*For Whom the Bell Tolls*), Catherine Bourne (*The Garden of Eden*), David Bourne (*Garden*), Marita (*Garden*).

4. Engage students in an exploration of the intersections of gender and sexuality with other social differences such as race, ethnicity, and dis/ability by asking them to (1) read some criticism on Hemingway's representations of one or more of these differences in his writing and then (2) argue for one position over another in regard to a specific character. A creative option to this assignment is to ask students to narrate (with some imagination to fill in the gaps) the story of one of these characters from that character's point of view. Among the possibilities: Bugs in "The Battler," the African American fighter in *The Sun Also Rises*, Robert Cohn in *The Sun Also Rises*, Trudy or Billy in "Fathers and Sons," Prudence Mitchell in "Ten Indians," the father who commits suicide in "Indian Camp," the Indian woman giving birth in "Indian Camp," the African servants in "The Snows of Kilimanjaro." Another option is to have students consider how racial identity or able-bodiedness functions in terms of the sex or gender identity of one of Hemingway's white protagonists, for example, Nick Adams, Jake Barnes, Brett Ashley, Frederic Henry, Robert Jordan, Catherine Bourne, David Bourne, Francis Macomber, or Margot Macomber.

Selected Research on Race and Hemingway:

Ann DuCille, "The Short Happy Life of Black Feminist Theory," *differences: A Journal of Feminist Cultural Studies* 21.1 (2010): 32–47.

Marc Dudley, *Hemingway, Race, and Art: Bloodlines and the Color Line* (Kent, OH: Kent State UP, 2012)

Carl Eby, "'Come Back to the Beach Ag'in, David Honey!': Hemingway's Fetishization of Race in *The Garden of Eden* Manuscripts," rpt. in The Garden of Eden: *Twenty-Five Years of Criticism*, ed. Suzanne del Gizzo and Frederic Svoboda (Kent, OH: Kent State UP, 2012), 237–54.

Essays on race by Gary Holcomb, Nghana Lewis, and Amy Strong in *Ernest Hemingway in Context*, ed. Debra Moddelmog and Suzanne del Gizzo (Cambridge: Cambridge UP, 2013), 307–31.

Gary Edward Holcomb and Charles Scruggs, eds., *Hemingway and the Black Renaissance* (Columbus: Ohio State UP, 2012).

Jeremiah M. Kitunda, "Hemingway's African Book: An Appraisal," *The Hemingway Review* 25.2 (2006): 107–13.

Philip Melling, "'There Were Many Indians in the Story': Hidden History in Hemingway's 'Big-Two-Hearted River,'" *The Hemingway Review* 28.2 (2009): 45–64.

Debra A. Moddelmog, "The Race of Desire and Hemingway's World-Traveling: Re-Placing Africa in *The Snows of Kilimanjaro* and Hemingway's African Safari, 1953–54," *Reading Desire: In Pursuit of Ernest Hemingway* (Ithaca, NY: Cornell UP, 1999), 100–19.

Toni Morrison, *Playing in the Dark: Whiteness and the Literary Imagination* (Cambridge: Harvard UP, 1992).

Ken Panda, "*Under Kilimanjaro:* The Multicultural Hemingway," *The Hemingway Review* 25.2 (2006): 128–31.

Amy Strong, *Race and Identity in Hemingway's Fiction* (New York: Palgrave Macmillan, 2008).

Cary Wolfe, "Fathers, Lovers, and Friend Killers: Rearticulating Gender and Race via Species in Hemingway," *boundary 2* 29.1 (2002): 223–57.

Selected Research on Ethnicity and Hemingway

Keith Gandal, *The Gun and the Pen: Hemingway, Fitzgerald, Faulkner and the Fiction of Mobilization* (Oxford: Oxford UP, 2008).

Jeremy Kaye, "Jews," *Ernest Hemingway in Context*, ed. Debra A. Moddelmog and Suzanne del Gizzo (Cambridge: Cambridge UP, 2013), 339–46.

Jeremy Kaye, "The 'Whine' of Jewish Manhood: Re-Reading Hemingway's Anti-Semitism, Reimagining Robert Cohn," *The Hemingway Review* 25.2 (2006): 44–60.

Ernest Lockridge, "'Primitive Emotions': A Tragedy of Revenge Called *The Sun Also Rises*," *The Journal of Narrative Technique* 20.1 (1990): 42–55.

Selected Research on Dis/ability and Hemingway

Miriam Marty Clark, "Hemingway's Early Illness Narratives and the Lyric Dimensions of 'Now I Lay Me,'" *Narrative* 12.3 (2004): 167–77.

Dana Fore, "Life Unworthy of Life? Masculinity, Disability, and Guilt in *The Sun Also Rises*," *The Hemingway Review* 26.2 (2007): 74–88.

Debra A. Moddelmog, "The Disabled Able Body and White Masculinity," in *Reading Desire: In Pursuit of Ernest Hemingway* (Ithaca, NY: Cornell UP, 1999), 119–30.

Appendix C

Sample Syllabi

Below is a selection of syllabi that include considerations of Hemingway and gender as a topic of study. From an introductory Women's Studies course to single-author senior capstone experience, these syllabi illustrate how the contributors to this volume have incorporated Hemingway into a range of courses. The syllabi have been edited for length and to highlight the information most relevant to readers of this volume.

Syllabus 1

English and Women's Studies and Gender Studies (cross-listed)
Topics in Feminist and Gender Studies
Adapted from Pamela L. Caughie and Erin A. Holliday-Karre

> Men and women are, of course, different. But they are not as different as day and night, earth and sky, yin and yang, life and death. In fact, from the standpoint of nature, men and women are closer to each other than either is to anything else—for instance, mountains, kangaroos, or coconut palms. . . . Far from being an expression of natural differences, exclusive gender identity is the suppression of natural similarities.
>
> —Gayle Rubin, "The Traffic in Women: Notes on the 'Political Economy' of Sex"

Theoretical Texts:
Bordo, Susan. *The Male Body* (Farrar, Straus, and Giroux, 1999)
Foucault, Michel. *Herculine Barbin* (Pantheon Books, 1980)
Kimmel, Michael. *Manhood in America: A Cultural History* (Free Press, 1996)
Roughgarden, Joan. *Evolution's Rainbow* (University of California Press, 2004)

Literature:
Boylan, Jennifer. *She's Not There: A Life in Two Genders* (Broadway Books, 2003)
Hemingway, Ernest. *The Garden of Eden* (Scribner, 1986)
Mazza, Cris. "Is It Sexual Harassment Yet?" (*Fiction Collective 2*, 1998)
Woolf, Virginia. *Orlando: A Biography* (Hogarth Press, 1928; Mariner Books Reprint edition 1973)

Film:
Boy Am I (2006), Dir. Sam Feder & Julie Hollar
Boys Don't Cry (1999), Dir. Kimberly Peirce
The Crying Game (1992), Dir. Neil Jordan
Transamerica (2005), Dir. Duncan Tucker

Articles:
Bartkey, Sandra Lee. "Foucault, Femininity, and the Modernization of Patriarchal Power." In *The Politics of Women's Bodies*. Ed. Rose Weitz (Oxford 2003): 25–45.

Butler, Judith. *Gender Trouble* (Routledge 1990): Preface (ix–xii); Part 3 (91–111); Conclusion (142–149)
Caughie, Pamela. "Passing as Modernism." *Modernism/modernity* (September 2005)
Frye, Marilyn. "Sexism." In *The Politics of Reality* (1983): 17–40.
Martin, Emily. "The Egg and the Sperm." *Signs* 16.3 (1991)
Selections from *The Nation* (TBA)
Anne Fausto-Sterling, "Two Sexes Are Not Enough," from *Sexing the Body*

Weekly Assignments

Feminist Studies

> "Feminism demands a theory of how we become sexed and gendered."
> —Nancy Chodorow, Feminism and Psychoanalytic Theory

> "In a culture which is in fact constructed by gender duality, however, one cannot simply be 'human'.... Our language, intellectual history, and social forms are 'gendered'; there is no escape from this fact and from its consequences in our lives.... One cannot be 'gender neutral' in this culture."
> —Susan Bordo, "Feminism, Postmodernism, and Gender-Skepticism"

Week 1: Introduction to Feminist and Gender Studies
 Frye, "Sexism"
 Selections from *The Nation* and *The New York Times*
 Discussion question: What characterizes these essays as *feminist*?

Week 2: Bordo, *The Male Body*: "In Hiding and On Display" and "Does Size Matter?"
 Bordo, *The Male Body*: "Fifties Hollywood" and "Gentleman or Beast?"
 Bordo, *The Male Body*: "The Sexual Harasser"

Week 3: Mazza, "Is It Sexual Harassment Yet?" and Caughie's introduction
 Martin, "The Egg and the Sperm"
 Bartky, "Foucault, Femininity, and the Modernization of Patriarchal Power"

 Work Due: Essay on issues in feminism

Gender Studies

"When we speak here of sexual difference, we must distinguish between opposition and difference. Opposition is two, opposition is man/woman. Difference on the other hand can be an indefinite number of sexes...."
—Jacques Derrida, "Women in the Beehive," Men in Feminism

Week 4: Butler, selections from *Gender Trouble*
Butler, selections from *Undoing Gender*

Week 5: Foucault, *Herculine Barbin*

Week 6: Hemingway, *The Garden of Eden*
Caughie, "Passing as Modernism"

Week 7: Kimmel, "Muscles, Money, and the M-F Test: Measuring Masculinity Between the Wars" from *Manhood in America: A Cultural History*
Kimmel, "The Masculine Mystique" and Epilogue, from *Manhood in America*

Work Due: Essay on issues in gender studies

Transgender studies

"If the state and legal system has an interest in maintaining only two sexes, our collective biological bodies do not."
—Anne Fausto-Sterling, Sexing the Body

"There are no transsexuals. We are all transsexuals."
—Judith Halberstam

Week 8: Fausto-Sterling, "Two Sexes Are Not Enough"
Roughgarden, selections from *Evolution's Rainbow*, chapters 18 and 22

Week 9: Terry Grande: Guest lecture on Roughgarden's *Evolution's Rainbow*
Boylan, *She's Not There*

Week 10: Woolf, *Orlando*

Week 11: *Boy Am I*, Dir. Sam Feder & Julie Hollar

Week 12: *Boys Don't Cry*, Dir. Kimberly Peirce

Week 13: *The Crying Game*, Dir. Neil Jordan

Week 14: *Transamerica*, Dir. Duncan Tucker

    Work Due: Essay on issues in transgender studies

    Exam

Syllabus 2

Advanced Seminar in a Major Author
Ernest Hemingway
Adapted from Carl P. Eby

Course Description and Learning Objectives:
By the end of this semester, students who successfully complete this course will be able to demonstrate a deep understanding of one of the twentieth century's most important and influential writers: Ernest Hemingway. Students will be able to understand Hemingway's individual works within the context of his entire life and career—and students should more generally appreciate how a deep knowledge of a writer's life and corpus can profoundly enhance their understanding and enjoyment of individual works by that author. Students will be able to place Hemingway's works within the tradition of modernism, and they will be able to explain how his works from the 1920s, '30s, and '40s exemplify American literature in those decades. Students will think critically about what Michel Foucault calls the "author function," and the class will explore Hemingway's development as an artist and his transformation into a popular American icon. We will explore the major themes in his work (aesthetics, the struggle to construct meaningful values in a world in which values are not a given, war, violence, courage, vulnerability, marriage, love, sexuality, loss, nature, spirituality, coming of age, and the writing life), and we will explore his work from multiple perspectives (textual, biographical, psychological, historical, political, intertextual, and semiotic). To capitalize on my own expertise, the class will pay particular attention to psychology and gender theory—areas which have dominated Hemingway criticism for the past two decades. Students will improve their abilities as close readers of literature, learn how to work with manuscripts, and develop their ability to conduct literary research and write professional research papers.

Required Texts:
Hemingway, Ernest. *The Sun Also Rises.* Scribner's, 1926.
Hemingway, Ernest. *A Farewell to Arms.* Scribner's, 1929.
Hemingway, Ernest. *Death in the Afternoon.* Scribner's, 1932.
Hemingway, Ernest. *For Whom the Bell Tolls.* Scribner's, 1940.
Hemingway, Ernest. *The Old Man and the Sea.* Scribner's 1952.
Hemingway, Ernest. *A Moveable Feast.* Scribner's, 1964. (posthumous)

Hemingway, Ernest. *The Garden of Eden*. Scribner's, 1986. (posthumous)
Hemingway, Ernest. *The Complete Short Stories of Ernest Hemingway. The Finca Vigía Edition*. Scribner's, 1986.

Students will also be required to read one Hemingway biography of their choice from the following list:
Baker, Carlos. *Ernest Hemingway: A Life Story*. Colliers, 1969.
Meyers, Jeffrey. *Hemingway: A Biography*. Harper, 1985.
Lynn, Kenneth. *Hemingway*. Simon and Schuster, 1987.
Mellow, James. *Hemingway: A Life without Consequences*. Addison Wesley, 1992.
Any two volumes from Michael Reynolds's five-volume biography (1986–1999) of Hemingway: (1) *The Young Hemingway*; (2) *The Paris Years*; (3) *The American Homecoming*; (4) *The 1930s*; (5) *The Final Years*.

Assignments & Grading:

Participation (10%):
Participation is essential to success in this class. This is a small class that meets only once per week. The quality of classroom discussion and the quality of your own experience depend upon your showing up for class regularly and on time and prepared to ask and answer an array of questions about the assigned reading.

Position Papers (20%):
Each student will be responsible for presenting four position papers—two-page arguments about some aspect of meaning in one of the texts assigned for a given day. One or more of these papers can serve as a seed for your seminar paper. (These papers will be distributed throughout the semester, with no more than two per class day, and students will sign up for dates on the first day of class.)

Presentation of Scholarship (10%):
Each student will present two 10-minute reviews of a scholarly article with relevance to a given day's reading. These reviews should both summarize and critique the articles under consideration. (These presentations will be distributed throughout the semester, with no more than one per class day, and students will sign up for dates on the first day of class.) Students should provide the class with copies of the article under consideration—but this can be done electronically at least two days in advance of that day's class.

Prospectus (10%):
Genuine research begins with a *research problem:* an authentic question, tension, or problem that calls your essay into being and that gives it a sense of purpose. You don't know what you're researching, what you want to argue, or why it matters until you can first define your research problem. (*Why does Hemingway keep doing x in his novels and stories? Why did Hemingway slice the ending off of . . . ? One aspect of text x pulls in one direction, while another aspect pulls in the opposite direction; to what extent can, or should, the opposing tendencies be reconciled . . . ?*) In a 3-page prospectus, do the following:
- define your research problem
- suggest some tentative lines of approach to that problem (biographical, psychological, historical, textual, ideological, etc.)
- suggest what might be at stake in the answer to your research problem (usually something specific about the broader meaning of a text or set of texts)
- suggest what *types* of sources might be useful for this project (biographies, letters, manuscripts, newspaper stories, criticism, reference works, etc.)

Attach a bibliography of sources that you plan to consult. I can't give you any artificial number of sources to consult. I want a robust list of sources that are relevant to your research problem.

Seminar Paper (50%): This 25-page essay gives you an opportunity to conduct guided in-depth research, apply what you have learned during the semester, and develop and practice your skills at writing a publication-length paper. You must engage with the current critical and theoretical scholarship, but you should engage with these sources only insofar as they help you to make an original argument of your own design. You will do a short presentation on your research at our mini-conference on the final day of class.

Schedule
  Week 1
    Roland Barthes, "The Death of the Author" ([Course Management System])
    Michel Foucault, "What Is an Author?" ([CMS])
    Stories and inter-chapters from *In Our Time* (1925) (In *The Complete Short Stories . . .*)
    "On the Quai at Smyrna" (see related newspaper coverage on [CMS])

"Indian Camp" (see "Three Shots"—original manuscript intro to "Indian Camp," [CMS])
"The Doctor and the Doctor's Wife"
"The End of Something"
"The Three-Day Blow"
"The Battler"
"A Very Short Story" (see also transcript of early manuscript draft, [CMS])
Inter-Chapters I–VI (see also Hemingway's original newspaper story, "A Silent, Ghastly Procession," & compare w/ "Chapter II," [CMS]; see also newspaper background for Chapter V; and see the vignettes as first published in *The Little Review*, 1923, [CMS])

Week 2

Stories and inter-chapters from *In Our Time* (1925) (In *The Complete Short Stories . . .*)
"Soldier's Home" (see related newspaper coverage, [CMS])
"The Revolutionist"
"Mr. and Mrs. Elliot" (see page from original typescript, [CMS])
"Cat in the Rain"
"Out of Season"
"Cross Country Snow"
"My Old Man"
"Big Two-Hearted River," parts I & II (see "On Writing"—original conclusion of "Big Two-Hearted River" mss., [CMS])
Inter-Chapters V–XIV
Robert Paul Lamb, selections from *Art Matters: Hemingway, Craft, and the Creation of the Modern Short Story* ([CMS])

Week 3

The Sun Also Rises (1926) (chapters I–XII, pages 11–130)

Week 4

The Sun Also Rises (1926) (chapters XIII–XV, pages 131–251)
(see also Hemingway's newspaper story, "Pamplona in July," *Toronto Star Weekly*, Oct. 27, 1923, [CMS])

Week 5

A Moveable Feast (1964)
Gertrude Stein, selection from *The Autobiography of Alice B. Toklas* ([CMS])
(see also transcription of typescript, "The Autobiography of Alice B. Hemingway," [CMS])

(see also Hemingway's newspaper story, "American Bohemians in Paris," *Toronto Star Weekly*, Mar. 25, 1922, [CMS])

Week 6

The Garden of Eden (1986) (chapters 1–16, pages 3–145)

(see assorted passages from *Eden* Manuscript, Item 422.1, JFK Library, [CMS])

Week 7

The Garden of Eden (1986) (chapters 17–29, pages 146–247)

Sigmund Freud, "Fetishism" and "Splitting of the Ego in the Defensive Process," [CMS]

D. W. Winnicott, from "Transitional Objects and Transitional Phenomena," [CMS]

Eby, Chapters 6 & 7, *Hemingway's Fetishism: Psychoanalysis and the Mirror of Manhood*, [CMS]

(see also "Provisional Ending" from *Eden* Manuscript, Item 422.1, JFK Library, [CMS])

(see also deleted chapters from *Islands in the Stream*, [CMS])

Week 8

A Farewell to Arms (1929) (chapters I–XXIV, pages 3–233)

(see also Newspaper Coverage of Retreat from Caporetto, [CMS])

Week 9

A Farewell to Arms (1929) (chapters XXV–XLI, page 237-conclusion)

(see also alternate endings of *A Farewell to Arms*, [CMS])

Thomas Strychacz, from *Hemingway's Theatres of Masculinity*, pp. 87–103, [CMS]

Judith Butler, passages from *Bodies that Matter*, [CMS]

Week 10

Stories from *Men Without Women* (1927) (In *The Complete Short Stories*...)

"The Undefeated"

"In Another Country"

"Hills Like White Elephants"

"The Killers"

"Che Ti Dice Le Patria?"

"Fifty Grand"

"A Simple Enquiry"

"Ten Indians"

"A Canary for One"

"An Alpine Idyll"

"Now I Lay Me"

Week 11
- *Death in the Afternoon* (1932) (chapters 1–16 & 20, pages 1–192 & 270–278)
- (see a bullfight, [CMS])
- (see transcription of typescript/manuscript of "A Natural History of the Dead," [CMS]—continues story on page 144 of *Death in Afternoon*)

Week 12
- Stories from *Winner Take Nothing* (1933) (In *The Complete Short Stories* . . .)
- "After the Storm"
- "A Clean Well-Lighted Place"
- "Light of the World"
- "God Rest You Merry, Gentlemen"
- "The Sea Change" (see related manuscript material, [CMS])
- "A Way You'll Never Be" (see manuscript material & related newspaper coverage, [CMS])
- "Homage to Switzerland"
- "Fathers and Sons"
- Manuscript Fragment #355a, John F. Kennedy Library ([CMS])
- Prospectus Due

Week 13
- Stories from *The First 49 Stories* (1938) (In *The Complete Short Stories* . . .)
- "The Short Happy Life of Francis Macomber"
- "The Snows of Kilimanjaro"
- "The Capital of the World"
- "The Last Good Country" (posthumous)

Week 14
- *For Whom the Bell Tolls* (1940) (chapters 1–17, page 1–224)

Week 15
- *For Whom the Bell Tolls* (1940) (chapters 18–43, pages 225–conclusion)

Week 16
- *The Old Man and the Sea*

Week 17
- Mini-Conference: Student Presentations of Research from Seminar Papers
- Seminar Papers Due

Syllabus 3

Special Topics Undergraduate Literature Seminar
Understanding America: Hemingway in a World of Discredited Values and Traditions
Adapted from John Fenstermaker

Overview:

Through the Roaring '20s, Great Depression, World War II, and the 1950s, Americans read Ernest Hemingway. Following World War I, in Hemingway's early adulthood, struggles developed over sexual freedom, economic independence, and political power. "Understanding America" will particularly interrogate gender relations in America and, among other critical subjects, Hemingway on war and nationalism and on racial, ethnic, and religious prejudice. Through the lenses of Hemingway biography, texts, and audience, we will investigate—in 32 stories and 4 novels—cultural and political issues and defining moments in twentieth-century America, questioning earlier moral/ethical quandaries that, today, continue to shape our culture, ourselves.

Five decades after his death, Hemingway remains a consistent presence in cultural debates describing twentieth-century America. His reputation as a "major American author" continues to grow. Biographer Scott Donaldson recalls: "Hemingway's passing was memorialized by the Kremlin and the White House, in the Vatican and the bullrings of Spain" (*Cambridge Companion*, 1). John Raeburn was struck by the editorializing of the *Louisville Courier Journal:* "It is almost as though the Twentieth Century itself has come to a sudden, violent, and premature end" (*Fame Became of Him,* 168). Indisputably, Hemingway became a polymath. Matthew Bruccoli's characterizations in *Hemingway and the Mechanism of Fame* (xix) are suggestive: "hunter, fisherman, soldier, aesthetician, patriot, military strategist, yachtsman, drinker, womanizer, gourmet, sportsman, philosopher, naturalist, intellectual, anti-intellectual, traveler, war correspondent, boxer, big-game hunter—and author," not to mention prize winner: a Pulitzer (1953); the Nobel (1954). Near century's end—in 1995—the Modern Language Association *Bibliography* recorded more published scholarship that year devoted to Hemingway than to any other American writer of the twentieth century. Notable further, *The Sun Also Rises* (1926), *A Farewell to Arms* (1929), and *For Whom the Bell Tolls* (1940) continue to rank among the top 100 banned and challenged American classics.

Background:

In addition to working with the Hemingway texts for the day, our classroom discussions will include background lectures (brief and introductory or supplemental) and additional assigned readings on reserve at the library. These materials will establish a historical/biographical frame of reference and, in part, develop the following details and points of emphasis:

Ernest Hemingway was born in 1899; he died in 1961. Many Hemingway readers in his time—individuals born roughly between 1890 and 1945—experienced radical revision of the WASP traditions and values of their parents and grandparents. These codes had been modified throughout the nineteenth century in the Anglo world by aggressive development of industrial capitalism, increasing religious tolerance, and, in the last quarter-century, an array of social and legal reforms affecting class and gender roles (e.g., feminized conceptions of masculinity and the genteel male, and the rise of the New Woman). In America, specifically, at century's turn, discontinuities and dislocations existed caused by urbanization, secularization, immigration, the advent of a consumer economy, and the rise of "Big Business"—the latter impacting, not least, formal religion.

Hemingway was present at the wars and revolutions of his time, an historical era defined by such violence: WWI (wounded in Italy, 1918); Greco-Turkish War (covered as journalist, 1922); on scene during revolution in Spain (1931) and overthrow of Machado in Cuba (1933), installing Batista (1934); Spanish Civil War (covered as journalist, 1937, 1938); War in China (covered as journalist, 1941); WWII (covered as journalist, Europe—including Normandy landing—1944); Cuban Revolution, 1959 (Castro appropriates Finca Vigía, Hemingway's home since 1940; he returned to Ketchum, Idaho, where he died 2 July 1961).

Hemingway wrote on major issues in his time: community, domestic, legal, patriotic, political, military, and religious. Within one of these—the domestic—he explored, in extraordinary breadth (most explicitly in ca. 17 "Nick Adams" stories) possibly his most important subject: male/female relationships.

Hemingway's dialogue nearly perfectly mimics actual speech; his words rarely require the common reader to seek a dictionary. His fictional realism—expressed in a complex-declarative sentence structure of everyday language free of abstractions, relatively free of adjectives and adverbs, and uniformly free of explicit authorial or ethical judgments—seems to capture everyday existence in his time: its dark moments—alienation, loneliness, disillusion, inarticulateness, irrationality, physical violence; its liberating elements—self-awareness, self-discipline, sensitivity, human solidarity, camaraderie, sport, the natural world.

Jake in *The Sun Also Rises* (1926), experiencing an existential darkness, formulates early the central Hemingway question (felt by many of Hemingway's contemporary readers): How does one discover in a world of discredited or otherwise destabilized values and traditions the way to live now?

Course Materials:

(the novels in Scribner's Paperback Library editions):
The Sun Also Rises
A Farewell to Arms
To Have and Have Not
The Old Man and the Sea
The Complete Short Stories (We will read 32), Finca Vigía Edition

Course Assignments:

Writing—You will write two short essays of 1,500–2,000 words each, take either the midterm *or* the final, and write a term paper of 3,000–3,500 words. Follow MLA style for all documentation.

Drawing upon scene, action, and dialogue in Hemingway's fiction, your essays will explore how literature records, for example, society's formal and informal rites and traditions, including setting and enforcing rules of identity and behavior, especially for characters on its margins. In several Hemingway short stories, young women—innocent, naïve, or otherwise vulnerable—are depicted in various stages of emotional or psychological growth following serious, sometimes violent, adversity. Interacting with such material will allow you to think creatively about complex *contemporary* issues, to address (integrate?) contradictory perspectives between societal (legal) and personal responsibility in debates over gender or ethnic or other pressing social controversies. Your writing will demonstrate awareness of the moral/ethical complexities of the larger world, where classroom debates touching both abstract intellectual issues and "nuts and bolts" writing and research methods must make sense and unfold in the context of humane values.

Paper 1 will deal with authors, editors, journalists, diarists/memoirists, artists, women's rights activists, or others explicitly involved with Hemingway's life or work and selected from a list (provided) of 125 names: Djuna Barnes, John Dos Passos, Nancy Cunard, T. S. Eliot, Scott Fitzgerald, Janet Flanner, Jane Heap, Robert McAlmon, Joan Miro, Ezra Pound, Gertrude Stein.... This essay will make palpable the times and places of Hemingway's life and writing. In your essay, you will "grab on to" concrete elements of these times and places as you explore the life of an individual who interacted substantively with Hemingway. In capturing this relationship in your essay, you will (a) give proper space to your subject's achievements in his/her own right and (b) make more real for yourself the broad era we are studying, even as we focus principally on Hemingway's life and writing.

Paper 2 will deal with a novel or story we are reading. You should define or delimit a crucial issue: e.g., prospects for obtaining an abortion in Europe in 1927 ("Hills Like White Elephants"); alteration of biographical facts of real-life models: e.g., for Marjorie or Bill ("The End of Something," "The Three-Day Blow"; see also, *The Sun Also Rises*); the lifestyles of American expatriates in the literary or art scene in Paris (*The Sun Also Rises*); formal and informal activities of American nurses serving with the Red Cross in Italy in 1918 or roles of women in the war effort at home in 1917–18 (*A Farewell to Arms*); attitudes toward gay men or lesbians ("A Simple Enquiry" or "The Sea Change"); the prevalence and typical experiences of wealthy women on safari in Africa in the 1930s ("The Short Happy Life of Francis Macomber," "The Snows of Kilimanjaro"); any other major Hemingway subject particularly centering upon fundamental American values in this era (e.g., "Soldier's Home").

Midterm or Final Exam. Sample Essay Question—"The world depicted by serious artists is morally and ethically complex. These artists challenge us to acknowledge this complexity and to extend compassion, tolerance, and sympathy to their characters (and, by extension, to those persons we must live among and deal with in our own lives). Discuss this moral or ethical complexity—with at least brief reference to our own time—in the specific worlds of three stories or *The Sun Also Rises*. Possible subjects of focus include class or race, male/female relations (such as marriage, family), religion, personal vs. social responsibility ...)."

Paper 3, the term paper, will focus on the general cultural moment of a significant literary or historical event/issue important during Hemingway's lifetime. Drawing upon newspapers, magazines, published letters, journals, and/or other contemporary records, you will explore cultural features shaping a selected event: one pertinent to Hemingway's biography, texts, and/or audience; one centering upon an intellectual or social issue prominent today.

Your essay will take as its anchoring historical moment—

Either:
Publication of a Hemingway novel or story or of Cather's *One of Ours*, Toomer's *Cane*, Stein's *The Autobiography of Alice B. Toklas*, Mitchell's *Gone with the Wind*, Steinbeck's *The Grapes of Wrath*, Faulkner's *Go Down Moses*, Mailer's *The Naked and the Dead*. ... or any other title through 1952.

> [Example: Select publication of *The Old Man and the Sea* (September 1, 1952). Shape a topic touching culture, here Cuba's obsession with a sport intimately tied to the societal values of the United States ... or ... research images of Joe DiMaggio drawn by contemporary sports writers (1940s-1950s) and descriptions of the real DiMaggio drawn by serious subsequent biographers. Using these details and the vision of DiMaggio full-blown in Santiago's imagination, what conclusions may be drawn comparing Hemingway's DiMaggio with that of the sports writers and of the biographers ... or ... using these details, explore what roles, if any, race, class, and culture—(i.e., Cuban fisherman Santiago and Italian immigrant DiMaggio)—play in Hemingway's fictional DiMaggio, in the author's concept of identity and heroism in this novel? More. ...]

Or:
publication of an article in *American Mercury, Atlantic Monthly, Better Homes and Gardens, Cosmopolitan, Good Housekeeping, Harper's, Ladies Home Journal, Motion Picture, Nation, New Republic, New Yorker, Photoplay, Reader's Digest, Saturday Evening Post, Scribner's Magazine, Smart Set, Vanity Fair* or *Vogue* about ... advertising (particularly as this defines maleness or masculinity or womanhood or femininity), censorship, racial issues, religious sects and

movements, the automobile, the telephone, the radio, new music and dance crazes, talking pictures or newsreels, the Stock Market crash, the Depression, the War . . . or, similarly, throughout the 1920s-1950s, about the impact upon male/female relationships and social roles of women working (assuming professional roles outside the home), living and traveling alone, drinking, smoking, using birth control, divorcing. . . .

Paper (3000–3500 words) will be due no later than the last day of class.

Syllabus 4

Senior Majors Capstone Project or Introductory Graduate Seminar
Hemingway's Short Fiction
Adapted from Hilary Kovar Justice

Context: After an initial seven weeks engaged in free-form intensive class discussion/analysis of the early stories "Indian Camp," "Three Shots," and "Out of Season," in which students are introduced to various archives and avenues available for scholarly research (including extant criticism, textual scholarship, biography, letters, etc.), students are challenged to become the world expert on a single short story (for one, brief, shining moment). To achieve a passing project grade, students must develop and document beginning graduate-level familiarity with all available archival and critical sources and present an original scholarly argument in a critical, theoretically informed essay.

Story Selection Process: Students are given a list of stories from which to select one for final project focus. This list is proscribed in order that students have time to read each story option at least three times and "sleep on it"; they are encouraged to "trust their gut" in making their choice. The list is provided in the second week of a 16-week semester; choices are due at mid-term. Stories on the syllabus for class discussion are deliberately off-limits for final projects (the syllabus continues with the longer two-parters "Big Two-Hearted River I & II" (and "On Writing") and "In Another Country"/"Now I Lay Me" [originally "In Another Country—II"]). Also off-limits is "The Snows of Kilimanjaro," which I often teach in my section of the introductory course for majors, which some (but not all) students may have taken. The purpose of the list is to level the playing field (no previous in-class discussion) and to provide students with a manageably knowable archive given time constraints.

In a recent section of this course, final project options were: "An Alpine Idyll," "Cat in the Rain," "A Clean, Well-Lighted Place," "Cross-Country Snow," "Hills Like White Elephants," "The Killers," "The Sea Change," and "Up in Michigan." This list offers both relatively neglected stories (e.g., "An Alpine Idyll") and stories at the epicenter of recent and emerging critical trends (i.e., gender and sexuality studies, environmental criticism, food studies).

Course Assessment: 50% class discussion and 50% final project [This distribution transitions students to the "final project = 100% of your grade" that often accompanies graduate study].

Project Assessment: 50%/25%/25% for three project sections: annotated bibliography, endnotes, and critical essay. The section earning the highest grade counts as 50% of the project grade. [This flexibility allows graduating seniors to take risks and to play to their strengths, curiosities, and passions. It serves our English Studies population especially well; our majors include English, English Education, Tech Writing, Linguistics, and Publishing, thus students' individual talents and prior coursework vary tremendously and may not include extensive practice with critical writing.]

Objectives: The project introduces professional scholarly research methodologies, providing excellent practice for students planning to begin graduate study or careers in secondary education (in which they may not always set their own syllabus and will thus be teaching works with which they are initially unfamiliar). The project requires an original scholarly argument. More ephemerally, but arguably most importantly, by its very nature, the project constitutes a daunting but manageable challenge with which to mark the culmination of undergraduate study and the opportunity to realize growth and evolution over the course of a college career. [Students find herein a benevolent yet absolute mandate to feel pride in their capabilities, training, accomplishments, and potential. "Done," I tell them, "is Good."]

Required Elements/Guidelines
1. Complete MLA bibliography listing for story. [Instructions are given in class; students are given two days to do their MLA searches and bring the print-outs to class for instructions regarding winnowing (if necessary).]
Note: A period of source acquisition will now ensue which will require professional courtesy and cooperation. You are allowed to work together on source acquisition (the books especially only exist in so many places). All written work is done independently; each student must summarize and assess the sources on their own.
2. Annotated bibliography. A summary and assessment of each critical source published after 1989. You must include the relevant chapter in Paul Smith's *A Reader's Guide to the Short Stories of Ernest Hemingway* (Boston: G.K. Hall 1989). Use Smith's section on "Critical Discussion" as a model for content and professional tone. Present your own work as a list: list the source, then

skip a line and include your short summary and assessment paragraph). You must include the relevant chapter in Smith.

Note: If you find yourself engaging more deeply with a source than a short summary and assessment, chances are excellent that you should include that source engagement in your critical essay.

Guidelines and Sample Entries:
  I. Your annotated bibliography must include:
     A. Everything you were able to get your hands on from your MLA bibliography searches. (If your "story + author / after 1989" search yields over 30 sources, email me; we'll work together to tailor it to your interests. Critical discussion of some stories has been sparse; of others, frequent and often intense. It depends on the story and on trends; not everyone will work with the same number of sources.)
     B. Any other sources you're using for your critical essay (with the exception of the story itself and other works of fiction). If a non-fiction work appears in your Works Cited, it must appear in your annotated bibliography.
        Note: That only works one way. Not everything in your annotated bibliography need appear in your Works Cited:
           Annotated Bibliography = MLA Search + Works Cited − Fictional Work
           Works Cited = Every source mentioned in Critical Essay
     C. Paul Smith's chapter on your story. (Full citation for Works Cited page: Smith, Paul. *A Reader's Guide to the Short Stories of Ernest Hemingway.* Boston: G.K. Hall, 1989.)

—

 II. Sample Annotated Entries (completely and utterly made up):
     A. Sample #1 (with example of descriptive assessment):
        Le Chien, Snoopy. "On the care and feeding of spotted dogs." *Beagle Quarterly.* III: 2 (Spring 2011 34–38).
        [Summary]: Le Chien outlines procedures for caring for and feeding spotted dogs. He particularly emphasizes kindness, socialization, and adequate protein intake.
        [Descriptive Assessment]: Although Le Chien's essay will be informative for the general reader, expert caregivers of spotted dogs will wish for more specific guidelines based on more (and more recent) scientific evidence. The only scientific work cited in his bibliography is dated 1910.

—

B. Sample #2 (with examples of evaluative assessment):
Barnes, Marita. "Everything you need to know about 'Ten Indians.'" *The Hemingway Review* IV: 3 (Fall 2011 50–78).

Summary #1: Barnes focuses entirely on the scene between Nick and his father in this story and forwards the theory that the Garners are Nick's imaginary friends.

Negative Assessment: Although Barnes's close reading of the actual dialogue in the scene is sensitive, thoughtful, and extremely logical, she does not effectively argue for the "imaginary friends" thesis on which her larger argument seems to rest. Had she considered Smith's discussion of the manuscripts, this would have been obvious. Also, one questions using Henry James's fiction as factual evidence for the existence of imaginary friends.

Summary #2: Barnes exhaustively considers all possible angles of approach to understanding, reading, and teaching this story in contemporary and current contexts.

Positive Assessment: Barnes gives balanced consideration to all major approaches to literary study (including gender studies, postcolonialism, manuscript study, close reading, and linguistics). Of particular use are her considerations of how pronoun usage in the story renders Dr. Adams a sympathetic character and how Other Scholar's arguments concerning gender construction help us read the absence of Nick's mother in the story.

3. Complete footnotes for story (1938 version). Must include translation of every term not in English with full explanation of its resonance (remember the "geld" discussion from "Out of Season") *and* every historical/cultural reference present in the story. Organization: cue it to page # and line # of the 1938 collection. (You will be assessed here on thoroughness, quality of sources, and clarity of explanation.)

4. Critical essay, informed by critical/theoretical school of your choice (Jonathan Culler's *Literary Theory: A Very Short Introduction*, 2nd ed. [Oxford: Oxford UP 2011] may be helpful here), situated within current critical discussion, forwarding your own argument. Your argument can be based on existing arguments or you can go in a new direction, but you must be absolutely clear on the shape of the existing discussion and your reader must be able to tell how you are reacting to and departing from that existing

discussion. This is a characteristic of all scholarly discourse and occurs at the beginning of your critical essay.
   A. As part of your discussion you must include and integrate:
      1. Extant critical discussion post-1989 (discussion pre-1989 is summarized by Smith).
         a. The "critical backstory" must begin within the first page of the essay.
         b. Organize the "backstory" section by focus, not year.
         c. You must include mention of the five most recent critical works whether or not they pertain directly to your argument.
         d. You may engage critical discussion throughout your essay as well.
         e. You may, if your argument warrants, refer also to discussions pre-1989.
      2. Evidence from the story's drafts (summarized in the Smith chapter).
      3. One chapter from *Hemingway in Context* (2012).
5. Relevant biographical information surrounding the context of the actual writing of the story and also for the years Hemingway's own age matched that of the protagonist(s). (Use the Reynolds biographies, on reserve.)
   A. Form of argument (two examples).
      1. Example #1: Apply new evidence and/or theoretical approach to an existing scholarly argument, either in refutation or extension.
         a. Engaging with the work of a single scholar: After establishing general scope of current discourse, engage closely with that scholar's essay (following his or her organization works well here), bringing in new evidence/approaches with each point.
         b. Engaging with the work of multiple scholars: After establishing general scope of current discourse, establish a particular facet in more depth, then continue as in "a" above. This approach is useful when there are multiple scholarly works using similar approaches and/or working on the same text(s). How you organize this kind of argument depends on several variables; email for an appointment to discuss options.
      2. Example #2: Identify a lacuna in extant scholarly discourse and, after establishing that lacuna, initiate a new critical direction by forwarding your own argument. (You can use various scholarly esays as touchstones throughout your argument; the organization of your argument will depend entirely on you.)

Syllabus 5

Undergraduate Literature Seminar in English and Women's Studies
(cross-listed)
Women & Literature
Adapted from Catherine R. Mintler

Representing Women: Sex and Gender in the Twentieth Century

Course Description

This upper level English/Women's Studies course will explore changes in how women have been represented by twentieth-century authors. More specifically, we will examine how novels written from the early 1900s through the 1990s have challenged normative, homogenous, & essentialist representations of the feminine gender and female sexuality. Course readings will engage issues involving women as sexual agents & sexual objects, explore how women have negotiated various "economies of exchange" like marriage, and examine how women have resisted different forms of social and economic objectification while at the same time redefining their image and roles as women. Some readings today may seem revolutionary in their frank accounts of sex or sexuality, while others speak to other underlying prejudices, such as racism or classism. Whether subtly or more obviously, they offer a critique of status quo representations of sex and gender, often as these identity categories relate to race and class. Taken together, these novels offer examples of the once-radical (but now more commonly accepted) theory that identity, including gender and sexuality, is socially constructed.

Readings
Barnes, Djuna. *Nightwood*. New Directions, 2006.
Chopin, Kate. *The Awakening*. Avon, 1982.
Hemingway, Ernest. *The Garden of Eden*. Scribner, 2003.
Hurston, Zora Neale. *Their Eyes Were Watching God*. Harper, 2006.
Keller, Nora Okja. *Comfort Woman*. Virago, 1998.
Lawrence, D. H. *Lady Chatterley's Lover*. Penguin Classics, 2006.
Maso, Carol. *The American Woman in the Chinese Hat*. Plume, 1995.
Obejas, Achy. *Memory Mambo*. Cleis Press, 1996.
Thurman, Wallace. *The Blacker the Berry*. Touchstone, 1996.

Woolf, Virginia. *Mrs. Dalloway.* Harcourt, 1989.
Shorter pieces that supplement our readings are available on electronic reserve

Course Schedule

Week I: Introductions; Read in class and discuss "The Yellow Wallpaper" by Gilman and "Patterns" by Lowell

Week II: *The Awakening* by Chopin; "Aunt Jennifer's Tigers" by Rich (electronic reserve); Response Paper #1

Week III: *Lady Chatterley's Lover* by Lawrence; "Cocksure Women and Hensure Men" (electronic reserve); RP #2

Week IV: *Lady Chatterley's Lover,* continued

Week V: *Their Eyes Were Watching God* by Hurston; "Girl" by Kincaid (electronic reserve); RP #3

Week VI: *The Blacker the Berry* by Thurman; RP #4

Week VII: *Mrs. Dalloway* by Woolf; excerpt from *A Room of One's Own* (electronic reserve); RP #5

Week VIII: *Nightwood* by Barnes; RP #6

Week IX: Analytical Paper Due; Midterm

Week X: *The Garden of Eden* by Hemingway; RP #7; Final paper/project proposals due; Brief final project idea presentations

Week XI: *The American Woman in the Chinese Hat* by Maso; excerpt from Maso essay (electronic reserve); RP #8

Week XII: *Memory Mambo* by Obejas; RP #9. Annotated Bibliography draft due

Week XIII: *Comfort Woman* by Keller; excerpt from *The Warrior Woman* by Hong Kingston (electronic reserve); RP #10; Annotated Bibliography due

Week XIV: Student-directed open forum discussion. Annotated Bibliographies returned with feedback

Week XV: Study week—sign up for Final Project conferences

Exam Week: Final Exams due Monday of Final Exam week; Final Project will be presented during scheduled exam time

Works Cited

Adelman, Janet. *Suffocating Mothers: Fantasies of Maternal Origin in Shakespeare's Plays, Hamlet to The Tempest.* New York and London: Routledge, 1992.

Alajalov, Constantin. "Vanity Fair's Own Paper Dolls—No. 5." *Vanity Fair* (March 1934): 29.

Aldridge, John. *After the Lost Generation: A Critical Study of the Writers of Two Wars.* New York: McGraw Hill, 1951.

Altman, Meryl. "Posthumous Queer: Hemingway Among Others." *The Hemingway Review* 30.1 (2010): 129–41.

Atkinson, Dwight. *Alternative Approaches to Second Language Acquisition.* New York: Routledge, 2011.

Bak, John S. *Homo Americanus: Ernest Hemingway, Tennessee Williams, and Queer Masculinities.* Madison, NJ: Fairleigh Dickinson UP, 2010.

Baker, Carlos. *Ernest Hemingway: A Life Story.* New York: Scribner's, 1969.

———. *Hemingway: The Writer as Artist.* Princeton, NJ: Princeton UP, 1972.

Barlowe, Jamie. "Hemingway's Gender Training." *A Historical Guide to Ernest Hemingway.* Ed. Linda Wagner-Martin. Oxford: Oxford UP, 2000. 117–53.

———. "Re-reading Women: The Example of Catherine Barkley." *The Hemingway Review* 12.2 (1993): 24–35.

Barnard, Rita. "Modern American Fiction." *The Cambridge Companion to American Modernism.* Ed. Walter Kalaidjian. Cambridge: Cambridge UP, 2005. 39–67.

Baym, Nina. "'Actually I Felt Sorry for the Lion': Reading Hemingway's 'The Short Happy Life of Francis Macomber.'" Rpt. *Feminism and American Literary History: Essays.* New Brunswick, NJ: Rutgers UP, 1992. 71–80.

Bederman, Gail. *Manliness and Civilization: A Cultural History of Gender and Race in the United States, 1880–1917.* Chicago: U of Chicago P, 1995.

Beegel, Susan F. "Conclusion: The Critical Reputation of Ernest Hemingway." *The Cambridge Companion to Ernest Hemingway.* Ed. Scott Donaldson. Cambridge: Cambridge UP, 1996.

———. "Santiago and the Eternal Feminine: Gendering *La Mar* in *The Old Man and the Sea.*" *Hemingway and Women: Female Critics and the Female Voice.* Ed. Lawrence R. Broer and Gloria Holland. Tuscaloosa: U of Alabama P, 2002. 131–56.

———. "Second Growth: The Ecology of Loss in 'Fathers and Sons.'" *New Essays on Hemingway's Short Fiction.* Ed. Paul Smith. Cambridge: Cambridge UP, 1998. 75–110.

Bell, Millicent. "*A Farewell to Arms:* Pseudoautobiography and Personal Metaphor." *Ernest Hemingway: The Writer in Context.* Ed. James Nagel. Madison: U of Wisconsin P, 1984. 107–28.

Bender, Bert. *Evolution and "The Sex Problem": American Narratives during the Eclipse of Darwinism.* Kent, OH: Kent State UP, 2004.

Berlant, Lauren. *The Female Complaint: The Unfinished Business of Sentimentality in American Culture.* Durham, NC: Duke UP, 2008.

Blackmore, David. "'In New York It'd Mean I Was a . . . ': Masculine Anxiety and Period Discourses of Sexuality in *The Sun Also Rises.*" *The Hemingway Review* 18.1 (1998): 49–67.

Bloom, Harold. "Character Profile." *Nick Adams.* Ed. Harold Bloom. Broomall, PA: Chelsea House Publishers, 2004.

Bonds, Patrick Blair. "Hemingway, Gender Identity, and the 'Paris 1922' Apprenticeship." *The Hemingway Review* 29.1 (2009): 123–33.

Booth, Wayne C. *The Vocation of a Teacher: Rhetorical Winner Take Nothing Occasions, 1967–1988.* Chicago: U of Chicago P, 1989.

Bordo, Susan. *The Male Body.* New York: Farrar, Straus, and Giroux, 1999.

Brandl, Klaus. *Communicative Language Teaching in Action: Putting Principles to Work.* Upper Saddle River, NJ: Pearson/Prentice Hall, 2009.

Brasch, James D., and Joseph Sigman. *Hemingway's Library: A Composite Record.* New York: Garland, 1981.

Brenner, Gerry. *Concealments in Hemingway's Works.* Columbus: Ohio State UP, 1983.

Broer, Lawrence R. *Vonnegut and Hemingway: Writers at War.* Columbia: U of South Carolina P, 2011.

Broer, Lawrence R., and Gloria Holland, eds. *Hemingway and Women: Female Critics and the Female Voice.* Tuscaloosa: U of Alabama P, 2002.

Brogan, Jacqueline Vaught. "Strange Fruits in *The Garden of Eden:* 'The Mysticism of Money,' *The Great Gatsby*—and *A Moveable Feast.*" *French Connections: Hemingway and Fitzgerald Abroad.* Ed. J. Gerald Kennedy and Jackson R. Bryer. New York: St. Martin's, 1998. 235–54.

Brown, Judith. *Glamour in Six Dimensions: Modernism and the Radiance of Form.* Ithaca, NY: Cornell UP, 2009.

Bruccoli, Matthew J. Introduction. *Hemingway and the Mechanism of Fame.* Ed. Bruccoli, with Judith S. Baughman. Columbia: U of South Carolina P, 2006. xvii–xxvi.

Buckley, J. F. "Echoes of Closeted Desires: The Narrator and Character Voices of Jake Barnes." *The Hemingway Review* 19.2 (2000): 73–87.

Buell, Lawrence. "Literary History without Sexism: Feminist Studies and Canonical Reconception." *American Literature* 59.1 (1987): 102–14.

Burkhalter, Nancy. "Women's Magazines and the Suffrage Movement: Did They Help." *Journal of American Culture* 19.2 (1996): 13.

Burwell, Rose Marie. *Hemingway: The Postwar Years and the Posthumous Novels.* Cambridge: Cambridge UP, 1996.

Butler, Judith. *Gender Trouble: Feminism and the Subversion of Identity.* 2nd ed. New York: Routledge, 1990.

Caughie, Pamela L. "'Passing' and Identity: A Literary Perspective on Gender and Sexual Diversity." *God, Science, and Sexual Diversity: An Interdisciplinary Approach to Christian Ethic*. Ed. Patricia Jung and Aana Vigen. Urbana: U of Illinois P, 2010. 195–216.

———. "Passing as Modernism." *Modernism/modernity* 12.3 (September 2005): 385–406.

Chu, C. Y. Cyrus, and Ruoh-Rong Yu. *Understanding Chinese Families: A Comparative Study of Taiwan and Southeast China*. New York: Oxford UP, 2010.

Cixous, Hélène. "The Laugh of the Medusa." Trans. Keith Cohen and Paul Cohen. *Signs* 1.4 (1976): 875–93.

Cohen, Peter F. "'I Won't Kiss You. . . . I'll Send Your English Girl': Homoerotic Desire in *A Farewell to Arms*." *The Hemingway Review* 15.1 (1995): 42–53.

Comley, Nancy R. "Hemingway: The Economics of Survival." *Novel: A Forum on Fiction* 12.3 (1979): 244–53.

———. "Women." *Ernest Hemingway in Context*. Ed. Debra A. Moddelmog and Suzanne del Gizzo. Cambridge: Cambridge UP, 2013. 409–17.

Comley, Nancy R., and Robert Scholes. *Hemingway's Genders: Rereading the Hemingway Text*. New Haven, CT: Yale UP, 1994.

Cuddy-Keane, Melba, Adam Hammond, and Alexandra Peat. "Woman, New Woman." *Modernism: Keywords*. Chichester, UK: Wiley-Blackwell, 2014. 238–45.

Curnutt, Kirk. "Review: Junk Bonds in a Jerrybuilt America." *The F. Scott Fitzgerald Review* 10 (2012): 154–63.

Davidson, Cathy N., and Arnold E. Davidson. "Decoding the Hemingway Hero in *The Sun Also Rises*." *New Essays on* The Sun Also Rises. Ed. Linda Wagner-Martin. New York: Cambridge UP, 1990. 83–107.

del Gizzo, Suzanne. "'Glow-in-the-Dark Authors': Hemingway's Celebrity and Legacy in *Under Kilimanjaro*." *The Hemingway Review* 29.2 (2010): 7–27.

del Gizzo, Suzanne, and Frederic J. Svoboda, eds. *Hemingway's* The Garden of Eden: *Twenty-Five Years of Criticism*. Kent, OH: Kent State UP, 2012.

Dell'Orto, Giovanna. "'Memory and Imagination Are the Great Deterrents': Martha Gellhorn as War Correspondent and Literary Author." *Journal of American Culture* 27.3 (2004): 303–14.

Dreger, Alice. *Intersex in the Age of Ethics*. Hagerstown, MD: University Pub. Group, 1999.

DuCille, Ann. "The Short Happy Life of Black Feminist Theory." *Differences: A Journal of Feminist Cultural Studies* 21.1 (2010): 32–47.

Dudley, Marc Kevin. *Hemingway, Race, and Art: Bloodlines and the Color Line*. Kent, OH: Kent State UP, 2012.

Duggan, Lisa, and Nan D. Hunter. *Sex Wars: Sexual Dissent and Political Culture*. New York: Routledge, 1995.

Earle, David M. *All Man! Hemingway, 1950s Men's Magazines, and the Masculine Persona*. Kent, OH: Kent State UP, 2009.

Eastman, Max. "Bull in the Afternoon." Rev. of *Death in the Afternoon*, by Ernest Hemingway. *New Republic* (7 June 1933): 94–96.

Eby, Carl. "'He Felt the Change So That It Hurt Him All Through': Sodomy and Transvestic Hallucination in Late Hemingway." *The Hemingway Review* 25.1 (2005): 77–95.

———. *Hemingway's Fetishism: Psychoanalysis and the Mirror of Manhood.* Albany: State U of New York P, 1999.

———. "Who Is 'The Destructive Type'? Re-Reading Literary Jealousy and Destruction in *The Garden of Eden*." *The Hemingway Review* 33.2 (2014): 99–106.

Ehrenreich, Barbara. *The Hearts of Men: American Dreams and the Flight from Commitment.* Garden City, NY: Anchor Press/Doubleday, 1984.

Elliott, Ira. "*A Farewell to Arms* and Hemingway's Crisis of Masculine Values." *LIT: Literary Interpretive Theory* 4.4 (1993): 291–304.

———. "Performance Art: Jake Barnes and 'Masculine' Signification in *The Sun Also Rises*." *American Literature* 63.1 (1995): 77–94. Rpt. in *Ernest Hemingway's* The Sun Also Rises*: A Casebook.* Ed. Linda Wagner-Martin. Oxford: Oxford UP, 2002. 65–80.

Ellis, Havelock. *Studies in the Psychology of Sex.* New York: Random House, 1936.

Faderman, Lillian. *Surpassing the Love of Men: Romantic Friendship and Love between Women from the Renaissance to the Present.* New York: William Morrow, 1981.

Fantina, Richard. *Ernest Hemingway: Machismo and Masochism.* New York: Palgrave Macmillan, 2005.

Faulkner, William. *As I Lay Dying.* New York: Vintage, 1990.

Fausto-Sterling, Anne. *Sexing the Body: Gender Politics and the Construction of Sexuality.* New York: Basic Books, 2000.

"Fears for Modern Woman." *New York Times.* 23 June 1921: 16.

Ferguson, Roderick A. *Aberrations in Black: Toward a Queer of Color Critique.* Minneapolis: U of Minnesota P, 2003.

Fetterley, Judith. "*A Farewell to Arms*: Hemingway's 'Resentful Cryptogram.'" *Journal of Popular Culture* 10.1 (1976): 203–14.

———. *The Resisting Reader: A Feminist Approach to American Fiction.* Bloomington: Indiana UP, 1978.

Fiedler, Leslie A. *Love and Death in the American Novel.* 1960. Rpt., Champaign, IL: Dalkey Archive Press, 2003.

Fleming, Robert E. "The Endings of Hemingway's *Garden of Eden*." *American Literature* 61.2 (1989): 261–70.

Fore, Dana. "Life Unworthy of Life? Masculinity, Disability, and Guilt in *The Sun Also Rises*." *The Hemingway Review* 26.2 (2007): 74–88.

Forter, Greg. "Melancholy Modernism: Gender and the Politics of Mourning in *The Sun Also Rises*." *The Hemingway Review* 21.1 (2001): 22–37.

Foucault, Michel. *Herculine Barbin.* New York: Pantheon Books, 1980.

———. *The History of Sexuality.* Vol. 1. New York: Vintage Books, 1990.

Freud, Sigmund. "Fetishism." *The Standard Edition of the Complete Psychoanalytic Works of Sigmund Freud.* Trans. James Strachey. Vol. 21. London: Hogarth, 1963.

———. "The Splitting of the Ego in the Defensive Process." *The Standard Edition of the Complete Psychoanalytic Works of Sigmund Freud.* Trans. James Strachey. Vol. 23. London: Hogarth, 1964.

Gallatin, Albert. "Plea for Old-Time Girls." *New York Times.* 22 Aug. 1926: 1.

Gandal, Keith. *The Gun and the Pen: Hemingway, Fitzgerald, Faulkner and the Fiction of Mobilization.* Oxford: Oxford UP, 2008.

Gareis, Elisabeth, Martine Allard, and Jackie Saindon. "The Novel as Textbook." *TESL Canada Journal* 26.2 (2009): 136–47.

Gellhorn, Martha. *The Face of War.* New York: Atlantic Monthly, 1994.

Gilbert, Sandra M. "Finding Atlantis: Thirty Years of Exploring Women's Literary Traditions in English." *Rereading Women: Thirty Years of Exploring Our Literary Traditions.* New York: W.W. Norton, 2011.

Gilbert, Sandra, and Susan Gubar. *The Madwoman in the Attic: The Woman Writer and the Nineteenth-Century Literary Imagination.* New Haven, CT: Yale UP, 1979.

———. *No Man's Land: The Place of the Woman Writer in the Twentieth Century, Volume II: Sexchanges.* New Haven, CT: Yale UP, 1991.

Gilman, Charlotte Perkins. *Women and Economics.* Mineola, NY: Dover, 1998.

Gladstein, Mimi. *The Indestructible Woman in the Works of Faulkner, Hemingway, and Steinbeck.* Ann Arbor: UMI P, 1986.

Glass, Loren Daniel. *Authors Inc.: Literary Celebrity in the Modern United States, 1880–1980.* New York: New York UP, 2004.

Gleeson-White, Sarah. "A Peculiarly Southern Form of Ugliness: Eudora Welty, Carson McCullers, and Flannery O'Connor." *The Southern Literary Journal* 36.1 (2003): 46–57.

Greenacre, Phyllis. *Emotional Growth: Psychoanalytic Studies of the Gifted and a Great Variety of Other Individuals.* 2 Vols. New York: International Universities P, 1971.

Hackett, Francis. "Hemingway: A Farewell to Arms." *Saturday Review of Literature* (6 Aug. 1949): 32–33.

Halberstam, Judith. *Female Masculinity.* Durham, NC: Duke UP, 1998.

Halperin, David. *Saint Foucault: Towards a Gay Hagiography.* Oxford: Oxford UP, 1995.

Hammond, Adam, Alexandra Peat, and Melba Cuddy-Keane. "Woman, New Woman." *Modernism: Keywords.* Chichester, UK: Wiley-Blackwell, 2014. 238–45.

Haralson, Eric. *Henry James and Queer Modernity.* Cambridge: Cambridge UP, 2003.

Harding, Brian. "Ernest Hemingway: Men With, or Without, Women." *American Declarations of Love.* Ed. Ann Massa. New York: St. Martin's, 1990. 104–21.

Hatten, Charles. "The Crisis of Masculinity, Reified Desire, and Catherine Barkley in *A Farewell to Arms.*" *Journal of the History of Sexuality* 4.1 (1993): 76–98.

Hausman, Bernice. "Recent Transgender Theory." *Feminist Studies* 27.2 (2001): 465–90.

Haytock, Jennifer. "Hemingway, Wilhelm, and a Style for Lesbian Representation." *The Hemingway Review* 32.1 (2012): 100–18.

Helstern, Linda Lizut. "Indians, Woodcraft, and the Construction of White Masculinity: The Boyhood of Nick Adams." *The Hemingway Review* 20.1 (2000): 61–78.

Hemingway, Ernest. *By-Line Ernest Hemingway: Selected Articles and Dispatches of Four Decades.* Ed. William White. New York: Scribner's, 1967.

———. *The Complete Short Stories of Ernest Hemingway: The Finca Vigía Edition.* New York: Scribner's, 1987.

———. *A Farewell to Arms.* New York: Scribner, 1995.

———. *The Garden of Eden.* New York: Scribner, 2003.

———. Letter to Maxwell Perkins. 8 October 1942. Charles Scribner's Sons Archive, Princeton University Library, Princeton, NJ.

———, ed. *Men At War: The Best War Stories of All Time.* New York: Crown, 1942.

———. *A Moveable Feast: The Restored Edition.* New York: Scribner, 2009.

———. "Nobel Prize Acceptance Speech." *Conversations with Ernest Hemingway.* Ed. Matthew J. Bruccoli. Jackson: UP of Mississippi, 1986.

———. *In Our Time.* New York: Scribners, 2003.

———. "The Short Happy Life of Francis Macomber." *Cosmopolitan.* (Sept. 1936): 30–33, 166–72.

———. *The Sun Also Rises.* New York: Scribners, 2003.

———. *To Have and Have Not.* New York: Scribner, 2003.

Hemingway, Hadley Richardson. Letter to Ernest Hemingway. 28 January 1921. John F. Kennedy Library, Boston.

Hemingway, Marcelline. *At the Hemingways: A Family Portrait.* Boston: Little, Brown, 1962.

Hemingway, Mary. *How It Was.* New York: Knopf, 1976.

"Hemingway Slaps Eastman in the Face." *New York Times.* 14 Aug. 1937. <www.nytimes.com>.

Henry, George W. *All the Sexes: A Study of Masculinity and Femininity.* New York: Rinehart, 1955.

Herbst, Josephine. *The Starched Blue Sky of Spain and Other Memoirs.* New York: HarperCollins, 1992.

Hewson, Marc. "A Matter of Love or Death: Hemingway's Developing Psychosexuality in *For Whom the Bell Tolls.*" *Studies in the Novel* 36.2 (2004): 170–84.

———. "'The Real Story of Ernest Hemingway': Cixous, Gender, and *A Farewell to Arms.*" *The Hemingway Review* 22.2 (2003): 51–62.

Holder, Alan. "The Other Hemingway." *Twentieth-Century Literature* 9.3 (1963): 153–57.

Jensen, Kimberly. *Mobilizing Minerva: American Women in the First World War.* Urbana: U of Illinois P, 2008.

Johnston, Kenneth J. "In Defense of the Unhappy Margot Macomber." *The Hemingway Review* 2.2 (1983): 44–47.

Josephs, Allen. "Hemingway's Out of Body Experience." *The Hemingway Review* 2.2 (1983): 11–17.

Justice, Hilary K. *The Bones of the Others: The Hemingway Text from the Lost Manuscripts to the Posthumous Novels.* Kent, OH: Kent State UP, 2006.

Katz, Jonathan Ned. *Gay American History: Lesbians and Gay Men in the U.S.A.* 1976. Rev. ed. New York: Meridian, 1990.

Kaye, Jeremy. "The 'Whine' of Jewish Manhood: Re-Reading Hemingway's Anti-Semitism, Reimagining Robert Cohn." *The Hemingway Review* 25.2 (2006): 44–60.

Kennedy, J. Gerald. "Hemingway's Gender Trouble." *American Literature* 63.2 (1991): 187–207.

Kennedy, X. J., and Dana Gioia, eds. *Backpack Literature: An Introduction to Fiction, Poetry, Drama, and Writing.* Boston: Pearson, 2012.

Kert, Bernice. *The Hemingway Women.* 1983. Rpt., New York: Norton, 1986.

Kilcup, Karen. "Embodied Pedagogies: Femininity, Diversity, and Community in Anthologies of Women's Writing, 1836–2009." *Legacy* 26.2 (2009): 299–328.

Kimmel, Michael. "Integrating Men into the Curriculum." *Duke Journal of Gender Law & Policy* 4 (1997): 181–95.

———. *Manhood in America: A Cultural History*. New York: Free Press, 1996.

Kimmel, Michael S., Jeff Hearn, and R. W. Connell, eds. *Handbook of Studies on Men & Masculinities*. Thousand Oaks, CA: Sage, 2005.

Kinsey, Alfred Charles, Wardell B. Pomeroy, and Clyde E. Martin. *Sexual Behavior in the Human Male*. Philadelphia: W. B. Saunders, 1948.

Kitunda, Jeremiah M. "Ernest Hemingway's African Book: An Appraisal." *The Hemingway Review* 28.1 (2008): 107–13.

———. "'Love Is a Dunghill . . . And I'm the Cock That Gets on It to Crow': Ernest Hemingway's Farcical Adoration of Africa." *Hemingway in Africa*. Ed. Miriam B. Mandel. Rochester, NY: Camden House, 2012. 121–48.

Knights, Ben, ed. *Masculinities in Text and Teaching*. Hampshire, UK: Palgrave Macmillan, 2008.

Kobler, J. F. "Hemingway's 'The Sea Change': A Sympathetic View of Homosexuality." *Arizona Quarterly* 26 (1970): 318–24.

Kosbia, Sara. "Dawn Powell: Hemingway's 'Favorite Living Writer.'" *The Hemingway Review* 29.2 (2010): 46–60.

Kosiba, Sara, and Tim Page. "Memories of Hemingway: A Letter from Dawn Powell to Carlos Baker, 10 May 1965." *The Hemingway Review* 30.1 (2010): 152–57.

Lacan, Jacques. *The Seminar of Jacques Lacan, Book XI: The Four Fundamental Concepts of Psycho-Analysis*. Trans. Alan Sheridan. New York: W. W. Norton, 1998.

Landers, James. *The Improbable First Century of* Cosmopolitan *Magazine*. Columbia: U of Missouri P, 2010.

Lansky, Ellen. "The Barnes Complex: Ernest Hemingway, Djuna Barnes, *The Sun Also Rises*, and *Nightwood*." *The Languages of Addiction*. Ed. Jane Lilienfeld and Jeffrey Oxford. New York: St. Martin's, 1999. 205–24.

Lawrence, D. H. "Cocksure Women and Hensure Men." *The Gender of Modernism: A Critical Anthology*. Ed. Bonnie Kime Scott. Bloomington: Indiana UP, 1990: 227–29.

Lebowitz, Alan. "No Farewell to Arms." *Uses of Literature*. Ed. Monroe Engel. Cambridge, MA: Harvard UP, 1973.

Lee, James, and Bill VanPatten. *Making Communicative Language Teaching Happen*. New York: McGraw-Hill, 2003.

Leff, Leonard J. *Hemingway and His Conspirators: Hollywood, Scribners, and the Making of American Celebrity Culture*. Lanham, MD: Rowman & Littlefield, 1999.

Leinwald, Gerald. *1927: The High Tide of the Twenties*. New York: Four Walls Eight Windows, 2001.

Leland, Jacob Michael. "Yes, That Is a Roll of Bills in My Pocket: The Economy of Masculinity in *The Sun Also Rises*." *The Hemingway Review* 23.2 (2004): 37–46.

Leslie, Edgar. "Masculine Women, Feminine Men." New York: Okeh Records, 1926.

Lewis, Nghana. "Truth, Lies, and Racial Consequences in Ernest Hemingway's *True at First Light: A Fictional Memoir*." *Comparative American Studies* 4.4 (2006): 459–70.

Lewis, Robert W. Jr. *Hemingway on Love*. Austin: U of Texas P, 1965.

Long, Samantha. "Catherine as Transgender: Dreaming Identity in *The Garden of Eden*." *The Hemingway Review* 32.2 (2013): 42–56.

Lynn, Kenneth. *Hemingway*. New York: Simon & Schuster, 1987.

Lyon, Janet. "Gender and Sexuality." *The Cambridge Companion to American Modernism*. Ed. Walter Kalaidjian. Cambridge: Cambridge UP, 2005. 221–41.
Mandel, Miriam B. "Ferguson and Lesbian Love: Unspoken Subplots in *A Farewell to Arms*." *The Hemingway Review* 14.1 (1994): 18–24.
———, ed. *Hemingway in Africa*. Rochester, NY: Camden House, 2012.
Marshall, Ian. "Rereading Hemingway: Rhetorics of Whiteness, Labor, and Identity." *Hemingway and the Black Renaissance*. Ed. Gary Edward Holcomb and Charles Scruggs. Columbus: Ohio State UP, 2012. 177–213.
Martin, Wendy. "Brett Ashley as New Woman in *The Sun Also Rises*." *Ernest Hemingway's* The Sun Also Rises: *A Casebook*. Ed. Linda Wagner-Martin. Oxford: Oxford UP, 2002. 47–62.
Martínez, Ernesto Javier. *On Making Sense: Queer Race Narratives of Intelligibility*. Stanford, CA: Stanford UP, 2013.
McGowan, Philip. *American Carnival: Seeing and Reading American Culture*. Santa Barbara, CA: Greenwood Press, 2001.
McLoughlin, Kate, ed. *The Cambridge Companion to War Writing*. Cambridge: Cambridge UP, 2009.
Mellow, James. *Hemingway: A Life Without Consequences*. Boston: Houghton Mifflin, 1992.
Merrill, Robert. "Demoting Hemingway: Feminist Criticism and the Canon." *American Literature* 60.2 (1988): 255–68.
Messent, Peter B. *Ernest Hemingway*. New York: St. Martin's, 1992.
Meyerowitz, Joanne. *How Sex Changed: A History of Transsexuality in the United States*. Cambridge, MA: Harvard UP, 2004.
Miller, Linda Patterson. "In Love with Papa." *Hemingway and Women: Female Critics and the Female Voice*. Ed. Lawrence R. Broer and Gloria Holland. Tuscaloosa: U of Alabama P, 2002. 3–22.
Moddelmog, Debra A. "Queer Families in Hemingway's Fiction." *Hemingway and Women: Female Critics and the Female Voice*. Ed. Lawrence R. Broer and Gloria Holland. Tuscaloosa: U of Alabama P, 2002. 297–324.
———. *Reading Desire: In Pursuit of Ernest Hemingway*. Ithaca, NY: Cornell UP, 1999.
———. "Sex, Sexuality, and Marriage." *Ernest Hemingway in Context*. Ed. Debra A. Moddelmog and Suzanne del Gizzo. New York: Cambridge UP, 2013. 357–66.
———. "'We Live in a Country Where Nothing Makes Any Difference': The Queer Sensibility of *A Farewell to Arms*." *The Hemingway Review* 28.2 (2009): 7–24.
Monteiro, George. "'This Is My Pal Bugs': Ernest Hemingway's 'The Battler.'" *New Critical Approaches to the Short Stories of Ernest Hemingway*. Ed. Jackson J. Benson. Durham, NC: Duke UP, 1990. 224–28.
Moreland, Kim. *The Medievalist Impulse in American Literature: Twain, Adams, Fitzgerald, Hemingway*. Charlottesville: U of Virginia P, 1996.
Morrison, Toni. *Playing in the Dark: Whiteness and the Literary Imagination*. Cambridge, MA: Harvard UP, 1992.
Mulvey, Laura. "Visual Pleasure and Narrative Cinema." *Screen* 16.3 (1975): 6–18.
Muñoz, José Esteban. *Disidentifications: Queers of Color and the Performance of Politics*. Minneapolis: U of Minnesota P, 1999.

Murdock, Catherine Gilbert. *Domesticating Drink: Women, Men, and Alcohol in America, 1870–1940*. Baltimore: Johns Hopkins UP, 1998.
Nolan, Charles J. "Hemingway's Women's Movement." *The Hemingway Review* 3.2 (1984): 14–22.
Nydell, Margaret K. *Understanding Arabs: A Guide for Westerners*. Yarmouth, ME: Intercultural Press, 2002.
Nyström, Anton Kristen. *The Natural Laws of Sexual Life: Medical-sociological Researches*. 3rd Swedish ed. Trans. Carl Sandzen. St. Louis: C. V. Mosby, 1919.
O'Brien, Sharon. "*Women and Death: Linkages in Western Thought and Literature*, and: *A Portrait of the Artist as a Young Woman: The Writer as Heroine in American Literature*, and: *Insatiable Appetites: Twentieth-Century American Women's Bestsellers*, and: *Fantasy and Reconciliation: Contemporary Formulas of Women's Romance Fiction*, and: *Reading the Romance: Women, Patriarchy, and Popular Literature* (Review)." *Modern Fiction Studies* 32.2 (1985): 353–58.
Palumbo-Liu, David. *The Deliverance of Others*. Durham, NC: Duke UP, 2012.
Parker, Dorothy. *The Portable Dorothy Parker*. New York: Penguin, 2006.
———. "Soldiers of the Republic." *Her War Story: Twentieth-Century Women Write about War*. Ed. Sayre P. Sheldon. Carbondale: Southern Illinois UP, 1999.
Parsons, Elsie Clews. "The Zuni *La'mana*" *American Anthropologist*. 18.4 (1916): 521–28.
Patterson, Martha H. *Beyond the Gibson Girl: Reimagining the American New Woman 1895–1915*. Urbana: U of Illinois P, 2005.
Pettipiece, Deirdre Anne McVicker. *Sex Theories and the Shaping of Two Moderns: Hemingway and H.D.* New York: Routledge, 2002.
Picken, Jonathan D. "Helping Foreign Language Learners to Make Sense of Literature with Metaphor Awareness-raising." *Language Awareness*, 14.2 (2005): 142–52.
Pollan, Michael. *The Omnivore's Dilemma: A Natural History of Four Meals*. New York: Penguin, 2006.
Powell, Dawn. *Turn, Magic Wheel*. New York: Library of America, 2001.
Pullin, Faith. "Hemingway and the Secret Language of Hate." *Ernest Hemingway: New Critical Essays*. Ed. A. Robert Lee. London and Totowa, NJ: Vision Press Limited and Barnes & Noble Books, 1983.
Putnam, Ann. "On Defiling Eden: The Search for Eve in the Garden of Sorrows." *Hemingway and Women: Female Critics and the Female Voice*. Ed. Lawrence R. Broer and Gloria Holland. Tuscaloosa: U of Alabama P, 2002.
Raeburn, John. *Fame Became of Him: Hemingway as Public Writer*. Bloomington: Indiana UP, 1984.
Rainey, Lawrence. "The Price of Modernism: Publishing *The Waste Land*." *Institutions of Modernism: Literary Elites and Public Culture*. New Haven, CT: Yale UP, 1998. 77–106.
Ramsey, Michele. "Selling Social Status: Women and Automobile Advertisements from 1910–1920." *Women and Language* 28.1 (2005): 26–38.
Reik, Theodor. *Of Love and Lust: On the Psychoanalysis of Romantic and Sexual Emotions*. New York: Farrar, Straus, and Cudahy, 1957.
Reynolds, Michael. *Hemingway: The 1930s*. New York: Norton, 1997.

———. *Hemingway: The American Homecoming*. Oxford: Blackwell, 1992.
———. *Hemingway: The Paris Years*. Oxford: Blackwell, 1989.
———. *Hemingway's Reading, 1910–1940: An Inventory*. Princeton: Princeton UP, 1980.
———. *The Young Hemingway*. Oxford and New York: Basil Blackwell, 1986.
Rogers, Katherine M. *The Troublesome Helpmate: A History of Misogyny in Literature*. Seattle: U of Washington P, 1966.
Rohy, Valerie. "A Darker Past in *The Garden of Eden*." *Anachronism and Its Others: Sexuality, Race, Temporality*. Albany: State U of New York P, 2009. 99–119.
———. "Hemingway, Literalism, and Transgender Reading." *Twentieth-Century Literature* 57.2 (2011): 148–79.
Rotundo, Anthony E. *American Manhood: Transformations in Masculinity from the Revolution to the Modern Era*. New York: Basic Books, 1993.
Sanderson, Rena. "Hemingway and Gender History." *The Cambridge Companion to Hemingway*. Ed. Scott Donaldson. Cambridge: Cambridge UP, 1996. 170–96.
———. "Hemingway's Literary Sisters: The Author through the Eyes of Women Writers." *Hemingway and Women: Female Critics and the Female Voice*. Ed. Lawrence R. Broer and Gloria Holland. Tuscaloosa: U of Alabama P, 2002. 276–94.
———. "Women in Fitzgerald's Fiction." *The Cambridge Companion to F. Scott Fitzgerald*. Ed. Ruth Prigozy. Cambridge: Cambridge UP, 2002. 143–63.
Scott, Bonnie Kime, ed. *The Gender of Modernism: A Critical Anthology*. Bloomington: Indiana UP, 1990.
Sedgwick, Eve Kosofsky. *Epistemology of the Closet*. Berkeley: U of California P, 1990.
Smith, Paul. *A Reader's Guide to the Short Stories of Ernest Hemingway*. Boston: G. K. Hall & Co., 1989.
Spanier, Sandra Whipple. "Catherine Barkley and the Hemingway Code: Ritual and Survival in *A Farewell to Arms*." *Modern Critical Interpretations:* A Farewell to Arms. Ed. Harold Bloom. New York: Chelsea, 1987. 131–48.
Spanier, Sandra, and Robert W. Trogdon, eds. *The Letters of Ernest Hemingway*. Cambridge: Cambridge UP, 2011, 2013, 2015, and forthcoming.
Spilka, Mark. "Hemingway's Barbershop Quintet: The Garden of Eden Manuscript." *Novel: A Forum on Fiction* 21.1 (1987): 29–55.
———. *Hemingway's Quarrel with Androgyny*. Lincoln: U of Nebraska P, 1990.
———. "The Importance of Being Androgynous." *Hemingway: Essays of Reassessment*. Ed. Frank Scafella. New York: Oxford UP, 1991. 201–12.
Stecopoulos, Harry, and Michael Uebel, eds. *Race and the Subject of Masculinities*. Durham, NC: Duke UP, 1997.
Stein, Gertrude. *The Autobiography of Alice B. Toklas*. New York: Harcourt, Brace, 1933.
Steinach, Eugen. *Sex and Life: Forty Years of Biological and Medical Experiments*. New York: Viking, 1940.
Stoller, Robert. *Observing the Erotic Imagination*. New Haven and London: Yale UP, 1985.
———. *Presentations of Gender*. New Haven, CT: Yale UP, 1992.
———. *Sexual Excitement: Dynamics of Erotic Life*. London: Karnac Books, 1986.
Stoneback, H. R. *Reading Hemingway's* The Sun Also Rises: *Glossary and Commentary*. Kent, OH: Kent State UP, 2007.

St. Pierre, Scott. "Bent Hemingway: Straightness, Sexuality, Style." *GLQ* 16.3 (2010): 363–87.

Strong, Amy L. *Race and Identity in Hemingway's Fiction*. New York: Palgrave Macmillan, 2008.

Strychacz, Thomas. *Dangerous Masculinities: Conrad, Hemingway, and Lawrence*. Gainesville: UP of Florida, 2008.

———. *Hemingway's Theaters of Masculinity*. Baton Rouge: Louisiana State UP, 2003.

———. "Masculinity." *Ernest Hemingway in Context*. Ed. Debra A. Moddelmog and Suzanne del Gizzo. Cambridge: Cambridge UP, 2013. 277–86.

Takeuchi, Masaya. "Frederic's Conflict between Homosociality and Heterosexuality: War, Marvell, and Sculpture in *A Farewell to Arms*." *Midwest Quarterly* 53.1 (2011): 26–44.

Tanimoto, Chikako. "Queering Sexual Practices in 'Mr. and Mrs. Elliot.'" *The Hemingway Review* 32.1 (2012): 88–99.

———. "Subversion of the In/Out Model in Understanding Hemingway's Texts." *Genders* 39 (2004).

Toomer, Jean. *Cane*. Ed. Rudolph P. Byrd and Henry Louis Gates Jr. New York: W. W. Norton, 2011.

Traber, Daniel S. "Performing the Feminine in *A Farewell to Arms*." *The Hemingway Review* 24.2 (2005): 28–40.

Trogdon, Robert W. *The Lousy Racket: Hemingway, Scribners, and the Business of Literature*. Kent, OH: Kent State UP, 2007.

Turner, Catherine. "Changing American Literary Taste: Scribner's and Ernest Hemingway." *Marketing Modernism Between the Two World Wars*. Amherst: U of Massachusetts P, 2003. 145–72.

Tyler, Lisa. "'How Beautiful the Virgin Forests Were before the Loggers Came': An Ecofeminist Reading of Hemingway's 'The End of Something.'" *The Hemingway Review* 27.2 (2008): 60–73.

Valis, Noël, ed. *Teaching Representations of the Spanish Civil War*. New York: Modern Language Association, 2007.

Vernon, Alex. *Hemingway's Second War: Bearing Witness to the Spanish Civil War*. Iowa City: U of Iowa P, 2011.

———. *Soldiers Once and Still: Ernest Hemingway, James Salter, and Tim O'Brien*. Iowa City: U of Iowa P, 2004.

Wadden, Paul. "Barefoot in the Hemlocks: Nick Adams' Betrayal of Love in 'Ten Indians.'" *Nick Adams*. Ed. Harold Bloom. Broomall, PA: Chelsea House Publishers, 2004.

Wagner-Martin, Linda. "Proudly and Friendly and Gently: Women in Hemingway's Early Fiction." *College Literature* 7.3 (1980): 239–47.

———. "The Romance of Desire in Hemingway's Fiction." *Hemingway and Women: Female Critics and the Female Voice*. Ed. Lawrence R. Broer and Gloria Holland. Tuscaloosa: U of Alabama P, 2002. 54–69.

Walcott, William H. *Knowledge, Competence, and Communication: Chomsky, Freire, Searle, and Communicative Language Teaching*. Toronto: Black Rose Books, 2007.

Walezak, Émilie. "The 'I' and the Voice: Interpreting the Narrator's Acronym in Ernest

Hemingway's 'The Light of the World.'" *Journal of the Short Story in English* 49 (2007): 137–47. <http://jsse.revues.org/864>.

Warner, Michael. *Fear of a Queer Planet: Queer Politics and Social Theory.* Minneapolis: U of Minnesota P, 1993.

Weinstein, Philip. *Unknowing: The Work of Modernist Fiction.* Ithaca, NY: Cornell UP, 2005.

Welty, Eudora. "Petrified Man." *The Collected Stories of Eudora Welty.* Orlando: Harcourt, 1994. 17–28.

———. "Place in Fiction." *The Eye of the Story: Selected Essays and Reviews.* New York: Vintage, 1979. 131–32.

Westling, Louise H. *The Green Breast of the New World: Landscape, Gender, and American Fiction.* Athens: U of Georgia P, 1996.

Weston, Jessie. *From Ritual to Romance.* New York: Cosimo Classics, 2005.

Westwood, Gordon [aka Michael George Schofield]. *Society and the Homosexual.* New York: Dutton, 1953.

Wexler, Joyce. "E.R.A. for Hemingway: A Feminist Defense of *A Farewell to Arms.*" *Georgia Review* 35.1 (1981): 111–23.

Whitlow, Roger. *Cassandra's Daughters: The Women in Hemingway.* Westport, CT: Greenwood Press, 1984.

Willingham, Kathy. "Hemingway's *The Garden of Eden:* Writing with the Body." *The Hemingway Review* 12.2 (1993): 45–61.

Wilson, Edmund. Rev. of "Ernest Hemingway: Bourdon Gauge of Morale." *Atlantic* 164 (July 1939): 36–46.

———. "Hemingway: Gauge of Morale." *The Wound and the Bow: Seven Studies in Literature.* 1941. Rpt., New York: Oxford UP, 1965. 174–97.

Winnicott, D. W. "Transitional Objects and Transitional Phenomena." *International Journal of Psycho-Analysis* 34.2 (1953): 89–97.

Wolfe, Cary. "Fathers, Lovers, and Friend Killers: Rearticulating Gender and Race via Species in Hemingway." *Boundary 2* 29.1 (2002): 223–57.

Woolf, Virginia. "An Essay in Criticism." *Ernest Hemingway: The Critical Reception.* Ed. Robert O. Stephens. New York: Burt Franklin, 1977.

———. *Orlando: A Biography.* New York: Harcourt Brace, 1928.

———. *A Room of One's Own.* 1929. Orlando, FL: Harvest/Harcourt, 1989.

Worden, Daniel. *Masculine Style: The American West and Literary Modernism.* New York: Palgrave, 2011.

Wright-Cleveland, Margaret E. "*Cane* and *In Our Time:* A Literary Conversation about Race." *Hemingway and the Black Renaissance.* Ed. Gary Holcomb and Charles Scruggs. Columbus: Ohio State UP, 2012. 151–76.

Yamani, Mai. "Saudi Identity: Negotiating between Tradition and Modernity." *Arab Society and Culture: An Essential Reader.* Ed. Samir Khalaf and Roseanne Saad Khalaf. St. Paul, MN: Saqi, 2009. 129–40.

Yellis, Kenneth A. "Prosperity's Child: Some Thoughts on the Flapper." *American Quarterly* 21.1 (1969): 44–64.

Young, Philip. *Ernest Hemingway.* New York: Rinehart, 1952.
———. *Ernest Hemingway: A Reconsideration.* New York: Harcourt, Brace & World, 1966.
———. Preface. *The Nick Adams Stories.* By Ernest Hemingway. New York: Scribner's, 1972.

Selected Bibliography and Suggestions for Further Reading

By Debra A. Moddelmog

Aldridge, John. *After the Lost Generation: A Critical Study of the Writers of Two Wars.* New York: McGraw Hill, 1951.
Altman, Meryl. "Posthumous Queer: Hemingway Among Others." *The Hemingway Review* 30.1 (2010): 129–41.
Bak, John S. *Homo Americanus: Ernest Hemingway, Tennessee Williams, and Queer Masculinities.* Madison, NJ: Fairleigh Dickinson UP, 2010.
Baker, Carlos. *Hemingway: The Writer as Artist.* Rev. ed. Princeton, NJ: Princeton UP, 1972.
Barlowe, Jamie. "Hemingway's Gender Training." *A Historical Guide to Ernest Hemingway.* Ed. Linda Wagner-Martin. Oxford: Oxford UP, 2000. 117–53.
———. "Re-reading Women: The Example of Catherine Barkley." *The Hemingway Review* 12.2 (1993): 24–35.
Baym, Nina. "'Actually I Felt Sorry for the Lion': Reading Hemingway's 'The Short Happy Life of Francis Macomber.'" 1990. *Feminism and American Literary History: Essays.* Rpt., New Brunswick, NJ: Rutgers UP, 1992. 71–80.
Bederman, Gail. *Manliness and Civilization: A Cultural History of Gender and Race in the United States, 1880–1917.* Chicago: U of Chicago P, 1995.
Beegel, Susan F. "Santiago and the Eternal Feminine: Gendering *La Mar* in *The Old Man and the Sea.*" *Hemingway and Women.* Ed. Lawrence R. Broer and Gloria Holland. Tuscaloosa: U of Alabama P, 2002. 131–56.
———. "Second Growth: The Ecology of Loss in 'Fathers and Sons.'" *New Essays on Hemingway's Short Fiction.* Ed. Paul Smith. Cambridge: Cambridge UP, 1998. 75–110.
Bell, Millicent. "*A Farewell to Arms*: Pseudoautobiography and Personal Metaphor." *Ernest Hemingway: The Writer in Context.* Ed. James Nagel. Madison: U of Wisconsin P, 1984. 107–28.
Bender, Bert. "'Night Song': Africa and Eden in Hemingway's Late Work." *Evolution and "the Sex Problem": American Narratives during the Eclipse of Darwinism.* Kent, OH: Kent State UP, 2004. 329–57.
Blackmore, David. "'In New York It'd Mean I Was a . . . ': Masculine Anxiety and Period Discourses of Sexuality in *The Sun Also Rises.*" *The Hemingway Review* 18.1 (1998): 49–67.
Bonds, Patrick Blair. "Hemingway, Gender Identity, and the 'Paris 1922' Apprenticeship." *The Hemingway Review* 29.1 (2009): 123–33.

Brasch, James D., and Joseph Sigman. *Hemingway's Library: A Composite Record.* New York: Garland, 1981.

Brenner, Gerry. *Concealments in Hemingway's Works.* Columbus: Ohio State UP, 1983.

Broer, Lawrence R. *Vonnegut and Hemingway: Writers at War.* Columbia: U of South Carolina P, 2011.

———, and Gloria Holland, eds. Introduction. *Hemingway and Women: Female Critics and the Female Voice.* Ed. Broer and Holland. Tuscaloosa: U of Alabama P, 2002. xix–xiv.

Buckley, J. F. "Echoes of Closeted Desires: The Narrator and Character Voices of Jake Barnes." *The Hemingway Review* 19.2 (2000): 73–87.

Buell, Lawrence. "Literary History Without Sexism: Feminist Studies and Canonical Reconception." *American Literature* 59.1 (1987): 102–14.

Butler, Judith. *Gender Trouble: Feminism and the Subversion of Identity.* 2nd ed. New York: Routledge, 1990.

Carter, Natalie. "'Always Something of It Remains': Sexual Trauma in Ernest Hemingway's *For Whom the Bell Tolls.*" *War, Literature, and the Arts: An International Journal of the Humanities* 25 (2013): 1–40.

Clifford, Stephen P. *Beyond the Heroic "I": Reading Lawrence, Hemingway, and Masculinity.* Lewisburg, PA: Bucknell UP, 1998.

Cohen, Peter F. "'I Won't Kiss You.... I'll Send Your English Girl': Homoerotic Desire in *A Farewell to Arms.*" *The Hemingway Review* 15.1 (1995): 42–53.

Comley, Nancy R. "Women." *Ernest Hemingway in Context.* Ed. Debra A. Moddelmog and Suzanne del Gizzo. Cambridge: Cambridge UP, 2013. 409–17.

———, and Robert Scholes. *Hemingway's Genders: Rereading the Hemingway Text.* New Haven, CT: Yale UP, 1994.

Davidson, Cathy N., and Arnold E. Davidson. "Decoding the Hemingway Hero in *The Sun Also Rises.*" *New Essays on* The Sun Also Rises. Ed. Linda Wagner-Martin. Cambridge: Cambridge UP, 1990. 83–107.

del Gizzo, Suzanne. "'Glow-in-the-Dark Authors': Hemingway's Celebrity and Legacy in *Under Kilimanjaro.*" *The Hemingway Review* 29.2 (2010): 7–27.

———, and Frederic J. Svoboda, eds. *Hemingway's* The Garden of Eden: *Twenty-five Years of Criticism.* Kent, OH: Kent State UP, 2012.

Diliberto, Gioia. *Hadley.* Boston: Ticknor and Fields, 1992.

DuCille, Ann. "The Short Happy Life of Black Feminist Theory." *Differences: A Journal of Feminist Cultural Studies* 21.1 (2010): 32–47.

Dudley, Marc Kevin. *Hemingway, Race, and Art: Bloodlines and the Color Line.* Kent, OH: Kent State UP, 2012.

Earle, David M. *All Man! Hemingway, 1950s Men's Magazines, and the Masculine Persona.* Kent, OH: Kent State UP, 2009.

Eastman, Max. "Bull in the Afternoon." Rev. of *Death in the Afternoon,* by Ernest Hemingway. *New Republic* (7 June 1933): 94–97.

Eby, Carl P. "'He Felt the Change so That It Hurt Him All Through': Sodomy and Transvestic Hallucination in Late Hemingway." *The Hemingway Review* 25.1 (2005): 77–95.

———. *Hemingway's Fetishism: Psychoanalysis and the Mirror of Manhood*. Albany: State U of New York P, 1999.

———. "Who Is the 'Destructive Type'? Re-Reading Literary Jealousy and Destruction in *The Garden of Eden*." *The Hemingway Review* 33.2 (2014): 99–106.

Elliott, Ira. "*A Farewell to Arms* and Hemingway's Crisis of Masculine Values." *LIT: Literary Interpretive Theory* 4.4 (1993): 291–304.

———. "In Search of Lost Time: Reading Hemingway's *Garden*." *Modernist Sexualities*. Ed. Hugh Stevens and Caroline Howlett. Manchester: Manchester UP, 2000. 251–66.

———. "Performance Art: Jake Barnes and 'Masculine' Signification in *The Sun Also Rises*." *American Literature* 63.1 (1995): 77–94. Rpt. in *Ernest Hemingway's* The Sun Also Rises: *A Casebook*. Ed. Linda Wagner-Martin. Oxford: Oxford UP, 2002. 65–80.

Faderman, Lillian. *Surpassing the Love of Men: Romantic Friendship and Love between Women from the Renaissance to the Present*. New York: William Morrow, 1981.

Ferguson, Roderick A. *Aberrations in Black: Toward a Queer of Color Critique*. Minneapolis: U of Minnesota P, 2003.

Fetterley, Judith. *The Resisting Reader: A Feminist Approach to American Fiction*. Bloomington: Indiana UP, 1978.

Fiedler, Leslie A. *Love and Death in the American Novel*. New York: Stein and Day, 1960; Dalkey Archive Press, 2003.

Fore, Dana. "Life Unworthy of Life? Masculinity, Disability, and Guilt in *The Sun Also Rises*." *The Hemingway Review* 26.2 (2007): 74–88.

Forter, Greg. "Melancholy Modernism: Gender and the Politics of Mourning in *The Sun Also Rises*." *The Hemingway Review* 21.1 (2001): 22–37.

Gandal, Keith. *The Gun and the Pen: Hemingway, Fitzgerald, Faulkner and the Fiction of Mobilization*. Oxford: Oxford UP, 2008.

Gladstein, Mimi. *The Indestructible Woman in the Works of Faulkner, Hemingway, and Steinbeck*. Ann Arbor, MI: UMI P, 1986.

Glass, Loren Daniel. *Authors Inc.: Literary Celebrity in the Modern United States, 1880–1980*. New York: New York UP, 2004.

Hackett, Francis. "Hemingway: *A Farewell to Arms*." *Saturday Review of Literature* 32 (6 Aug. 1949): 32–33.

Halberstam, Judith. *Female Masculinity*. Durham, NC: Duke UP, 1998.

Halperin, David. *Saint Foucault: Towards a Gay Hagiography*. Oxford: Oxford UP, 1995.

Haralson, Eric. "'The Other Half Is the Man': The Queer Modern Triangle of Gertrude Stein, Ernest Hemingway, and Henry James." *Henry James and Queer Modernity*. Cambridge: Cambridge UP, 2003. 173–204.

Harding, Brian. "Ernest Hemingway: Men With, or Without, Women." *American Declarations of Love*. Ed. Ann Massa. New York: St. Martin's Press, 1990. 104–21.

Hatten, Charles. "The Crisis of Masculinity, Reified Desire, and Catherine Barkley in *A Farewell to Arms*." *Journal of the History of Sexuality* 4.1 (1993): 76–98.

Haytock, Jennifer. "Hemingway, Wilhelm, and a Style for Lesbian Representation." *The Hemingway Review* 32.1 (2012): 100–18.

Hemingway, Hadley Richardson. Letter to Ernest Hemingway. 28 January 1921. John F. Kennedy Library, Boston.
Hemingway, Mary. *How It Was*. New York: Knopf, 1976.
Hewson, Marc. "A Matter of Love or Death: Hemingway's Developing Psychosexuality in *For Whom the Bell Tolls*." *Studies in the Novel* 36.2 (2004): 170–84.
———. "'The Real Story of Ernest Hemingway': Cixous, Gender, and *A Farewell to Arms*." *The Hemingway Review* 22.2 (2003): 51–62.
Holcomb, Gary Edward, and Charles Scruggs, eds. *Hemingway and the Black Renaissance*. Columbus: Ohio State UP, 2012.
Holder, Alan. "The Other Hemingway." *Twentieth-Century Literature* 9.3 (1963): 153–57.
Johnston, Kenneth J. "In Defense of the Unhappy Margot Macomber." *The Hemingway Review* 2.2 (1983): 44–47.
Justice, Hilary K. *The Bones of the Others: The Hemingway Text from the Lost Manuscripts to the Posthumous Novels*. Kent, OH: Kent State UP, 2006.
Kale, Verna. *Ernest Hemingway*. London: Reaktion, 2016.
Katz, Jonathan Ned. *Gay American History: Lesbians and Gay Men in the U.S.A.* 1976. Rev. ed. New York: Meridian, 1990.
Kaye, Jeremy. "The 'Whine' of Jewish Manhood: Re-Reading Hemingway's Anti-Semitism, Reimagining Robert Cohn." *The Hemingway Review* 25.2 (2006): 44–60.
Kempton, Daniel. "Sexual Transgression and Artistic Creativity in Hemingway's *The Garden of Eden*." *The Hemingway Review* 65.3 (1998): 136–42.
Kennedy, J. Gerald. "Hemingway's Gender Trouble." *American Literature* 63.2 (1991): 187–207.
———. "Life as Fiction: The Lure of Hemingway's *Garden*." *The Southern Review* 24.2 (1988): 451–61.
Kert, Bernice. *The Hemingway Women*. 1983. Rpt., New York: Norton, 1986.
Kimmel, Michael. *Manhood in America: A Cultural History*. New York: Free Press, 1996.
Kitunda, Jeremiah M. "Ernest Hemingway's African Book: An Appraisal." *The Hemingway Review* 28.1 (2008): 107–13.
———. "'Love Is a Dunghill. . . . And I'm the Cock that Gets on It to Crow': Ernest Hemingway's Farcical Adoration of Africa." *Hemingway in Africa*. Ed. Miriam B. Mandel. Rochester, NY: Camden House, 2012. 121–48.
Kobler, J. F. "Hemingway's 'The Sea Change': A Sympathetic View of Homosexuality." *Arizona Quarterly* 26 (1970): 318–24.
Lebowitz, Alan. "No Farewell to Arms." *Uses of Literature*. Ed. Monroe Engel. Cambridge, MA: Harvard UP, 1973. 187–204.
Leff, Leonard J. *Hemingway and His Conspirators: Hollywood, Scribners, and the Making of American Celebrity Culture*. Lanham, MD: Rowman & Littlefield, 1999.
Lewis, Nghana. "Truth, Lies, and Racial Consequences in Ernest Hemingway's *True at First Light: A Fictional Memoir*." *Comparative American Studies* 4.4 (2006): 459–70.
Lewis, Robert W., Jr. *Hemingway on Love*. Austin: U of Texas P, 1965.
Long, Samantha. "Catherine as Transgender: Dreaming Identity in *The Garden of Eden*." *The Hemingway Review* 32.2 (2013): 42–56.
Lynn, Kenneth. *Hemingway*. New York: Simon & Schuster, 1987.

Mandel, Miriam B. "Ferguson and Lesbian Love: Unspoken Subplots in *A Farewell to Arms*." *The Hemingway Review* 14.1 (1994): 18–24.
Marshall, Ian. "Rereading Hemingway: Rhetorics of Whiteness, Labor, and Identity." *Hemingway and the Black Renaissance* Ed. Holcomb and Scruggs. 177–213.
Martin, Wendy. "Brett Ashley as New Woman in *The Sun Also Rises*." *Ernest Hemingway's* The Sun Also Rises: *A Casebook*. Ed. Linda Wagner-Martin. Oxford: Oxford UP, 2002. 47–62.
Martínez, Ernesto Javier. *On Making Sense: Queer Race Narratives of Intelligibility*. Stanford, CA: Stanford UP, 2013.
Mellow, James. *Hemingway: A Life Without Consequences*. Boston: Houghton Mifflin, 1992.
Merrill, Robert. "Demoting Hemingway: Feminist Criticism and the Canon." *American Literature* 60.2 (1988): 255–68.
Messent, Peter B. "Gender Role and Sexuality." *Ernest Hemingway*. New York: St. Martin's Press, 1992. 83–123.
Moddelmog, Debra A. "Queer Families in Hemingway's Fiction." *Hemingway and Women*. Ed. Broer and Holland. 297–324.
———. *Reading Desire: In Pursuit of Ernest Hemingway*. Ithaca, NY: Cornell UP, 1999.
———. "Sex, Sexuality, and Marriage." *Ernest Hemingway in Context*. Ed. Debra A. Moddelmog and Suzanne del Gizzo. 357–66.
———. "Telling Stories from Hemingway's FBI File: Conspiracy, Paranoia, and Masculinity." *Modernism on File: Modernist Writers, Artists, and the FBI, 1920–1950*. Ed. Claire Culleton and Karen Leick. New York: Palgrave Macmillan, 2008. 53–72.
———. "'We Live in a Country Where Nothing Makes Any Difference': The Queer Sensibility of *A Farewell to Arms*." *The Hemingway Review* 28.2 (2009): 7–24.
———. "'Who's Normal? What's Normal?': Teaching Hemingway's *The Garden of Eden* through the Lens of Normalcy Studies." *The Hemingway Review* 30.1 (2010): 142–51.
———, and Suzanne del Gizzo, eds. *Ernest Hemingway in Context*. Cambridge: Cambridge UP, 2012.
Moreland, Kim. *The Medievalist Impulse in American Literature: Twain, Adams, Fitzgerald, Hemingway*. Charlottesville: UP of Virginia, 1996.
Morrison, Toni. *Playing in the Dark: Whiteness and the Literary Imagination*. Cambridge, MA: Harvard UP, 1992.
Muñoz, José. *Disidentifications: Queers of Color and the Performance of Politics*. Minneapolis: U of Minnesota P, 1999.
Nesmith, Chris L. "'The Law of an Ancient God' and the Ending of Hemingway's *Garden of Eden*." *The Hemingway Review* 10.2 (2001): 16–36.
Nissen, Axel. "Outing Jake Barnes: *The Sun Also Rises* and the Gay World." *American Studies in Scandinavia* 31.2 (1999): 42–57.
Nolan, Charles J. "Hemingway's Women's Movement." *The Hemingway Review* 3.2 (1984): 14–22.
Pettipiece, Deirdre Anne McVicker. *Sex Theories and the Shaping of Two Moderns: Hemingway and H.D.* New York: Routledge, 2002.
Prescott, Jeryl J. "Liberty and Just(us): Gender and Race in Hemingway's *To Have and*

Have Not." *CLA Journal* 37.2 (1993): 176–88.
Pullin, Faith. "Hemingway and the Secret Language of Hate." *Ernest Hemingway: New Critical Essays*. Ed. A. Robert Lee. London and Totowa, NJ: Vision Press Limited and Barnes & Noble Books, 1983. 172–92.
Raeburn, John. *Fame Became of Him: Hemingway as Public Writer*. Bloomington: Indiana UP, 1984.
Reynolds, Michael S. *Hemingway: The 1930s*. New York: Norton, 1997.
———. *Hemingway: The American Homecoming*. Oxford: Blackwell, 1992.
———. *Hemingway: The Final Years*. New York: Norton, 1999.
———. *Hemingway: The Paris Years*. Oxford: Blackwell, 1989.
———. *Hemingway's Reading, 1910–1940: An Inventory*. Princeton, NJ: Princeton UP, 1980.
———. *The Young Hemingway*. Oxford: Basil Blackwell, 1986.
Rogers, Katherine M. *The Troublesome Helpmate: A History of Misogyny in Literature*. Seattle: U of Washington P, 1966.
Rohy, Valerie. "A Darker Past in *The Garden of Eden*." *Anachronism and Its Others: Sexuality, Race, Temporality*. Albany: State U of New York P, 2009. 99–119.
———. "Hemingway, Literalism, and Transgender Reading." *Twentieth-Century Literature* 57.2 (2011): 148–79.
Rotundo, E. Anthony. *American Manhood: Transformations in Masculinity from the Revolution to the Modern Era*. New York: Basic Books, 1993.
Rudat, Wolfgang E. H. "Hemingway on Sexual Otherness: What's Really Funny in *The Sun Also Rises*." *Hemingway Repossessed*. Ed. Kenneth Rosen. Westport, CT: Praeger Publishers, 1994. 169–79.
———. "Hemingway's *The Sun Also Rises*: Masculinity, Feminism, and Gender-Role Reversal." *American Imago* 47.1 (1990): 43–68.
———. *A Rotten Way to Be Wounded: The Tragicomedy of* A Sun Also Rises. New York: Peter Lang, 1990.
———. "Sexual Dilemmas in *The Sun Also Rises*: Hemingway's Count and the Education of Jacob Barnes." *The Hemingway Review* 8.2 (1989): 2–13.
Sanderson, Rena. "Hemingway and Gender History." *The Cambridge Companion to Hemingway*. Ed. Scott Donaldson. Cambridge: Cambridge UP, 1996. 170–96.
Sedgwick, Eve Kosofsky. *Epistemology of the Closet*. Berkeley: U of California P, 1990.
Silbergleid, Robin. "Into Africa: Narrative and Authority in Hemingway's *The Garden of Eden*." *The Hemingway Review* 27.2 (2008): 96–116.
Spanier, Sandra Whipple. "Catherine Barkley and the Hemingway Code: Ritual and Survival in *A Farewell to Arms*." *Modern Critical Interpretations: A Farewell to Arms*. Ed. Harold Bloom. New York: Chelsea, 1987. 131–48.
———. "Hemingway's Unknown Soldier: Catherine Barkley, the Critics, and the Great War." *New Essays on* A Farewell to Arms. Ed. Scott Donaldson. Cambridge: Cambridge UP, 1990. 75–108.
Spilka, Mark. *Hemingway's Quarrel with Androgyny*. Lincoln: U of Nebraska P, 1990.
St. Pierre, Scott. "Bent Hemingway: Straightness, Sexuality, Style." *GLQ* 16.3 (2010): 363–87.

Stecopoulos, Harry, and Michael Uebel, eds. *Race and the Subject of Masculinities*. Durham, NC: Duke UP, 1997.
Stein, Gertrude. *The Autobiography of Alice B. Toklas*. New York: Harcourt, Brace, 1933.
Strong, Amy F. *Race and Identity in Hemingway's Fiction*. New York: Palgrave Macmillan, 2008.
Strychacz, Thomas. *Dangerous Masculinities: Conrad, Hemingway, and Lawrence*. Gainesville: UP of Florida, 2008.
———. *Hemingway's Theaters of Masculinity*. Baton Rouge: Louisiana State UP, 2003.
———. "Masculinity." *Hemingway in Context*. Moddelmog and del Gizzo. 277–86.
Takeuchi, Masaya. "Frederic's Conflict between Homosociality and Heterosexuality: War, Marvell, and Sculpture in *A Farewell to Arms*." *Midwest Quarterly* 53.1 (2011): 26–44.
Tanimoto, Chikako. "Queering Sexual Practices in 'Mr. and Mrs. Elliot.'" *The Hemingway Review* 32.1 (2012): 88–99.
———. "Subversion of the In/Out Model in Understanding Hemingway's Texts." *Genders* 39 (2004).
Traber, Daniel S. "Performing the Feminine in *A Farewell to Arms*." *The Hemingway Review* 24.2 (2005): 28–40.
Trogdon, Robert W. *The Lousy Racket: Hemingway, Scribners, and the Business of Literature*. Kent, OH: Kent State UP, 2007.
Turner, Catherine. "Changing American Literary Taste: Scribner's and Ernest Hemingway." *Marketing Modernism Between the Two World Wars*. Amherst: U of Massachusetts P, 2003. 145–72.
Tyler, Lisa. "'How Beautiful the Virgin Forests Were Before the Loggers Came': An Ecofeminist Reading of Hemingway's 'The End of Something.'" *The Hemingway Review* 27.2 (2008): 60–73.
Vernon, Alex. *Hemingway's Second War: Bearing Witness to the Spanish Civil War*. Iowa City: U of Iowa P, 2011.
———. *Soldiers Once and Still: Ernest Hemingway, James Salter, and Tim O'Brien*. Iowa City: U of Iowa P, 2004.
Wagner-Martin, Linda. *Ernest Hemingway: A Literary Life*. New York: Palgrave Macmillan, 2007.
———. "Proudly and Friendly and Gently: Women in Hemingway's Early Fiction." *College Literature* 7.3 (1980): 239–47.
———. "The Romance of Desire in Hemingway's Fiction." *Hemingway and Women*. Ed. Broer and Holland. 54–69.
Warner, Michael. *Fear of a Queer Planet: Queer Politics and Social Theory*. Minneapolis: U of Minnesota P, 1993.
Wexler, Joyce. "E.R.A. for Hemingway: A Feminist Defense of *A Farewell to Arms*." *Georgia Review* 35.1 (1981): 111–23.
Whitlow, Roger. *Cassandra's Daughters: The Women in Hemingway*. Westport, CT: Greenwood Press, 1984.
Willingham, Kathy G. "Hemingway's *The Garden of Eden*: Writing with the Body." *The Hemingway Review* 12.2 (1993): 46–61.

———. "The Sun Hasn't Set Yet: Brett Ashley and the Code Hero Debate." *Hemingway and Women*. Ed. Broer and Holland. 43–58.

Wilson, Edmund. "Hemingway: Gauge of Morale." *The Wound and the Bow: Seven Studies in Literature*, 174–97. 1941. Rpt. New York: Oxford UP, 1965. Rev. of "Ernest Hemingway: Bourdon Gauge of Morale," *Atlantic* 164 (July 1939): 36–46.

Wolfe, Cary. "Fathers, Lovers, and Friend Killers: Rearticulating Gender and Race via Species in Hemingway." *Boundary 2* 29.1 (2002): 223–57.

Wolfe, Susan J. "Women's Speech in Hemingway's Novels." *South Dakota Review* 46.4 (2008): 73–83.

Woolf, Virginia. "An Essay in Criticism." *Ernest Hemingway: The Critical Reception*. Ed. Robert O. Stephens. New York: Burt Franklin, 1977. 54.

Worden, Daniel. "A Discipline of Sentiments: Masculinity in Ernest Hemingway's *Death in the Afternoon*." *Masculine Style: The American West and Literary Modernism*. New York: Palgrave, 2011. 107–26.

Wylder, Delbert E. "The Two Faces of Brett: The Role of the New Woman in *The Sun Also Rises*." *Kentucky Philological Assn. Bulletin* (1980): 27–33.

Contributors

Pamela L. Caughie is professor of English at Loyola University Chicago and past president of the Modernist Studies Association. Her books include *Virginia Woolf and Postmodernism* (1991), *Passing and Pedagogy: The Dynamics of Responsibility* (1999), *Virginia Woolf in the Age of Mechanical Reproduction*, ed. (2000), *Disciplining Modernism*, ed. (2009), and *Virginia Woolf Writing the World*, coed. (2015). She has contributed to *Modernism and Theory: A Critical Debate* (2009), *The Edinburgh Companion to Virginia Woolf* (2010), and *The Cambridge History of the Modernist Novel* (2015), among others. She is codirector of Modernist Networks, a consortium of digital projects in modernist studies.

Crystal Gorham Doss, assistant teaching professor at University of Missouri Kansas City, teaches American literature from 1865 to the present. She is currently working on a book about drinking, masculinity, and Prohibition-era literature.

Carl P. Eby is professor of English and department chair at Appalachian State University. Before coming to Appalachian State, he taught for many years at the University of South Carolina Beaufort, where as a Carolina Trustee Professor, he was twice named Professor of the Year and twice the recipient of the South Carolina Governor's Distinguished Professor Award. He is author of *Hemingway's Fetishism: Psychoanalysis and the Mirror of Manhood* (1999) and coeditor of *Hemingway's Spain: Imagining the Spanish World* (Kent State University Press, 2015). He has published more than a dozen articles on Hemingway and modernism in such journals as *The Hemingway Review, Twentieth-Century Literature*, and *Arizona Quarterly*.

John Fenstermaker, Fred L. Standley Professor of English, emeritus, at Florida State University, has recently published essays on Hemingway in *Literature and Journalism* (2013), *War and Ink: New Perspectives on Ernest Hemingway's Early Life and Writings* (Kent State University Press, 2014), and the *South Atlantic Review*. He is currently researching Hemingway as a "banned author."

Joseph Fruscione, author of *Faulkner and Hemingway: Biography of a Literary Rivalry* (2012) and numerous essays and reviews, taught American literature and first-year writing for fifteen years at George Washington University, Georgetown University, and the University of Maryland, Baltimore County. He's also been the editor of *Teaching Hemingway and Modernism* (Kent State University Press, 2015) and the "Adjuncts Interviewing Adjuncts" column for Inside Higher Ed. He's currently a freelance copy editor and proofreader, as well as cofounder and communications director for PrecariCorps, a nonprofit that supports adjunct professors.

Sarah B. Hardy is Elliott Professor of English at Hampden-Sydney College where she teaches courses on the short story, William Faulkner, postcolonial literature, modern fiction, popular culture, and gender/men's studies. She has published articles on topics ranging from *Mrs. Dalloway* to science fiction, and coedited the collection *Motherhood and Space: Configurations of the Maternal though Politics, Home, and the Body* (2005) with Caroline Wiedmer.

Erin A. Holliday-Karre, an assistant professor of twentieth-century literature and theory at Qatar University, has published a series of articles that articulate an unacknowledged current of seduction running throughout feminism, from Joan Rivière and Virginia Woolf in the modernist era to Hélène Cixous and Donna Haraway in the postmodern era.

Hilary Kovar Justice, associate professor of English and director of Undergraduate Studies at Illinois State University, is author of *The Bones of the Others* (Kent State University Press, 2006) and *A Groundling's Guide to Shakespeare's* Hamlet (2014); her other works on Hemingway include contributions to *Hemingway in Context, Hemingway and Women, A Companion to Hemingway's* Death in the Afternoon, *The Hemingway Review, Resources for American Literary Study, The Mailer Review,* and *North Dakota Quarterly*. Her forthcoming works include *A Reader's Guide to* Green Hills of Africa and a study of gender and trauma in *The Lord of the Rings* and *Game of Thrones*.

Verna Kale, visiting assistant professor in rhetoric at Hampden-Sydney College, has published articles and shorter pieces on Hemingway in *The Hemingway Review, Ernest Hemingway in Context* (2012), and *Ernest Hemingway and the Geography of Memory* (Kent State University Press, 2010). Her critical biography, *Ernest Hemingway* (2016), challenges a number of long-held assumptions about the author's relationships with his mother and wives and about his late-career literary experiments.

Sara Kosiba is an associate professor of English at Troy University, Montgomery. In addition to researching the life and work of Ernest Hemingway, she has published articles on women writers, including Josephine Herbst, Dawn Powell, and Meridel Le Sueur, and she wrote the introduction to the first American printing of John Herrmann's 1926 novel *What Happens* (2015).

Catherine R. Mintler, who teaches in the Expository Writing Program at the University of Oklahoma, specializes in American and British modernism. She is currently at work on a book that explores the connections between sartorial culture and formal innovation in the modernist novel and the effects of that coalescence in representing modern identity. Her work on Fitzgerald and dandyism has appeared in the *F. Scott Fitzgerald Review*. Mintler is the recipient of a National Endowment for the Humanities Fellowship, an Annette Kolodny Award, and a Smith Reynolds Founders Fellowship from the Ernest Hemingway Foundation and Society.

Debra A. Moddelmog is professor and chair of English at the Ohio State University, specializing in twentieth-century American fiction, modernism, and sexuality studies. She is author of essays on American fiction, film, and pedagogy published in journals such as *American Literature, Modern Fiction Studies, The Hemingway Review, The Journal of Popular Film and Television,* and *Pedagogy* as well as in collections such as *Hemingway and Women: Female Critics and the Female Voice*. Her book *Reading Desire: In Pursuit of Ernest Hemingway* (1999) has been translated into Japanese, and she is coeditor (with Suzanne del Gizzo) of *Ernest Hemingway in Context* (2012).

Douglas Sheldon is an instructor at DePaul University's English Language Academy in Chicago. He is currently performing research on transnational empathy and second language learning.

Joshua Weiss lives in Washington, DC, and teaches at Prince George's Community College, specializing in transatlantic modernism, theology, and queer theory. He is currently at work on a project exploring the mutually critical correlation between the Catholic sacraments and emergent forms of sexuality in modernist literature, focusing on how these potent religious rituals and symbols enabled modernists to express homosexuality and other forms of queerness despite the Church's disapproval.

Belinda Wheeler, assistant professor of English at Claflin University, divides her scholarship between early twentieth-century American literature and Australian Aboriginal literature. Her articles on female magazine editors from the modernist period have appeared in *PMLA*, on Cary Nelson's *MAPS* website, and in Cherene Sherrard-Johnson's *The Blackwell Companion to the Harlem Renaissance*. Wheeler is currently completing several books: *Gwendolyn Bennett: The Harlem Renaissance's Quintessential Poet, Artist, Editor, Educator, and Columnist; A Companion to the Works of Kim Scott;* and *A Companion to the Works of Alexis Wright*. She is also the editor of *A Companion to Australian Aboriginal Literature* (2013).

Index

NOTE: Page references in *italics* refer to figures.

Across the River and into the Trees (Hemingway), 56
"Actually, I Felt Sorry for the Lion" (Baym), 47–48
Adelman, Janet, 37n6
advertising, portrayal of women by, 51–54
afición, defining, 93, 94, 99–101
"African Book" (Hemingway), 16, 20–21
agape (brotherly love), 14
Aldridge, John, 12
Allard, Martine, 88
All Man! Hemingway, 1950s Men's Magazines, and the Masculine Persona (Earle), 6n1
"An Alpine Idyll" (Hemingway), 66, 69n2
Altman, Meryl, 17
American Periodicals Online, 133
"(You Make Me Feel Like) A Natural Woman" (Franklin), 45
Anderson, Sherwood, 150
androgyny, 16, 40
Arkell-Smith, Valerie (Barker), 40
artistic production, feminine, 115–26
As I Lay Dying (Faulkner), 28, 31, 32–33
Atkinson, Dwight, 81
At the Hemingways (Sanford), 23n8
Au Bonheur des Dames (Zola), 124n1
The Autobiography of Alice B. Toklas (Stein), 7, 28, 31
The Awakening (Chopin), 28, 31, 125n5

Bak, John S., 18
Baker, Carlos, 12, 86, 143–44
Barker, Victor (Arkell-Smith), 40
Barlowe, Jamie, 8, 14
Barnard, Rita, 31, 34
Barthes, Roland, 153
Bartky, Sandra, 39
"The Battler" (Hemingway), 30, 36n2, 63

Baym, Nina, 3, 4, 14, 47–48, 57n1, 58
The Bedford Glossary of Critical and Literary Terms (Murfin, Ray), 150
Beegel, Susan, 2, 21, 59, 154–55, 158
Beerbohm, Max, 161
Bell, Millicent, 12
Bender, Bert, 16
"Berdache," 40
Berlant, Lauren, 6, 130–31
Beyond the Gibson Girl (Patterson), 46n3
"Big Two-Hearted River" (Hemingway), 66
Blackmore, David, 18
Bloom, Harold, 72
"Bona and Paul" (Toomer), 32
Bonds, Patrick Blair, 17
"The Book of the Grotesque" (Anderson), 150
Booth, Wayne, 58
Bordo, Susan, 39, 41
Boswell, James, 164n2
Brenner, Gerry, 8
Broer, Lawrence R., 14, 16
Brogan, Jacqueline Vaughn, 120
Brown, Judith, 50
Bruccoli, Matthew J., 59
Buckley, J. F., 18
Buell, Lawrence, 13
bullfights, sexual themes of, 96, 97–98
Burkhalter, Nancy, 141n3
Burwell, Rose Marie, 16, 17, 23n8
Butler, Judith, 9, 39, 45
"The Butterfly and the Tank" (Hemingway), 56
By-Line (Hemingway), 145, 146

The Cambridge Companion to American Modernism, 34
Cambridge University Press, 21
Cane (Toomer), 28, 31, 32, 36n2, 37n5
"*Cane* and *In Our Time*" (Wright-Cleveland), 37n5

INDEX   237

Cassandra's Daughters (Whitlow), 13–14
"Cat in the Rain" (Hemingway), 13, 28, 29, 30, 31, 33, 60
Caughie, Pamela L., 4, 5
Chopin, Kate, 28, 33, 125n5, 135, 142
The Chronicle of Higher Education, 163
Chu, C. Y. Cyrus, 84
Cixous, Hélène, 120, 126n10
"A Clean, Well-Lighted Place" (Hemingway), 56, 142, 149
Clefs pour l'imaginaire ou l'autre scène (Mannoni), 114n20
Coca-Cola, 51
"code heroes": male protagonists and, 11–12; in *The Nick Adams Stories* (Hemingway), 75; women as, 13
Cohen, Peter F., 18
Comley, Nancy R., 2, 16, 21, 30–31, 72, 85, 124
The Common Law (Gibson), 131
Complete Short Stories (Hemingway), 60–69
Connell, R. W., 58
Cosmopolitan, 49–54, 50, 53, 56
Cowles, Virginia, 144
Crandell, Bradshaw, 49–50
"Cross-Country Snow" (Hemingway), 28, 29, 30, 32, 65
cross-dressing, transvestism compared to, 113n6
Cuddy-Keane, Melba, 135
Curnutt, Kirk, 2
A Curtain of Green (Welty), 150

"Damned Women" (Rodin), 125n7
Dangerous Masculinities (Strychacz), 17–18, 77
"A Darker Past" (Rohy), 18
Davidson, Arnold, 18
Davidson, Cathy, 18
"A Day's Wait" (Hemingway), 66–67, 69n2
Death in the Afternoon (Hemingway), 18, 153
"The Death of the Author" (Barthes), 153
Debba (Hemingway's African "fiancée"), 21
del Gizzo, Suzanne, 8, 20
Dell'Orto, Giovanna, 144–45
"The Doctor and the Doctor's Wife" (Hemingway), 30, 31, 36n2, 61
domestic relationships, portrayal of, 58–69
Doss, Crystal Gorham, 6
Dreger, Alice, 39–40
duCille, Ann, 19, 47
Dudley, Marc, 20
Duff Twysden, Lady, 119
Duggan, Lisa, 102n2

Earle, David M., 6n1, 8
Eastman, Max, 7–8, 151n1
Eby, Carl, 5; "He Felt the Change So That It Hurt Him All Through," 17, 20, 111–12n2; *Hemingway's Fetishism*, 16, 17, 18, 20, 105, 110, 111n1, 113n7, 125–26n7, 125n3; "Who Is the Destructive Type," 112n2
economic power, gender and, 115–26
ego, splitting of, 105, 110
Ehrenreich, Barbara, 41
Elbe, Lili (Wegener), 46n3
Eliot, T. S., 48, 102n1
Elliot, Ira, 18
Ellis, Havelock, 9, 16, 46n2
Emotional Growth (Greenacre), 113n8
"The Endings of Hemingway's *Garden of Eden*" (Fleming), 42, 44–45
"The End of Something" (Hemingway), 29, 31, 32, 33, 62
English as second language (ESL), teaching students of, 80–89
Epistemology of the Closet (Sedgwick), 103n7
Ernest Hemingway (Young), 11–12
Ernest Hemingway: A Life Story (Baker), 86
Ernest Hemingway: A Reconsideration (Young), 11–12
eros (romantic and sexual love), 14–15
"erotic scenario," 104
Esquire, 56
"An Essay in Criticism" (Woolf), 7

The Face of War (Gellhorn), 145, 151n3
Faderman, Lillian, 9
Fantina, Richard, 16
A Farewell to Arms (Hemingway): dispelling Hemingway's misogynist reputation and, 159; fetishism and, 104–14; modern women and, 138; overview, 5, 12–13, 18; portrayal of women and domestic relationships, 58; teaching to ESL learners, 85
"Fathers and Sons" (Hemingway), 5, 19, 66–67, 73, 75–78
Faulkner, William, 27, 28, 31, 32, 160
Fausto-Sterling, Anne, 39
"Fears For Modern Woman" (*New York Times*), 135
femininity: artistic production and economic power, 115–26; genres of femininity, defined, 130–31 (*see also* modern women); portrayal of women and, 54; sexual identity and, 40–42. *See also* gender roles
Fenstermaker, John, 4–5
Ferguson, Roderick, 11

fetishism, 104–14
Fetterley, Judith, 1, 12–13, 138
Fiedler, Leslie, 2, 12, 58
fiesta of Saint Fermin, 96–101
"Finding Atlantis" (Gilbert), 147
"The First Glimpses of War" (Hemingway), 145
Fitzgerald, F. Scott, 28
Fitzgerald, Zelda, 7, 119, 126n9
"The Flapper" (Leyendecker), 133
flappers, 132–35, 133, 134, 140
Fleming, Robert, 42, 44–45
Fore, Dana, 21
Forter, Greg, 17
For Whom the Bell Tolls (Hemingway), 12, 18
Foucault, Michel, 39, 40, 45
"Foucault, Femininity, and the Modernization of Patriarchal Power" (Bartky), 39
Franklin, Aretha, 45
Freud, Sigmund, 9, 106, 109, 112n2
From Ritual to Romance (Weston), 102n1
Fruscione, Joseph, 4

Gallatin, Albert, 135
Gandal, Keith, 19
García Márquez, Gabriel, 27
"garden of cultural acceptability," defined, 41
The Garden of Eden (Hemingway): economic power and, 115–26; fetishism and, 104–14; gender and culture in, 27–28; gender and sexual identity in, 38–46; overview, 2, 4, 5, 11, 15–17, 18, 19
Gareis, Elisabeth, 88
"Gauge of Morale" (Wilson), 12
Gautier, Théophile, 114n13
Gellhorn, Martha, 6, 119, 143, 144–45, 151n3
gender roles: artistic production and economic power, 118–24; cross-cultural attitudes of, 80–89; cultural acceptability of, 38–46; domestic relationships and, 58–69; gender identity exploration, 73; in gender studies, 8–12, 15–19; In Our Time (Hemingway), 27–37. See also masculinity; sexuality; women, portrayal of; women writers
gender studies, 7–23; gender roles, 8–12, 15–19; Hemingway's image and, 7–8, 21–22; love, 14–15; masculinity as performance, 17–18; overview, 10; publication of Hemingway's letters by Cambridge University Press, 21; race, 11, 19–21; sexuality, 9–12; women as portrayed by Hemingway, 12–14

Gender Trouble (Butler), 39
genres of femininity, defined, 130–31. See also modern women
Gibson, Charles Dana, 131
"Gibson girls," 131, 132, 135, 140
Gilbert, Sandra M., 118, 147
Gilman, Charlotte Perkins, 135
GLAAD Media Reference Guide, 113n7
Gladstein, Mimi, 12
Glass, Loren Daniel, 8
Gleeson-White, Sarah, 150
"Glow in the Dark" (del Gizzo), 8
Gohrbandt (doctor), 46n3
The Great Gatsby (Fitzgerald), 28
Greenacre, Phyllis, 113n8
Gubar, Susan, 118

Hackett, Francis, 12
Halberstam, Judith, 9
Hall, Radclyffe, 125n5
Halperin, David, 9–10
Hammond, Adam, 135
Haralson, Eric, 21
Harding, Brian, 14
Hardy, Sarah, B., 5
Hatten, Charles, 18
Hausman, Bernice, 38
Haytock, Jennifer, 16
Hearn, Jeff, 58
Hearst's International, 49, 50
The Hearts of Men (Ehrenreich), 41
"He Felt the Change So That It Hurt Him All Through" (Eby), 17, 20, 111–12n2
Hellman, Lillian, 143, 144
Helstern, Linda, 76
Hemingway (Lynn), 125n4
Hemingway: The 1930s (Reynolds), 144
Hemingway, Ernest: African "fiancée" of, 21; alternate endings in stories by, 44; archives (JFK Library), 17; archives (Scribner), 16; dispelling reputation as misogynist, 153–64; image of, 1, 7–8, 21–22, 70–71, 115, 142 (see also masculinity); interpreting characters as representative of, 139–40; magazine publications, 49–53, 50, 53, 56; marriages of, 119, 143; newspaper articles by, 96; relationship with von Kurowsky, 86, 86–87; relationship with women writers, 143; sister of, 23n8, 108; state of field publication of Hemingway's letters, 21; war injury of, 94, 110
Hemingway, Ernest, works by: Across the River and into the Trees, 56; "African

Book," 16, 20–21; "An Alpine Idyll," 66, 69n2; "The Battler," 30, 36n2, 63; "Big Two-Hearted River," 66; "The Butterfly and the Tank," 56; "Cat in the Rain," 13, 28, 29, 30, 31, 33, 60; "A Clean, Well-Lighted Place," 56, 142, 149; *Complete Short Stories*, 60–69; "Cross-Country Snow," 28, 29, 30, 32, 65; "A Day's Wait," 66–67, 69n2; *Death in the Afternoon*, 18, 153; "The Doctor and the Doctor's Wife," 30, 31, 36n2, 61; "The End of Something," 29, 31, 32, 33, 62; *A Farewell to Arms*, 5, 12–13, 18, 58, 85, 104–14, 138, 159; "Fathers and Sons," 5, 19, 66–67, 73, 75–78; "The First Glimpses of War," 145; *For Whom the Bell Tolls*, 12, 18; *The Garden of Eden*, 2, 4, 5, 11, 15–17, 18, 19, 27–28, 38–46, 104–14, 115–26; "Hills Like White Elephants," 2, 13, 32, 58, 156; "In Another Country," 64; "Indian Camp," 5, 29, 30, 31, 56, 61, 67, 73–76, 78, 162–63; *In Our Time*, 4, 27–37, 60, 62–63, 64, 65–66, 80–89, 142; *Islands in the Stream*, 11, 16, 18, 159; *Under Kilimanjaro*, 11; "The Killers," 63–64; "A Lack of Passion," 16; "The Last Good Country," 11; "The Light of the World," 63, 150; *Men at War*, 147; *Men Without Women*, 7, 61, 63, 64, 66; "The Mother of a Queen," 16; *A Moveable Feast*, 11, 16, 17, 110; "Mr. and Mrs. Elliot," 16, 30, 31, 60; "My Old Man," 60; "A New Kind of War," 146; "Now I Lay Me," 64–65; *The Old Man and the Sea*, 14, 27; "On the Quai at Smyrna," 27, 29, 36, 60; "Out of Season," 30, 58, 60, 161; "The Revolutionist," 60; "The Sea Change," 16, 27–28, 30, 58; "The Short Happy Life of Francis Macomber," 3, 4, 12, 19, 47–57, 53, 58, 77; "A Simple Enquiry," 16; "The Snows of Kilimanjaro," 13, 19, 129–30, 137; "Soldier's Home," 31, 60; *The Sun Also Rises*, 5, 7, 15, 18, 58, 68, 77, 93–103, 103n6, 116, 119, 122, 129–30, 131, 136, 137, 138, 142, 148, 157; "Ten Indians," 19, 61, 162–63; "The Three-Day Blow," 29, 30, 31, 33, 62–63; *To Have and Have Not*, 15; *True at First Light*, 11, 20; *Under Kilimanjaro*, 11, 20; "Up in Michigan," 12; "A Very Short Story," 5, 60, 80–89; " A Way You'll Never Be," 64–65; *Winner Take Nothing*, 63, 64, 66, 150
Hemingway, Grace Hall (mother), 8, 23n8
Hemingway, Marcelline (sister), 23n8, 108
Hemingway, Mary (wife), 20, 125–26n7, 126n9; *How It Was*, 17

"Hemingway, Literalism, and Transgender Reading" (Rohy), 18
"Hemingway and Gender History" (Sanderson), 15
Hemingway and the Black Renaissance (Holcomb and Scruggs, eds.), 37n5
Hemingway and Women (Broer and Holland), 14, 69n2
Hemingway Collection (JFK Library), 17
Hemingway Collection (Scribner's archives), 16
Hemingway & Gellhorn (film), 142
Hemingway in Context (Moddelmog), 87
The Hemingway Review, 102n3, 111n2, 145, 154
The Hemingway Review (Beegel), 59
"Hemingway's Barbershop Quartet" (Spilka), 126n9
Hemingway's Fetishism (Eby), 16, 17, 18, 20, 23n8, 105, 110, 111n1, 113n7, 125–26n7, 125n3
Hemingway's Genders (Comley and Scholes), 16, 30
"Hemingway's Gender Training" (Barlowe), 8
"Hemingway Slaps Eastman in the Face" (*New York Times*), 151n1
"Hemingway's Literary Sisters" (Sanderson), 143
Hemingway's Quarrel (Spilka), 17, 125n4, 125n7
Hemingway's Second War (Vernon), 18
Hemingway's Theaters (Strychacz), 17–18, 21, 74, 140–41n1
"Hemingway's Women's Movement" (Nolan), 14
Herbst, Josephine, 6, 144, 145–46, 151n3
Herculine Barbin (Foucault), 39, 40
Hewson, Marc, 18
"Hills Like White Elephants" (Hemingway), 2, 13, 32, 58, 156
Hinkle, Jim, 154
Hirschfeld, Magnus, 46n2
The History of Sexuality (Foucault), 39, 40
Holder, Alan, 13
Holland, Gloria, 14
Holliday-Karre, Erin A., 4, 5
homosexuality: in *The Garden of Eden* (Hemingway), 40, 41, 46n2, 46n3; sexuality and religion, 93–103. *See also* sexual identity; sexuality
How It Was (Hemingway, Mary), 17
Hunter, Nan D., 102n2

Images of Women in Literature (Baym), 57n1
"In Another Country" (Hemingway), 64

"Indian Camp" (Hemingway): dispelling Hemingway's misogynist reputation and, 162–63; gender and culture in, 29, 30, 31; masculinity and, 73–76, 78; overview, 5; portrayal of women and domestic relationships, 56, 61, 67
"In Love With Papa" (Miller), 155
In Our Time (Hemingway): "A Very Short Story" and cross-cultural attitudes toward gender, 80–89; gender and culture in, 27–37; overview, 4; portrayal of women and domestic relationships, 60, 62–63, 64, 65–66; women writers and, 142
"Integrating Men into the Curriculum" (Kimmel), 71, 79
Islands in the Stream (Hemingway), 11, 16, 18, 159
"Ivory," significance of, 108

Jenks, Tom, 42, 43, 44–45, 124
Jenson, Kimberly, 85
Johnson, Samuel, 164n2
Johnston, Kenneth, 14
Joseph d'Arimathie, 102n1
Journal of American Culture, 141n3
Joyce, James, 48, 125n5
Justice, Hilary Kovar, 6, 16, 68n1

Kafka, Franz, 164n2
"Karintha" (Toomer), 32
Katz, Jonathan Ned, 9
Kaye, Jeremy, 20, 102n3
Kennedy, J., 16, 17
Kilcup, Karen, 151
"The Killers" (Hemingway), 63–64
Kimmel, Michael, 41, 58, 71, 79
King Lear (Shakespeare), 37n6
Kitunda, Jeremiah, 20–21
Knights, Ben, 71, 79
Kobler, J. F., 16
Kosiba, Sara, 6, 144
Krafft-Ebing, Richard von, 46n2
Künstlerroman, 117–19, 123–24

Lacan, Jacques, 103n5
"A Lack of Passion" (Hemingway), 16
Lansky, Ellen, 140n1
"The Last Good Country" (Hemingway), 11
"The Laugh of the Medusa" (Cixous), 126n10
Lawrence, D. H., 41
Lebowitz, Alan, 12
Leff, Leonard J., 8

Leinwald, Gerald, 135
Leland, Jacob Michael, 119
The Letters of Ernest Hemingway (Spanier), 6n2
Lewis, Nghana, 21
Lewis, Robert, 14
Leyendecker, Frank Xavier, 133
Life of Samuel Johnson (Boswell), 164n2
"The Light of the World" (Hemingway), 63, 150
Long, Samantha, 18
Love and Death (Fiedler), 12
"Love is a Dunghill" (Kitunda), 21
Lynn, Kenneth, 17, 125n4
Lyon, Janet, 27–28, 30, 34

Mademoiselle de Maupin (Gautier), 114n13
The Male Body (Bordo), 41
Mandel, Miriam B., 18
Manhood in America (Kimmel), 41
Mannoni, Octave, 114n20
marriage: domestic relationships and, 58–69; economic power and, 115; gender and culture, 29–30
Marshall, Ian, 19
Martin, Emily, 39
Martin, Wendy, 15
Martínez, Ernesto Javier, 11
Masculinities in Text and Teaching (Knights), 71
masculinity: Hemingway's construction of hyper-masculine image, 154; masculine exchange economies and economic power, 115–26; masculinity studies, overview, 10; *The Nick Adams Stories* (Hemingway), 70–79; *In Our Time* (Hemingway) and, 29–30; overview, 17–18. See also gender roles; homosexuality
"Masculinity" (Strychacz), 2
Mason, Jane, 126n9
"Matter of Love or Death" (Hewson), 18
McGowan, Philip, 138–39
McLoughlin, Kate, 146
The Medievalist Impulse in American Literature (Moreland), 103n6
Mellow, James, 23n8
Men at War (Hemingway), 147
Mencken, H. L., 134
Men Without Women (Hemingway), 7, 61, 63, 64, 66
Merrill, Robert, 13
Messent, Peter B., 16
Meyer, Jeffrey, 126n9

Midnight in Paris (film), 142
Miller, Linda Patterson, 59, 154, 164
Mintler, Catherine R., 5–6
misogyny: dispelling Hemingway's reputation as misogynist, 153–64; economic power and, 115–16
Mobilizing Minerva (Jenson), 85
Moddelmog, Debra A.: *Hemingway in Context*, 87; overview, 4; "Queer Families in Hemingway's Fiction," 69n2; *Reading Desire*, 16, 18, 19, 21, 41, 42, 45, 85–86, 124
"Modern American Fiction" (Barnard), 31
Modernism: Keywords (Cuddy-Keane, Hammond, and Peat), 135
Modern Man magazine, 6n1
modern women, 129–41; flappers as, 132–35, *133*, *134*, 140; genres of femininity, defined, 130–31; "Gibson girls" as, *131*, 132, 135, 140; Hemingway's characters as, 129–30, 135–40
Monteiro, George, 63
Moreland, Kim, 12, 14, 103n6
Morrison, Toni, 19, 20
"The Mother of a Queen" (Hemingway), 16
A Moveable Feast (Hemingway), 11, 16, 17, 110
"Mr. and Mrs. Elliot" (Hemingway), 16, 30, 31, 60
Mulvey, Laura, 37n4, 103n5
Muñoz, José Esteban, 11
Murdock, Catherine Gilbert, 132
Murfin, Ross, 150
"My Old Man" (Hemingway), 60

Native Americans, "Berdache" of, 40
"A New Kind of War" (Hemingway), 146
New Republic, 7–8
The New Yorker, 147
New York Times, 135
The Nick Adams Stories (Hemingway): gender and culture, overview, 27; masculinity represented in, 70–79; portrayal of women and domestic relationships in, 58–69
Nolan, Charles J., 14
No Man's Land (Gilbert and Gubar), 118
Novel (Spilka), 126n9
"Now I Lay Me" (Hemingway), 64–65
Nydell, Margaret K., 84

O'Brien, Sharon, 117
Observing the Erotic Imagination (Stoller), 111n1, 114n11
The Old Man and the Sea (Hemingway), 14, 27

The Omnivore's Dilemma (Pollan), 164n1
"On the Quai at Smyrna" (Hemingway), 27, 29, 36, 60
Orlando (Woolf), 40
"The Other Hemingway" (Holder), 13
"Out of Season" (Hemingway), 30, 58, 60, 161

Page, Tim, 144
Palumbo-Liu, David, 88
The Paris Years (Reynolds), 17
Parker, Dorothy, 135, 143, 144, 145, 147, 151n3
Parsons, Elsie Clews, 46n3
Patterson, Martha H., 46n3
Peat, Alexandra, 135
"Performance Art" (Elliot), 18
"peri-text," 71
peritraumatic dissociation, 110
Perkins, Maxwell, 144, 148
"Petrified Man" (Welty), 150
Pettipiece, Deirdre Anne McVicker, 16
Pfeiffer, Pauline, 112n3, 119, 126n9
Picken, Jonathan, 88
"Place in Fiction" (Welty), 149
"Plea for Old-Time Girls" (Gallatin), 135
Pollan, Michael, 164n1
The Portable Dorothy Parker (Parker), 145
Porter, Katherine Anne, 135
A Portrait of the Artist as a Young Man (Joyce), 125n5
Powell, Dawn, 6, 143–44, 148
Presentations of Gender (Stoller), 111–12n2
"The Price of Modernism" (Rainey), 48
Der Prozess (Kafka), 164n2
Psychopathia Sexualis (Krafft-Ebbing), 46n2
Pullin, Faith, 12–13
Putnam, Ann, 1–2

"Queer Families in Hemingway's Fiction" (Moddelmog), 69n2
"Queering" (Tanimoto), 19
queer theory, overview, 10–11

race: gender studies and, 11, 19–21; masculinity and, 76–77, 79
Raeburn, John, 8
Rainey, Lawrence, 48
Ramsey, Michele, 52
Ray, Supryia M., 150
A Reader's Guide to the Short Stories of Ernest Hemingway (Smith), 69n6
Reading Desire (Moddelmog), 16, 18, 19, 21, 41, 42, 45, 85–86, 124
"Real Story" (Hewson), 18

religion, sexuality and, 93–103
The Resisting Reader (Fetterley), 1, 12–13, 138
"The Revolutionist" (Hemingway), 60
Reynolds, Michael, 9, 15, 17, 58, 86, 144
Richardson, Hadley, 9
Rodin, Auguste, 125n7
Rogers, Katherine M., 12
Rohy, Valerie, 18
A Room of One's Own (Woolf), 117–18
Roughgarden, Joan, 39

Saindon, Jackie, 88
Saint Fermin of Amiens, 96–101
St. Pierre, Scott, 21
Sanderson, Rena, 15, 59, 136, 143
Sanford, Marcelline Hemingway, 23n8, 108
"Santiago" (Beegel), 21
Scholes, Robert, 16, 21, 30–31, 72, 85
Scott, Bonnie Kime, 28
Screen, 103n5
Scribner, 16
Scribner's Magazine, 56, 132
"The Sea Change" (Hemingway), 16, 27–28, 30, 58
"secondary transsexuals," 111–12n2
"Second Growth" (Beegel), 21
second language learners (of English), 80–89
Sedgwick, Eve Kolofsky, 9, 103n7
The Seminar of Jacques Lacan, Book XI (Sheridan, tr.), 103n5
Sexchanges (Volume II) (Gilbert, Gubar), 118
Sexual Excitement (Stoller), 104, 111n1
sexual identity: androgyny, 16, 40; cultural acceptability of, 38–46; homosexuality, 40, 41, 46n2, 46n3, 93–103; overview, 10–11, 15–19; "secondary transsexuals," 111–12n2; sexuality studies, overview, 10; transgender theory, 38–46; transvestism and fetishism, 105, 106
Sexual Inversion (Ellis), 46n2
sexuality: economic power and gender, 115–26; fetishism and, 104–14; field of study, 7, 9–12; religion and, 93–103. *See also* sexual identity
Sex Wars (Duggan and Hunter), 102n2
Shakespeare, William, 2, 27, 37n6
Sheldon Douglas, 5
Sheridan, Alan, 103n5
"The Short Happy Life of Francis Macomber" (Hemingway): domestic relationships in, 58; masculinity in, 77; overview, 3, 4, 12, 19; portrayal of women in, 47–57; as short story in *Cosmopolitan*, 49–54, 53, 56
"A Simple Enquiry" (Hemingway), 16
Smart Set, 134, 134
Smith, Bill, 9
Smith, Paul, 69n6, 156
"The Snows of Kilimanjaro" (Hemingway), 13, 19, 129–30, 137
"Soldier's Home" (Hemingway), 31, 60
"Soldiers of the Republic" (Parker), 147
Soldiers Once (Vernon), 85
Spanier, Sandra, 6n2, 13, 21, 59
The Spanish Earth (film), 151n3
Spilka, Mark: on androgyny, 16; "Hemingway's Barbershop Quartet," 126n9; *Hemingway's Quarrel*, 17, 125n4, 125n7; "Importance," 140n1; *Novel*, 126n9
"The Splitting of the Ego in the Defensive Process" (Freud), 112n2
The Standard Edition of the Complete Psychoanalytic Works of Sigmund Freud (Stratchey, tr.), 112n2
The Starched Blue Sky of Spain (Herbst), 145–46
Stecopoulos, Harry, 9
Stein, Gertrude, 7, 28, 31, 143
Stoller, Robert, 104, 106, 111–12n2, 111n1, 114n11
Stoneback, H. R., 94, 102n2
"The Storm" (Chopin), 142
"The Story of an Hour" (Chopin), 135
Stratchey, James, 112n2
Strong, Amy L., 20
Strychacz, Thomas, 2, 17–18, 21, 74, 77, 140–41n1
Subjects and Strategies: A Writer's Reader, 80
Suburban Civics and Equal Suffrage Club, 8
"Subversion" (Tanimoto), 19
Suffocating Mothers (Adelman), 37n6
The Sun Also Rises (Hemingway): dispelling Hemingway's misogynist reputation and, 157; domestic relationships in, 58, 68; economic power and, 116, 119, 122; masculinity in, 77; modern women and, 129–30, 131, 136, 137, 138–40; overview, 5, 7, 15, 18; sexuality and religion, 93–103; teaching works by women writers with, 142, 148

Takeuchi, Masaya, 18
Tanimoto, Chikako, 19
Teaching Representations of the Spanish Civil War (Valis), 144
"Ten Indians" (Hemingway), 19, 61, 162–63

"Theater" (Toomer), 32
"The Three-Day Blow" (Hemingway), 29, 30, 31, 33, 62–63
A Time to Be Born (Powell), 148
To Have and Have Not (Hemingway), 15
Toomer, Jean, 28, 31, 36n2
Toronto Star, 96
Traber, Daniel S., 18
transatlantic review, 56
transgender theory, *The Garden of Eden* (Hemingway) and, 38–46
transsexuals, "secondary," 111–12n2
transvestism, fetishism and, 105, 106
Trogdon, Robert W., 8
True at First Light (Hemingway), 11, 20
Turn, Magic Wheel (Powell), 148
Turner, Catherine, 8
Tyler, Lisa, 21

Uebel, Michael, 10
Uncle Tom's Children (Wright), 36n2
Under Kilimanjaro (Hemingway), 11, 20
Understanding Arabs: A Guide for Westerners (Nydell), 84
Understanding Chinese Families (Chu and Yu), 84
Undoing Gender (Butler), 39
Unknowing (Weinstein), 141n4
"Up in Michigan" (Hemingway), 12

Valis, Noël, 144, 151n3
Vanity Fair, 7
Vernon, Alex, 18, 85
"A Very Short Story" (Hemingway), 5, 60, 80–89
"Visual Pleasure and Narrative Cinema" (Mulvey), 37n4, 103n5
von Kurowsky, Agnes, 86, 86–87

Wadden, Paul, 78
Wagner-Martin, Linda, 13, 14–15, 23n5, 59
Walcott, William H., 81
Walezak, Émilie, 150
Warner, Michael, 9
The Waste Land (Eliot), 102n1
"A Way You'll Never Be" (Hemingway), 64–65
Wegener, Einar (Elbe), 46n3
Weinstein, Philip, 141n4
Weiss, Joshua, 5
"We Live in a Country" (Moddlemog), 16, 18
The Well of Loneliness (Hall), 125n5

Welty, Eudora, 6, 149, 150
Westling, Louise H., 1
Weston, Jessie, 102n1
Wexler, Joyce, 13
Wheeler, Belinda, 4
"The 'Whine' of Jewish Manhood" (Kaye), 102n3
Whitlow, Roger, 13–14
"Who Is the Destructive Type" (Eby), 112n2
Willingham, Kathy, 120, 123, 124, 126n10
Wilson, Edmund, 12
Winesburg, Ohio (Anderson), 150
Winner Take Nothing (Hemingway), 63, 64, 66, 150
Winnicott, D. W., 106
Wolfe, Cary, 20
women, portrayal of: cross-cultural attitudes toward gender and, 82, 84, 85–88, 86; dispelling Hemingway's reputation as misogynist, 153–64; domestic relationships in *The Nick Adams Stories* (Hemingway) and, 58–69; gender studies and, 12–14; as modern women, 129–41; *In Our Time* (Hemingway) and, 32; "The Short Happy Life of Francis Macomber" (Hemingway) and, 47–57. *See also* women writers
"Women's Magazines and the Suffrage Movement" (Burkhalter), 141n3
women writers, 142–52; American short stories, 149–50; modern American writers, 147–49; teaching courses about, with Hemingway's works, 142–44, 150–51; on war, 144–47. *See also individual names of women writers*
Woolf, Virginia, 7, 27, 40–41, 117–18, 125n6
Worden, Daniel, 18
Wright, Richard, 36n2
Wright-Cleveland, Margaret E., 37n5
The Writer as Artist (Baker), 12

Yamani, Mai, 84
Yellis, Kenneth, 132
"The Yellow Wallpaper" (Gilman), 135
Young, Philip, 11–12, 27, 68–69n2, 140
The Young Hemingway (Reynolds), 9, 15, 58, 86
Yu, Ruoh-Rong, 84

Zola, Emile, 124n1
"The Zuni *La'mana*" (Parsons), 46n3

www.ingramcontent.com/pod-product-compliance
Lightning Source LLC
Chambersburg PA
CBHW021838220426
43663CB00005B/301